SACRED ENERGIES

Of the Golden Cities

ALSO BY LORI TOYE

A Teacher Appears

Sisters of the Flame

Fields of Light

The Ever Present Now

New World Wisdom Series

I AM America Atlas

Points of Perception

Light of Awakening

Divine Destiny

Freedom Star Book

I AM America Map

Freedom Star Map

6-Map Scenario

US Golden City Map

Sacred Energies

of the Golden Cities

GOLDEN CITY SERIES
BOOK FOUR

Lori Adaile Toye

I AM AMERICA PUBLISHING & DISTRIBUTING
P.O. Box 2511, Payson, Arizona, 85547, USA.
www.iamamerica.com

© (Copyright) 2017 by Lori Adaile Toye. All rights reserved. ISBN: 978-1-880050-22-4. All rights exclusively reserved, including under the Berne Convention and the Universal Copyright Convention. No part of this book may be reproduced or translated in any language or utilized in any form or by any means, electronic or mechanical, including photocopying, recording, or by any information storage and retrieval system, without written permission from the publisher. Published in 2017 by I AM America Seventh Ray Publishing International, P.O. Box 2511, Payson, Arizona, 85547, United States of America.

I AM America Maps and Books have been marketed since 1989 by I AM America Seventh Ray Publishing and Distributing, through workshops, conferences, and numerous bookstores in the United States and internationally. If you are interested in obtaining information on available releases please write or call:
I AM America, P.O. Box 2511, Payson, Arizona, 85547, USA. (928) 978-6435, or visit:
www.iamamerica.com

Graphic Design and Typography by Lori Toye
Host and Questions by Lenard Toye
Editing by Elaine Cardall and Betsy Robinson

Love, in service, breathes the breath for all!

Print On Demand Version

10 9 8 7 6 5 4 3 2 1

*"White Fire Mother Earth, Resurrecting Light.
White Fire in us all, Freedom is our right.
Burning bright through the night,
Perfecting our Christ Light.
Being ONE holds our sight
As Freedom's taking flight."*

~ from *Ceremony of Songs*

Contents

LIST OF ILLUSTRATIONS	xi
FOREWORD by Lee Gardner	xiii
PREFACE	xvii

CHAPTERS:

1. Communion	23
Study Guide for Communion	37
2. The Next Level	49
Study Guide for The Next Level	63
3. Golden Ray Stream Forth!	75
Study Guide for Golden Ray Stream Forth!	85
4. For Everything There is a Time	93
Study Guide For Everything There is a Time	106
5. Secret Teachings on the Map of Rings	119
Study Guide for Secret Teachings on the Map of Rings	131
6. A New Reality	147
Study Guide for A New Reality	159
7. The Golden Cities	172
Study Guide for The Golden Cities	184
8. Integrating Golden City Energies	191
Study Guide for Integrating Golden City Energies	198
9. Golden Ray Compassion	213
Study Guide for Golden Ray Compassion	225

SPIRITUAL LINEAGE OF THE VIOLET FLAME	247
GLOSSARY	249
BIBLIOGRAPHY	261
DISCOGRAPHY	265
INDEX	267
ABOUT LORI AND LENARD TOYE	281
ABOUT I AM AMERICA	284

List of Illustrations

FIGURE 1-B
Sidereal Conjunctions of Jupiter and Saturn to 2040 64

FIGURE 2-B
The Rapture: One in the Field 68

FIGURE 3-B
Arjuna and his Charioteer Krishna Confronts Karna 73

FIGURE 1-C
Starry Night by Vincent van Gogh 87

FIGURE 2-C
The City Rises by Umberto Boccioni 88

FIGURE 3-C
The Gold Ray and the Human Energy System 89

FIGURE 1-D
Experience of Time 110

FIGURE 2-D
Buddha Meditating Under the Bodhi Tree 111

FIGURE 3-D
The Indian Mystic Ramakrishna in Trance 112

FIGURE 4-D
Rosicrucian Rose 116

FIGURE 1-E
The Exhortation to the Apostles 132

FIGURE 2-E
Aphrodite from Pompeii 133

FIGURE 3-E
The Birth of Venus 134

FIGURE 4-E
Mercury 134

FIGURE 5-E
The Dream of Saint Joseph 135

FIGURE 6-E
The Ancient of Days 136

FIGURE 7-E
Merlin and the Knight 137

FIGURE 8-E
The Cycle of the Elements 138

FIGURE 9-E
Kuan Yin 139

FIGURE 10-E
Map of Rings 140

FIGURE 11-E
Humans and Elementals 140

FIGURE 12-E
Golden City of Gobean Northern Door with Map of Rings 141

FIGURE 1-F
Seeking the Tao 163

FIGURE 2-F
Saint Michael and Souls 164

FIGURE 1-G
The Four Doorways of a Golden City and Human Energy 185

FIGURE 1-H
Golden Cities through the Dimensions 199

FIGURE 2-H
Photon Hologram 201

FIGURE 3-H
Golden City Gateway Adjutant Point 202

FIGURE 4-H
Golden City Gateway Lei-line 203

FIGURE 5-H
Peak Adjutant Point 204

FIGURE 6-H
Peak Adjutant Lei-line 205

FIGURE 7-H
Slope of Land towards Energy Flow of a Golden City Lei-line 209

FIGURE 8-H
Creation of Bright Hall to Capture Golden City Energies 210

FIGURE 9-H
Cascading Bright Hall for Energy Collection 212

FIGURE 1-I
The First Layer of the Human Aura also known as the Electronic Blueprint 229

FIGURE 2-I
Layers of the Human Aura and the Seven Chakras 231

FIGURE 3-I
The Monad within the Eight-Sided Cell of Perfection 236

Foreword

The journey of our lives, the human experience in consciousness, presents us with an incredible array of choices and the free will to decide on what actions to take, if any. Although this freedom of choice is one of our greatest gifts, few really investigate the subtle (and sometimes not-so-subtle) forces behind the scenes that present the stimulus for us to choose. Lori Toye and her husband Lenard have produced numerous landmark books—channeled work of Saint Germain and other Ascended Masters—including *Sacred Energies*, which give us a rich meta-narrative of a hierarchical universe, our place in it, and the way out of duality. Most of us need only reflect and contemplate the paths our lives have taken to see that there is Divine assistance guiding us, urging us onward in our evolution. And as hard as these experiences may sometimes be, many people (myself included) have claimed these challenges prompt a much-needed change, a shift for the better.

So if we accept that it is natural to have both free will and outside forces at play in our lives, how can we make sense of it all and be in harmony and peace with life? And more importantly, how can we develop ourselves to our highest potential—mentally, emotionally, physically, and spiritually? These are some of the questions of the ages and perhaps the answers are the true Holy Grail and golden treasure that so many of us seek.

History shows that ancient mystery schools existed since the days of Atlantis to impart comprehensive, time-tested teachings, techniques, and trainings to help an aspirant achieve integration of mind, body, spirit, and beyond—enlightenment and Ascension. Lodges, mystery schools, and brotherhoods/sisterhoods such as Druidic, Delphinian, Egyptian, Hermetic, Vedic, Rosicrucian, and Freemasonry, just to name a few, were numerous, generally secretive to all but the worthy, and went underground when the political-religious climate was unfavorable. Today it is generally understood that all spiritual information is to be shared with those who will be open to seeing and hearing Truths. Paradoxically our current social paradigm has clouded our focus and direction by being hell-bent on sensual gratification and materialism, closing itself off to what might be freely received. But sacred energies are striking our planet, urging us ever-upward, and everywhere this crush of humanity is waking up and hungry for Spiritual Light. Thankfully, we have this ever-growing Divine Spark of Lori and Lenard Toye's Ascended Master teachings—a modern-day mystery school of its own in the Western Shamballa Tradition. We can receive it freely as a living template of the way to Enlightenment and Ascension.

My own experience of these "spiritual forces" and mystery schoolroom began in my early teens with visions and dreams of massive social upheaval and destruction. In reaction, I found myself seeking in the time-honored tradition of the day by getting my meditation mantra from Maharishi Mahesh Yogi in the seventies. After many years of yoga classes, meditation, and other "gurus," I slipped into my professional years to pursue money and materialism. Funny thing was the scattered spiritual path I'd been on wasn't working and now chasing money definitely didn't do it either. I couldn't find any peace or happiness and was starving for the Light—like so many of us. One of my Indian Teachers, Swami Jyotir Maya Nanda, told me as I was leaving for lala land, "You know, once you get the taste of Truth, you can never turn your back on it." Boy was he right. I tumbled through a couple of decades of fragmented spiritual work, with some partying and striving for wealth tossed in—but it was never complete, balanced, or in the harmony that my heart and soul hungered for.

Later, when I found my beloved, Tesha, she was also already very learned in spiritual tenets and traditions, and she introduced me to the first Saint Germain book, *Unveiled Mysteries*. She told me that when she'd been young, she'd had an encounter with a man at the foot of her bed who looked exactly like Saint Germain, and while he never spoke, she said it seemed he was scanning her intently.

I found the Ascended Master teachings, of which there are many traditions, to embrace all the great world traditions. I liked this for its purity and equanimity. Too much war and confusion has been promulgated by the old "my God is better than your God" struggle, and I found this inclusive approach refreshing. Saint Germain's teachings were of our culture and conveyed in a way that was not foreign to the Western mind. But what finally led Tesha and me to Lori's specific lineage of Ascended Master teachings was our time working with the great shamans of the Amazon in Ayahuasca ceremonies. After nearly fifteen years of work with the plant teacher medicines of the Amazon Basin, I began to get teachings during each ceremony explaining our Oneness, urging us to drop our attachments, to embrace the eternal flame of Divinity that we are, and prepare for Ascension. They would say very poetic things like, "We are your family of Light and are guiding you to your awakening—to the destiny that you chose and came here for," and, "So long as you follow the way of the ONE, your life will be ever nourished, protected, and thrive." They showed me the place to move to, which unknown to me at that time, was near the Golden City of Wahanee, one of the five Golden Cities of protection and spiritual upliftment that Saint Germain channeled to Lori Toye. Finally, once Tesha and I returned from the Amazon, in perfect synchrony, we found Lori's books and discovered this connection: the teachings in her books were almost exactly what I was told in the Amazon.

The Laws of Synchronicity and Attraction are all around us, and I am beginning to see the connections in my life, and the influences—thanks to the template of study that is the Ascended Masters teachings. Like all the other time-honored mystery schools, Lori Toye's books are rich in narrative, teachings, and techniques—no matter what level you are at. The living document you now hold in your hands, *Sacred Energies*, is a magical culmination of all the past teachings, the Violet Flame, the Shamballa lineage, the positive significance of Earth Change Prophecy, the Golden City Vortices, and Ascended Master and Hermetic Laws. But perhaps most illuminating is the introduction of the Golden Ray, the energy striking the planet that nearly all teachings speak of—and the integration this Ray brings when understood and used correctly.

I am honored and humbled to be a student in this modern-day Western Shamballa Tradition mystery school, and I know this body of knowledge, which now includes *Sacred Energies,* has created a template for our path to Ascension and a new Earth—Unana. My heartfelt love, thanks, and blessings go to Saint Germain, Sananda, Sanat Kumara, Serapis Bey, Kuthumi, Kuan Yin, Mother Mary, and so many other Masters who guide us through the layers of our consciousness and evolution—and to Lori and Len Toye, who give so much of themselves so that we may receive it in this schoolroom—Earth.

Lee Emerson

Lee Emerson grew up in Miami, Florida, and studied psychology and Eastern philosophy at University of Florida with a minor in business. He entered into the family accounting business which continues as a financial vehicle to enable him to pursue other holistic interests such as environmental leadership, shamanic practices, and yoga teaching. He was president of Sierra Club, Save our Suwannee, and other groups that teach respect and protection for our fragile planet, and he became an exploratory cave diver to map out precious fresh-water resources. His shamanic work led him to the great shamans of the Amazon and for more than fifteen years he has worked with the master plant teacher Ayahuasca. His wife, Tesha, born in Imlay City, Michigan, came to Florida more than twenty years ago and is a master chef and yoga teacher. She was the personal chef to Yogi Amrit Desai and teaches Ayurvedic cooking. She has her own yoga studio and together Lee and she teach Ascended Master studies, yoga, organic gardening, and nutrition, and they lead shamanic ceremonies.

Preface

Sacred Energies is an in-depth study regarding the metaphysics of the Golden Cities—specific sites where our spiritual growth can be expedited. How can we connect with the sublime energies of these places? The answers come via the channeled spiritual teacher Saint Germain, who also shares timely advice for a world divided between darkness and light, personal evolution and societal decay, higher vibration and moral stagnation, the old ways and the new. Offered in this book is Earth's much-needed intervention, which is both divine and human and led by the spiritual precepts of courage, love, and tolerance. What specifically are these Golden Cities? They are large Vortex areas that are disbursed over fifty-one locations on our planet. And according to the spiritual teachers in this book, they are also prophesied havens of safety, preserved in this ongoing *Time of Testing* and tumultuous change so we can carefully continue our spiritual growth and readily engage a transformative liberation process—the Ascension.

Throughout the last twenty-some years, I have received dozens of letters and emails from Ascended Master students and readers who have embraced the transcendent energies discussed in this book. One of the first inquiries came from an Australian mystic who had recently ceremonially activated *Angelica*, the *Golden City of Divine Love*. When I read his letter I was sincerely touched by his devotion to the Golden Cities, whose nascent energies can sometimes be a bit difficult to perceive if you have not yet developed "the eyes to see, and the ears to hear"—that is, the ability to sense Golden City energies in their many dimensions, doorways, and power spots. This, however, was not a problem at all for Patrick, a young scientist and researcher who contacted me in the late nineties after I had been channeling the Ascended Masters for a decade and had published three books of their teachings. He had just returned from Russia with a stockpile of unusual Vortex-sensing equipment and he immediately applied this technology in the Golden City of Malton (Illinois and Indiana). He accurately identified the arterial lei-lines that gave birth to the city's sizeable force field with the

Vortex center located at Walnut State Park, near Mattoon and Paris, Illinois. His research also suggested that the New Madrid fault line fed vital energies to the Vortex, and that a larger, more central lei-line surged from it with energies towards *Denasha*, the *Golden City of Scotland*. He wrote about "loud points" and "zero points"—the idea that Vortex energies can be chaotic or abound with the presence of calm, benefic nature spirits, and further identified Vortices as "Interdimensional wormholes that allow higher consciousness to flow into our dimension at a rate of energy that can be absorbed by the (human) aura."

My dear friend Elaine Cardall reiterated similar experiences after she parked her Airstream trailer near a soft-flowing river, and settled just northwest of Mattoon, Illinois. Then she forged a critical physical connection to the Vortex by traveling throughout its four energy calibrating doorways and explored its vital Star (apex) energies. Before long she began to integrate and memorize the spiritual symmetry contained in a Golden City Vortex with its unique subtleties and qualities. Then she embarked on a world tour, traveling overseas in her light bodies to the European and African Golden City Vortices, and onward into the locations of Tibet, China, and India. She later penned a small flyer, "The Ceremony of Songs." This booklet contains verses that honor each of the fifty-one Golden Cities that she and her study group members sang every week.

Several months after Elaine passed away, she contacted me in a dream. I heard her voice speaking over a telephone. It was clear, concise, and determined as she stated, "The Golden Cities are much, much larger than you think!" Her message didn't make sense until weeks later as I researched the actual height of a Golden City. Using the figures Saint Germain shared with the prophetic *I AM America Map* delineating Earth's coming changes, a Golden City is just over 248 miles high (400 kilometers). Interestingly, this reaches well into the Thermosphere, and a Golden City's extraterrestrial significance likely contacts the upper limits of Earth's atmosphere. At this level, Saint Germain claims, the Golden Cities connect us to other planets and solar systems through an interfacing *Galactic Web*.

About fifteen years ago, my husband I set out on our own trip throughout the *Golden City of Gobean*. It was part research and part fun—yet we were serious about the potential of Spiritual Migration and its ability to further initiate and deepen our Ascension process. First we traveled to the

Hopi Reservation, where I photographed a nature deva playfully dancing at our ceremonial site. Then we traveled to the next point, located on a dirt road in the Northern regions of the Navajo Reservation. Through a series of innocent mistakes, our four-wheel drive pickup nearly careened off an ice-slickened one hundred fifty-foot drop-off. After ordering me out of the vehicle, Len carefully backed the truck up inches at a time, while we laboriously placed rocks under the back wheels to gain traction. Finally the road widened and we could safely turn around. After the ordeal we both asked ourselves, "Are we really ready for this?" My point is that apparently the Golden Cities do not just contain benefic, angelic forces. They are vital, strong, and powerful energies that can instantly mirror their counterpart back to you, swift and stinging, like the lash of a whip. And if you are not prepared . . . well, you're not ready. Later, my teacher of Taoist tradition would call this type of teaching "wrathful."

The underlying infrastructure of all Golden Cities is the *Map of Rings*, described by the grandfather teacher, Sanat Kumara. This Map is common, and you can find versions of it in almost every culture and religious tradition, including mysterious crop circles, ancient Egyptian and Assyrian art, even Leonardo da Vinci's *Vitruvian Man*. In fact, I have a framed doily that was hand crocheted by my Prussian great grandmother hanging in our living room. My aunt called it a "Pineapple Print" when she gave me the family heirloom. But I recognize it as the *Flower of Life*, a universal symbol of creation. Its creative cycle of elements assists, nourishes, and generates life; its destructive cycle brings difficulties, ruin, even obliteration. Its inherent mystery reminds me a bit of Ecclesiastes 3: "To every thing there is a season . . . a time to be born, and a time to die; a time to plant; a time to pluck up that which is planted . . ." This energy of the cycles is also present in Golden Cities and its esoteric knowledge combines with the heavenly pulse of lei-lines.

As I mentioned before, wrathful teaching was one of the first lessons we learned in working with Golden City energies. As we walked with our Feng Shui teacher along the Little Colorado River that adjoins the three hundred-acre parcel where my husband and I plan to build a Golden City Community, we learned about benefic landforms that gather nourishing energies, contrasted by intense and somewhat agitating rock formations that required solemn respect or altogether avoidance. Our teacher, proficient in Chinese Feng Shui—the traditional art of living in harmony with our environment—gently reminded us that everything in our physical, living environments affects and calibrates our level of consciousness. And since consciousness creates our reality, attention to our outer landscape can prove invaluable. A picturesque, long horizon of rolling hills may enhance wealth, while a restricted view is just that—a confined and restricted level of consciousness. The last two chapters of *Sacred Energies* address this type of hidden knowledge, and how one can potentiate Golden City energies and capture their unique benefic, spiritual force.

Perhaps the most important guidance that is described and reiterated throughout almost every chapter of this book is the vital practice, cultivation, and connection to our own personal, inner landscape. Of course we can do this through a number of disciplines, including meditation and contemplation, the visualization of an inner garden that literally guards the spiritual growth of our soul, and above all, the human transcending aspects of the Sacred Fire—the practice of mercy, compassion, and forgiveness. According to the teachings in *Sacred Energies*, the Law of Love is highly valued as it can heal the societal division that breeds intolerance at every level: sexual, racial, and religious. In this current time of great division, of scathing political derisiveness and seemingly insurmountable cultural polarity, the Golden Ray appears. Yes, its arrival creates shadows and defines darkness, but in contrast it also lights a path so we may move out of darkness and into conscious light through its innate attributes of unity, brotherhood, balance, and peace. Saint Germain teaches, "When darkness seems to produce an all-time low, it is also the greatest opportunity for light. May light move forward in full measure!"

May you discover and embrace your most divine, sacred energy and light,

Lori Toye

for Elaine

1

Communion
Saint Germain

Greetings, Beloved chelas, in that mighty Violet Flame, I AM Saint Germain and I request permission to come forward.

Response: *Please, Saint Germain, come forward. You are most welcome.*

The work upon the Earth Plane and Planet is indeed one that is worrisome, is it not, Dear chelas of mine? There are many plans, many schedules, many things that should be brought forward into understanding and into their own evolutions. You see, Dear ones, the work of Earth Changes Prophecy is indeed incomplete. This work was originally intended to bring forth a voice for beloved Babajeran, who is also known as the Earth Mother. Those whose eyes and ears were open, upon hearing this voice, would indeed change their hearts.

This work was also brought forward to give a greater understanding of the work of prophecy and the evolution that is brought about by addressing the changes within the heart. This evolution is spiritual in its orientation and inevitably leads to the liberation of the Ascension. The liberation of the Ascension is indeed one of the most important aspects of this work. The work that we have brought forward, which is seen in Earth Changes Prophecy, was not brought forward to just improve conditions of life on Earth, but to expand, shall we say, in complete understanding, the purpose and the evolution of the souls that are incarnated in this schoolroom.

Dear ones, Dear hearts, the Violet Flame has been brought forward to bring complete liberation from all circumstance, from all things that bring you worry, and from anything that is in your life that you feel is a burden. For you see, the Violet Flame has been brought forward as that most refreshing drink. It is that mighty law in action that brings the Law of ultimate Forgiveness, complete and total understanding, and Divine Grace and Intervention in any circumstance or situation. When one begins to understand that it is through this mighty Law in action of Mercy and ultimate Forgiveness, Divine Intervention in its greatest role begins to align all wills involved in any situations. When you call upon that mighty Violet Flame for a situation, which you believe only involves yourself, you're also asking for this mighty law in its vibration and frequency to affect all of those involved. As I have stated before, "things do not happen to one person but happen with many simultaneously."

The Violet Flame in its ultimate wisdom and jurisdiction upon this Earth Plane and Planet then is able to come forward in its mighty brilliance, in its mighty transcendence, and bring a transformation of the gloomiest and dire of circumstances. It is indeed that ultimate sacrifice that has been made for you by many others prior. It was the sacrifice that was made by beloved Jesus Sananda, the Christ. It was the sacrifice made by the beloved Buddha in your Earth Plane. It was the sacrifice that has been made by all of the Avatars . . . by all of the Saviors . . . by all of the Messiahs. Of course, I will not go on and name those of other religions, but indeed they do exist. I mention these two for these are two that you would immediately understand within your own belief system. Dear ones, Dear hearts, know this great sacrifice has been made for you. Know that at any moment you can call this in, this mighty law in action, and use it to bring ultimate forgiveness and ultimate transformation into any circumstance or situation.

Now today, I would like to bring forth a discourse about the Golden City Vortices. For you see, Dear ones, this information, as you know, is still incomplete and many will be coming to you and asking, "How shall I serve? Where is a safe place to live? How do I move forward within these times?"

You see, Dear ones, many upon the Earth Plane and Planet have very little concern about their spiritual evolution but are indeed concerned about their basic needs of survival . . . to have enough money . . . to have food to eat . . . to have water to drink and a safe place for their children to move forward in their evolution upon the Earth Plane and Planet. But those who have the eyes to see and the ears to hear, shall we say, their heart beats to a different drummer. Those who really understand the subtle energies as they exist upon the Earth Plane and Planet at this time, are indeed those who are ready to move beyond survival issues. For they see that their soul is immortal and they are a drop of that eternal bliss of the ocean of all of life. They understand that it is the evolution of the soul that is most important.

It is evolution moving forward that propels the soul forward into its own memory of itself, of who it is, and where it is going. This is what we call the Divine Inheritor, the one who is in tune with the forces of nature, the forces of the universe, and the force of its own being. Dear ones, Dear hearts, the Golden Cities have been brought forth to ensure this evolution and provide, shall we say, that backdrop, so that there can be those energies infused at this most important time of Spiritual Awakening. Of course, spiritual and sacred energies have always existed upon the Earth, for the Earth is a great being of light . . . a great being beyond that of the Ascended Master, who now offers itself in service to that mighty Oneship. But in order to avoid any more confusion, let us talk at very basic levels.

The first sacred site that existed upon the Earth in your history was that of Shamballa. As we have said in many past discourses, this was an energy that was built through the cooperation of those who align their wills with beloved Babajeran. This created a great and mighty force. From this great and mighty force, the energies were able to collect, gather, and circulate in the same circular motion that exists within the human Chakra System, known as a Vortex. This great and mighty Vortex of energy also created the City of White Light, known as Shamballa. This city was used then by other beings who were coming to the Earth Plane and Planet at that time to bring spiritual evolution forward. This was created, you see, Dear ones, Dear hearts, through the Laws of complete Harmony and Cooperation. The great beings of light who came at that time for the evolution of the Earth Plane and Planet, came at a time before the Age of Kali Yuga. It was a time when the consciousness was in a descending order but at a higher frequency than you would understand presently. This consciousness was also brought forward at that time so that those who would be traveling in this present time - souls learning, growing, and understanding in the time of Kali Yuga - would still have the great opportunity to move into the realms of light.

Dear ones, Dear hearts, these beloved beings coming forward at that time, they too brought great sacrifices, sacrifices which you would understand to be of their energies. They worked tirelessly and with great effort to bring about the complete and total understanding of the great divinity and the liberation of the Ascension. For you see, Dear ones, as you understand, grow, and learn in this time of Spiritual Awakening, you will see that you are so much more than a physical body . . . so much more than a series of lifetimes . . . indeed, much more even than the memories of those past lifetimes. Simultaneously and together, you are much, much more even beyond that. This I have pointed out before in the previous discourse of "Point of Perception." There is that being who is the oversoul and there are these occurrences of simultaneous embodiments, the splitting of energies to achieve the goal at hand. But let me explain even more about the energies of sacred sites, or in this case, of a Golden City Vortex.

A Golden City Vortex is a special type of energy that is brought through in harmony and complete and total cooperation with beloved Babajeran. It is held through the conscious will of the Earth Planet itself and comes forward in a complete alignment to that mighty will in action. The great city of Shamballa held a consciousness through these higher beings of light, bringing forward a series of teachings which have evolved throughout the course of time and helped thousands of others reach their eternal freedom and liberation. This again, is the purpose of the Golden City Vortices as presented in the I AM America material. Of course, this information has been presented along catastrophic geographical changes, but understand that while these changes are still happening upon the Earth Plane and Planet, it is most important to put the emphasis upon the spiritual message. It is the spiritual message of the change within the heart itself and of understanding the true divinity that lies within.

The Golden City Vortices, as a most unique energy, help to create, at first, a communion with the great Inner Self. This allows a communion not only with the oversoul but also with the great Akashic Record that exists for every soul in incarnation. This great Akashic Record carries the memory and record of all embodiments. It also carries the record of all future embodiments; for you see, Dear ones, Dear hearts, to liberate yourself from the dual worlds also means to liberate yourself from the concept of time itself. Again, I would suggest to review "Point of Perception," in order to understand this concept in its totality.

The Golden City Vortices bring forward first this communion within the great Inner Self. Of course, the soul in its sojourn and journey in the Earth Plane and Planet is chasing that ever-present desire for its own Source. Yet, in the beginning stages, the soul will ask, "How do I fulfill myself? How do

I achieve this particular goal for myself?" This of course is very important and that is why the Golden City Vortices carry energies to manifest, or shall we say, carry instant-thought-manifestation. Instant-thought-manifestation will bring a consciousness of all desires to the individual. Until individuals are ready to face, understand, and take complete responsibility for their own desires, it will be almost impossible for them to liberate themselves from the Wheel of Karma, that is, the wheel of actions.

The Golden City Vortices allow the human in its evolutions to express these desires and to live these desires to the fullest. That is why the emotional bodies have been developed, so that desires can be sensed . . . desires can be felt . . . desires can be heard . . . desires can be seen and touched. You see, Dear ones, this is a most important step. When these desires, in their manifestation processes are suppressed, or shall we say, not expressed or understood to their fullest capability, the soul enters into a backward spiral and the evolutionary process then does not move forward in its own perfection.

There are many desires that a soul within itself has created and not lived through. The Golden City Vortices bring these desires into their manifestations. Name any desire that you may have—any desire. Is it to have all the riches of the Earth? Is it to have complete and total knowledge of all information that has ever existed? Is it even to just, in one case, obtain an object of desire that is within your own grasp or ability to bring into manifestation? Northern Doors of Golden City Vortices have been brought forward for this purpose; however, Dear hearts, Dear ones, in your understanding and applications of the Ray Forces, you'll understand that the five Golden Cities of the United States each have a particular nuance, a subtle overtone, so to speak.

In the Golden City of Gobean, for instance, desires are brought through Harmony, Cooperation, and Peace. Desires are brought through with complete cooperation with all those around them. When desires are brought through complete and absolute harmony, peace is the end result.

In the Golden City of Malton, the overtone of the Ruby and Gold Ray brings forth the manifestation of desires into complete and absolute fruition. Now when I say this, it is a manifestation of that desire into a physical manifestation. If there are those who require money . . . if there are those who would like to see the birth of a child . . . if there are those who would like to see the manifestation of a new home, all of these desires that we hold in physical incarnation are then brought to their physical manifestation.

Now, those who travel to Wahanee bring their manifestation for united Brotherhood and Sisterhood. If a desire is, shall we say, to bring forth a mission of world peace . . . a mission for world diplomacy . . . a mission for ultimate forgiveness among nations, you see how this works. This desire manifests upon that scale. Now take the same principle and put it into the measure of the family as a societal unit and this would bring this desire forward. To bring harmony within a family itself, to bring true Brotherhood and Sisterhood within a family, it would bring this desire into complete and absolute manifestation.

Desires manifesting in the Golden City of Shalahah would have that great overtone of the Green Ray, which brings an essence of active intelligence. Desires for complete and total healing . . . desires for the understanding of this healing . . . desires for complete and total abundance. Now when I say abundance, this is the principle that all who are touched by that abundance bring into a complete manifestation of prosperity for all, which is a Golden Age principle.

In the Golden City of Klehma is the overtone of the White Ray. Desires then are brought into complete and absolute purification and aligned to that of that mighty White Ray of Ascension. Those who have the desire for Ascension and complete liberation may bring this desire one step further to its goal in the Northern Door of Klehma.

Now before I proceed on additional teaching upon this subject, do you have questions?

Answer: *No, not at this time. Please continue.*

These Ray Forces are very important, indeed. It is important to understand how each of them works at this great Time of Testing. Now of course, any desire within itself is brought into manifestation to some degree in any Golden City at any time. I have outlined for you, Dear ones, Dear hearts, the specifics of how this does indeed work.

Now let us talk about healing. Healing comes, of course, always from the Southern Door energies, for the Golden City Vortices have been brought forth for the healing of all the nations of the Earth. Within Golden City Vortices, healing is of all types: body, spirit, mind . . . any problem that ails a relationship . . . any problem that ails one from within . . . any problem that ails the physical body, can be brought into greater union and balance through time spent in a Golden City Vortex. Of course, any location in the Vortex will bring this process and enable it further but the greatest condensation of the Ray Force to bring about healing collects and is located in what is known as the Southern Door or the gateway. This brings, of course, an understanding of vibration.

Healing is vibrational. As you have understood, certain diseases, parasites, or other ailments that happen to the physical within itself, reside first at a vibrational level. Healing that is brought, shall we say, at a mental level is also vibrational in nature. This is what we call perception; being able to see something from all points of view also involves the principle of vibration.

There have been those who say that when they listen to this information over and over again, that they gain a new perception. What is happening is they are infused with the vibration itself and from this principle of vibration are able to move and to understand with greater depth. This depth of learning, this depth of insight, is gained in all Southern Doors. This is most important in all healing; for you see, when one comes with the expression of disease or lack of understanding of their own experience, it takes a shift, a vibrational shift within the perception itself, to understand and perceive why one is continuously creating this situation and circumstance of disease.

Of course, Gobean and the forces of Gobean are very good for those who are beginning this journey of understanding the science of the self. Particularly in the arena of finding healing, the energies of Gobean and the Blue Ray are well sorted to bring that shift in perception. That shift is needed to bring harmony, transformation, and ultimate peace in understanding. This will affect the physical body in many ways which are beneficial. In the beginning of using Golden City energies and particularly those of all of the gateways, or Doorways as they are known, it is important to understand this principle of vibrational shifting. In the beginning, these energies are very subtle and may not even be noticed but one of the first clues in understanding this is a high frequency pitch or ring. That is the indication of the vibrational shifting.

Now, as we move on into Malton, again it is the same principle as seen through that Ruby and Gold Ray of complete and absolute ministration, devotion, and ultimate fruition. Again, the principle of desire is also presented in the Southern Door of Malton but it brings this desire into manifestation for complete and absolute healing. There are those who tread the path of healing and yet never fully experience that state. You have known this person very often as the unhealed healer . . . that healer who moves forward throughout society offering up to others all that is needed . . . that one who gives of that most refreshing drink, over and over again, but yet cannot receive it unto itself. The Southern Door of Malton's energies are well suited for the unhealed healer, for it instantaneously brings energies into balance and alignment so the experience of healing within itself can be completely, instantly, and uniquely experienced by those who are willing.

To bring about a complete and total transformation, along with the healing vibration of that mighty Violet Ray in action, travel to the Southern Door of Wahanee. There, I myself will give assistance to those who seek healing at the Alchemical level. As I have stated before, many Akashic Records reside within the energies of the Golden Cities. Each Master Teacher, with his own energy and influence of his own chelas, has brought this information forward through that collective will of beloved Babajeran. Those who have developed a greater understanding of meditation and peace, assisted through beloved El Morya and that mighty Blue Ray, will be able then to access many of the alchemical powers, many of the alchemical formulas, and many of the alchemical mysteries of nature in the Akashic Records of Wahanee. You see, Dear ones, alongside Beloved Kuthumi of the Golden City of Malton, the Nature and the Deva Kingdoms are aligning together with Malton and Wahanee to bring forth this energy. Each mineral and each vegetable upon the Earth Plane and Planet has a healing property and these healing properties, when properly understood and applied, do indeed bring such great assistance and an end to the suffering of all disease. These formulas are held eternally in the Akashic Records of Wahanee.

Onward now, to the soothing and healing energies of beloved Lord Sananda, held in the Shalahah Vortex. You see, Dear ones, to bring about true and complete healing also, as I have described before, brings a vibrational shifting which prepares the soul for ultimate forgiveness of self, ultimate transmutation of all past karma, into that state of acceptance and at-one-ment. This at-one-ment is the energy that is held in the Southern Door of Shalahah. The at-one-ment process, or what has been known as atonement, is the absolute acceptance and surrendering to the Eternal Will of the Divine. It is important, Dear ones and Dear hearts, to understand that the Southern Door of Shalahah brings about a complete and total preparation for the Ascension Process.

The Southern Door of Shalahah is a wonderful place for all healers to go to physically renew and rejuvenate themselves. This will bring about a greater understanding for themselves personally; to recharge their own energy bodies, to bring about this greater assistance. For the soul that is working on its own personal path, this is where some of the final trials can be understood and also healed within the soul itself. Therefore, visits to the Southern Door of Shalahah will bring immediate recall of many traumatic injuries that the soul has suffered throughout many successive embodiments upon the Earth itself. There they are brought for instant healing in the same way that there is instant-thought-manifestation. Instant healing is brought about in the Southern Door of Shalahah of all of the many wounds of the past.

Before I proceed, are there any more questions?

Answer: *No, not at this time. The discourse on the Doorways is quite, quite enlightening.*

The final capstone, shall we say, is the Southern Doorway of Beloved Serapis Bey's Vortex energies of Klehma. There, the purification becomes complete within itself and divinity is accepted as "from within, so without." The soul then meets, shall we say, the secret chamber, that mighty witness that sees all things, the all-seeing eye that speaks the whisper of the mysteries within the ear. This brings, shall we say, at a healing level, the soul in complete and total alignment to accept and honor its own Adeptship. There, it becomes united with the mighty mysteries of nature and brought to an even finer cooperation and understanding of the great purification. Now, I shall open the floor for your questions.

Question: *Since you have covered the Northern Doors and the Southern Doors, did you want to continue at this time with the Eastern and Western Doors?*

No, Dear heart, I shall continue that discourse at a later date.

Question: *As you wish. One of the questions that I would like to pose is about personal guidance. Many people know they have inner guidance and spirit guides. Is there a difference between a spirit guide and an Ascended Master in that relationship? Could you explain that to everyone?*

It is difficult of course for you see that many who come to this material are at different vibratory levels. As I have explained before, each must be accompanied by that vibration that best suits them. For instance, you do not take the first grader and place them into the accelerated classes, for they are not ready yet to understand. The same way, you do not take a being from, shall we say in reference to the lesson of today, from Shamballa and thrust them into the lowest, darkest pitches of Kali Yuga. You do not take that one from Kali Yuga and thrust them immediately into the higher vibrational pitches of Shamballa. Such it is with spirit guides, inner guidance, and moving forward in your own spiritual evolution. Of course, the foremost and most important aspect of this work is to bring the soul into complete communion with that mighty I AM Presence. The I AM Presence is guiding and directing the individual at all times. It is bringing forward the essence of the Rays and their qualities, which command and demand the actions that will take place in that individual's life. This, along side the Divine Purpose, will move it forward.

You see, Dear ones, Dear hearts, there are many spirit guides that do exist, but of course, it is most important to forge that identity first with that mighty I AM Presence. It is from there that you hear that voice that will give you the direction that says turn left instead of right, purchase this book and not that book. You see, it is that which brings a guidance, which prepares the soul later on for stewardship. There are indeed many spirit guides that do exist. These are forged, of course, through those great bonds of love. For instance, a grandparent, a special aunt, a favorite brother, or a favorite sister may stay after their embodiment and decide, in choosing, so to speak, to assist and help that particular soul move in its evolution for a period of time.

It is highly unusual though for a spirit guide to stay with one individual throughout an entire incarnation. A spirit guide indeed may come forward and serve you for a period of time, for five years, two years, or maybe even six months. That spirit guide, within itself, serves through a mutual desire, that mutual desire of course is known to the human as love. Now, there are those rare instances where a spirit guide will stay with an individual for twenty-five, thirty, maybe even fifty years. When I speak of years, I speak of that in a human timeframe. But it is most important to understand that it is the bond with the mighty I AM Presence that we work to bring forward, that we wish to see strengthened. It is through this complete and total communion that the soul is then readied to meet the Master Teacher. When the light of the I AM Presence shines so bright, that light cannot be held off, then, when the student is indeed ready, the Master appears.

Master Teachers have many appearances, you see, Dear ones. They may appear first in a book of teachings. They may appear first as a kind hand that helps you along the way. They may appear first in a dream and eventually, in the same way that the essence and the energy of the I AM Presence was brought forward and strengthened. It is the same with the Master Teacher. But know this, that the student does not choose the Master Teacher, the Master Teacher chooses the student. Questions?

Question: *I do see the difference. So in a sense, the I AM Presence could also be termed the Holy Spirit?*

The Holy Comforter. The I AM THAT I AM is an ever pervading light essence, another manifestation of the God source that exists. The I AM Presence contains within it a more individualized consciousness that is unique to the soul in its incarnation.

Question: *Then, would the I AM Presence be similar to the Oversoul?*

It is indeed. It is connected to that oversoul. It is that great, shall we say, ambassador to the oversoul itself. Union with the oversoul is obtained during the Ascension Process, you see, so let us not confuse the oversoul now with the I AM Presence.

Question: *I see. So in a certain sense the Presence is an individualization of the oversoul?*

It is that great mediator. It is that Holy Christ self. It is that Holy Buddha self. I give again these two names so you can identify.

Question: *I understand and so it is the I AM Presence that is actually responsible for the individualization of the soul and the path that each soul takes in embodiment after embodiment?*

It brings, shall we say, the pulses and the impulses that lead the soul in its evolution and its journey. So make no mistake, it will fulfill its destiny.

Response: *I see. So it is varying layers of responsibility and stewardship in the evolution.*

This is so, Dear ones, Dear hearts. And the soul then grows in its consciousness and understanding of its path on the Earth Plane and Planet. Then, as it grows in understanding, it must gain the assistance of an ascended being to bring it over to this understanding of the oversoul; however, this understanding must be fed again as milk is fed to a new baby.

Question: *Very interesting. So it truly is a step-by-step evolutionary process?*

As I have stated before, it is a vibrational process.

Question: *And vibration is the movement of light?*

Indeed it is, alongside the movement of sound.

Response: *So when you speak of the Akashic Records, you speak of how the records are there for every previous embodiment of each individual and every embodiment yet to be, as if this were a course program that the soul was going through.*

And then the Master Teacher brings this union to the oversoul, brings the union to the great mediator, to bring a complete and total understanding to anchor this as consciousness in the individualized incarnation.

Question: *So, through the element of the Divine Plan, the individual soul having many embodiments to learn and grow, are there times when things are left incomplete and are carried over to the next embodiment?*

It is rare in the Divine Plan that ever anything is left incomplete; however, the perception of the human would see it as such and thus through desire, again, the soul is thrust into the wheel of duality to find completeness.

Question: *So everything is right on schedule, regardless of our perceptions?*

Everything is always within that Divine Plan.

Response: *I see. So even this appointed moment in our conversation with you . . .*

Is brought forward on that light and sound ray of vibration in its most perfect harmony.

Question: *So would you say that a secret of life is to consider that the Divine Plan is always functioning, no matter what?*

Of course, Dear ones, Dear hearts; however, one may not see it in the present individualized moment of the current perception that they are now holding. It takes that shift in perception, that shift in vibration, to understand and see that there is a more complete picture. All is within its own unique accordance and timing.

Question: *There are those who wish to travel to and live in a safe place; is there preferably a Doorway to start in?*

Always within the Eastern Doorways, Dear ones and beloveds; however, I shall give that information in the next discourse.

Question: *I see. That is most interesting. I would be very appreciative if in that next discourse, I could also ask personal questions for others who have made requests.*

So be it; it is now done.

Response: *Then I thank you. I have no further questions at this moment.*

I shall take my leave now from your vibration.

Response: *I thank you very much for your courtesy and generosity.*

Study Guide for Communion

Topics:
The Violet Flame and Spiritual Liberation
Sacrifice and the Mighty Law
The Divine Inheritor
Insights on the Golden Cities
The Oversoul
Instant-thought-manifestation
Gateways of Healing in the Golden Cities
Teachings on the I AM

Spiritual Liberation

The process whereby the soul gains freedom from the Wheel of Karma, and the need to reincarnate in a physical body on Earth. In Ascended Master Teachings, spiritual liberation is known as *Ascension*. Depending on the spiritual level and evolution of each soul, after spiritual liberation from the Earth Plane the soul travels onward into higher levels of Astral or Causal Planes, where yet another liberation process ensues. This new level of consciousness and spiritual evolution may include Earth or other planets. In Hinduism, spiritual liberation is known as *moksha*, which is the release from suffering, and the cycle of death and rebirth. It is claimed that the soul is released from duality as the concept of self expands into the sublime realization of the *I AM* and the soul merges with the *I AM Presence*. This also includes the realization of the Christ Consciousness or birth of the Quetzalcoatl energies as the soul enters Fourth and Fifth Dimensional Awareness. This perfected state of consciousness realizes the Earthly Plane as illusion or *Maya* and exists without separation from the God Source, the spiritually free at-one-ment. The late, spiritual teacher, Choa Kok Sui, writes about this process:

> "When the person merges with the brilliant white light, he passes through a tunnel of light, which is actually the spiritual cord. In some cases, the incarnated soul may unite with the

higher soul immediately. Or it may just simply stay in heaven or the higher world for a certain period of time and then later unite with the higher soul. This depends on the degree of spiritual development of the soul. During meditation, a yogi may also see the tunnel of light and pass through it.

Physical death can be transformed into spiritual liberation. It is a priceless, spiritual opportunity to achieve illumination and oneness with one's higher soul. Such an opportunity should not be missed. If the person is not aware of this spiritual opportunity, then he will have to spend time in the lower astral world for purging or purification. This can be (a) relatively short or long period of time, depending on the quality of life the person had lived." [1]

There are many techniques that one may employ to assist one's Ascension or spiritual liberation process. The Ascended Masters suggest the use of the sacred fire or Violet Flame to initiate the soul into the alchemic transmutation of karma. Meditation, visualization, mantra, decree, and specifically Kriya Yogas (breath techniques, also known as pranayama) discipline both mind and body while spiritually preparing the chela for spiritual liberation. It is claimed that certain diets assist the Ascension Process. These are diets that exclude animal products of all types, including eggs and dairy. The spiritual teacher Saint Germain suggests a plant-based diet that assists spiritual development, promotes ahisma (nonviolence), and in this *Time of Change* helps to assist longevity and personal health.

Refreshing Drink
A metaphor for the Universal Supply of Life. It is alleged that the elixir or soma offered by Saint Germain helps one to spiritually awaken.

Saint Germain's Teachings on the Violet Flame
1. The Violet Flame is a spiritual liberation technique which transmutes and lifts burdens of all types.
2. The Violet Flame is an aspect of the forgiveness process—which is claimed to be a Universal Law. Through the application of forgive-

ness in difficult situations, the wills of those involved in conflict begin to align to the Divine Plan.
3. Saint Germain suggests that no one is ever a victim and that, "things do not (randomly) happen to a person," but certain situations and unusual circumstances often appear due to simultaneous karmas.
4. The Violet Flame, in one form or another, has been practiced to achieve liberation by Jesus Christ, the Buddha, and many other messiahs and avatars of Earth's various religions. Due to the preeminence of the Violet Flame, it has achieved "Jurisdiction on Earth," a form of collective authority to transmit transformation and transcendence among humanity.

Jurisdiction

To understand this term from a spiritual point of view, one must first understand its Latin etymology, which comes from *"ius"* which means "law," and the word *"dicere"* which means "to speak."[2] When Saint Germain affirms that the Violet Flame has achieved jurisdiction, this spiritual practice has gained sufficient impetus and recognition in the Collective Consciousness with the power to be heard and act with determination by administering forgiveness, mercy, grace, and the Divine Intervention of transcendence.

Through the principle of sacrifice, the Violet Flame has gained momentum and power to intervene in dire situations and transform our spiritual growth and evolution.

Sacrifice

The spiritual ideal that through giving selflessly, or taking a short-term loss, there is a greater long-term return for others created. The Hindu spiritual ceremony known as both *puja* and *yagna* is founded from this principle. The ceremony is known as a form of "bloodless sacrifice" which is offered to appease certain Gods or planetary afflictions to change the course of events.[3]

Allegedly the Violet Flame gained its momentum through the great avatars who sacrificed their human frailties through burning them ceremonially with a mental visualization of the Violet Fire. The sacrifice of duality inevitably creates unity, or entrance into Unity Consciousness, and our world is purified and made whole again. Joseph Campbell explains the spiritual concept of sacrifice and bliss:

> "Out of the rocks of fallen wood and leaves, fresh sprouts arise from which the lesson appears to have been that from death springs life, and out of death new birth. And the grim conclusion drawn was that the way to increase life is to increase death. Accordingly, the entire equatorial belt of this globe has been characterized by a frenzy of sacrifice—vegetable, animal, and human sacrifice." [4]

Through the Violet Flame, the rituals of sacrifice evolved to a level of consciousness, where the old patterns and paradigms of thoughts and feelings are offered to the sacred fire to initiate a new way, led through the process of transmutation into transcendence.

Bliss of the Eternal Ocean or Ocean of Eternal Bliss

All Masters encourage their students to move forward (spiritually) into the state of consciousness that immerses the individual into constant bliss. This forward evolutionary process is often referred to as the "Bliss of the Eternal Ocean," or "Ocean of Eternal Bliss." It is a state sometimes entered into with apprehension for fear of the loss of ourselves, our desires, and identity. Sri Ramakrishna once said, "Don't you want to plunge into this blissful ocean called God? One would not lose one's consciousness. Man does not lose his consciousness by being mad about God." [5]

Divine Inheritor

According to Ascended Master Teachings, as we immerse our consciousness into the Bliss of the Eternal Ocean we enter into a new, lighted understanding that affirms our status as a Divine Inheritor. The Islamic Prophet Muhammed once said, "Seek (spiritual) knowledge from cradle to grave, verily the men of knowledge are the inheritors of the Prophets." Divine Knowledge is also known as *Gnosis*, which is Greek for spiritual knowledge, or enlightenment.

Saint Germain's insights on the Golden Cities
1. The Golden Cities help to initiate our consciousness into the bliss of God (enlightenment) and reaffirm humanity's status as Divine Inheritors.
2. Mother Earth—Babajeran—is a great being of light and assists the formation of the Golden Cities.
3. Shamballa was the first sacred site on Earth that was built with the assistance of Babajeran.
    a. Its creation came through the conscious construction of a powerful, circular force—a Vortex.
    b. Shamballa assisted many on Earth to spiritually evolve during the period it was physically present on Earth.
    c. Shamballa's existence was during another epoch in Earth's spiritual history, before the darkness of Kali Yuga.
4. Each Golden City Vortex works on the spiritual principles of harmony and cooperation, held in the conscious will of Mother Earth.
5. Golden City Vortices help individuals to establish contact with the inner self. This helps to later establish communion with the Oversoul and personal Akashic Records. This instigates several processes for the chela:
    a. Desire to contact the Source, and the beginning of identifying desires of all types.
    b. The desire to set new goals for spiritual growth and development.

Oversoul

A metaphysical term coined in the nineteenth century by philosopher Ralph Waldo Emerson, while he was a student at Harvard University. The Oversoul refers to the soul in its relationship to the ONE, which is infinite, and from which finite souls draw sustenance and light. The Oversoul is analogous to the I AM Presence, and from Emerson's viewpoint is a "Celebration of the human soul in matter." [6]

Golden City Vortices and Instant-Thought-Manifestation

As you become more perfectly aligned and in harmony with your thoughts, feelings, and actions, your individual focused, directed desires may quickly manifest. This Co-creative activity is known by the Master Teachers as *Instant-Thought-Manifestation* and moves the *Initiate* to the beginning stages of *Arhat*. As initiates perfect this process, they may notice that the period of time between thoughts and manifestations diminishes; this is a common quality of HU-man development. Golden City Vortices purposely allow desires to quickly manifest in order to free the chela from the karmic wheel and chelas encounter desires that have been held for many lifetimes. The level and degree of this technique depends on the intensity of the desire, your position (location) within a Golden City, and the amount of time spent in a Golden City Vortex. Several spiritual formulas for instant-thought-manifestation follow:

Northern Door Formula

Instant-thought-manifestation is perhaps at its greatest level of clarity in this Golden City Doorway. However, it is important to remember that each Golden City Vortex will produce distinctive overtones of spiritual experience.

- *Gobean Northern Door*: The Co-creation with desires for Harmony, Cooperation, and Peace; this manifests especially on an inner, individual level.
- *Malton Northern Door*: Manifestation of desires into the physical plane of experience.
- *Wahanee Northern Door*: The Co-creation of Brotherhood and Sisterhood in families, groups, and on a larger scale in government, nations, and worldwide politics.
- *Shalahah Northern Door*: The Co-creation and manifestation of abundance (as richness and complexity) especially regarding the development of active intelligence. It is claimed that this newfound intelligence taps into the chela's desires for healing and manifestation of prosperity (good fortune and success in all endeavors.)
- *Klehma Northern Door*: Co-creation towards the Ascension Process through spiritual purification. Purification can manifest through all

aspects of personal experience: physical, emotional, and mental. It is suggested that to cope with this process that the chela focus on the spiritual techniques taught in the I AM America Teachings: Write and Burn techniques, breathwork, removal of Subjective Energy Bodies (the Closure Ceremony), meditation and prayer—especially the use of the Awakening Prayer and the Candle Meditation, use of Violet Flame decrees and meditation upon the Violet Fire, Cellular Awakening techniques, energy balancing, and Cup Ceremonies (especially powerful during the seasonal opening of Shamballa).

Gateway of Healing Formulas

Physical, emotional, and spiritual regeneration is said to accelerate in the Southern Doors of Golden City Vortices. The Ascended Masters claim that the Ray of the Golden City qualifies in the southern gateway especially for this purpose; hence, the following spiritual techniques are known as the *Gateway of Healing Formulas*. These techniques are claimed to alter vibration and instigate healing processes which may be physical, emotional, mental, or spiritual. The process may only include one of these aspects, or a combination of all of them. According to the Master Teachers, this first involves our perceptions, beliefs, and attitudes, which must first be adjusted in order to shift our viewpoint of the *dis-ease* process and into the experiential depth of healing.

- *Gobean Gateway of Healing*: Best for understanding the Science of Self, and needed shifts in self-perception to experience transformation, harmony, and inner peace. This often involves the process of Vibrational Shifting, and an opening towards the Fourth Dimension.
- *Malton Gateway of Healing*: This energy is said to help those who work in the professional healing fields, as it is said to rapidly restore and physically rejuvenate. This is an energy best suited for the *unhealed healer*, since Malton's energies can quickly balance and align auric light-fields. Because of their ability to quickly manifest, heal, and balance light energy fields, the southern doors of Malton are claimed to quickly assist the problems of the unhealed healer. Please remember, no one is perfect! Healers need time for self-reflection and honesty

to release and purify to avoid projection of their personal issues and emotional wounds.

- *Wahanee Gateway of Healing*: The healing energies of the southern door of Wahanee are alchemical in nature, and it is claimed this is the best location to use physical supplements, elixirs, and medicines for healing. The Akashic records of the Wahanee southern door are alleged to contain the healing medicine and cures of ancient times, so be prepared to meditate when you enter its healing energies.
- *Shalahah Gateway of Healing*: The vibrational shifting of Malton prepares the chela to enter the soothing, yet calm processes of at-one-ment in Shalahah. This is the birth of the Christ Consciousness (the Master Healer) which integrates acceptance and surrender to the Divine Will. The Master Teachers allege that the Shalahah southern door is the ideal location for integrated healers to physically renew their bodies and rejuvenate mentally and spiritually. The energies of the Shalahah gateway re-charge the healer, and assist the healing of the soul. It is claimed that the healing energies are so intense in this area that traumatic past life injuries are easily recalled, transformed, and healed. This is also known as instant-healing-manifestation.
- *Klehma Gateway of Healing*: The southern door of Klehma is considered the capstone of the five gateways within the United States Golden Cities, and purification manifests the inner Divine Being. This process is both metaphysical and hermetic. Serapis Bey oversees the process as an expression of the macrocosm and microcosm: "From within, so without." This initiates the spark of perfection and divinity within the Eight-sided Cell to witness and experience the great mystery of life. Healing is not only accepted and self-realized, and the soul opens to the allegorical Eye of Providence and is initiated into the Ninth and Tenth Pyramids of Adeptship and Mastery. [See *Divine Destiny*.] This Great Mystery is embedded with the spiritual principles of honor, cooperation, and purification which manifest as Divine Protection, Divine Intervention, and Divine Guidance. These are also known as the *Three Refuges* which comprise the Unfed Flame, and are integrated through the Tenth Jurisdiction, Faith. [Editor's Note: For more information on the *Twelve Jurisdictions*, see *New World Wisdom, Book One*.]

The Unhealed Healer

In order to help or assist others upon the path of healing, the healer must have already found within himself the wellspring of healing energy and power, and integrated this experience in all worlds: mental, emotional, and physical. However, many healers are unhealed themselves, and while they may inspire many upon the path to self-healing, they have yet to self-actualize the healing forces that they share with others. This ambiguous and somewhat contrary predicament is metaphysically referred to as the *unhealed healer*. No doubt, there are many different levels and types of healers for every diverse stage of consciousness—some healers are quite advanced and esoteric, while others deal with simplistic disease issues. It is important that a healer has indeed healed himself first, before assisting others with similar issues. The problem is that until one has healed the vital issues—emotionally, mentally, and physically—surrounding the disease they purport to know, the unhealed healer activates and is eluded by ego. Ozodi Osuji, Phd.—a synthesizer of Western, Asian, and African philosophies writes about the dangerous ego of the unhealed healer:

> "An unhealed healer cannot heal other persons; he must first heal himself before he can help other persons to heal themselves (the atonement is first for one before one shares it); each human being is responsible for healing himself (for each human being sentenced himself to the hell or world of separation we live in); he cannot directly heal other person(s) but when one is healed he can help those who want to heal themselves do so.
>
> To the contrary, an unhealed person sees himself as a victim of circumstances; he sees himself tossed around by events that he believes he has no hand in making.
>
> One is saved, healed, redeemed and delivered from the ego when one accepts that one made one's ego up and takes responsibility for what one's ego does. The healed healer, having taken responsibility for constructing his ego, lets go of it and does not blame other persons for what his ego delivered to him." [7]

Spirit Guides

A spiritual ancestor or teacher who gives individual guidance and teaching at critical junctures for spiritual growth and evolution. According to the Master Teachers, it is most important to first forge and develop a relationship with the I AM Presence, and from there develop, if necessary, an ancillary relationship with a spirit guide. The spirit guide may be ascended or unascended, and most always has a close relationship with the individual, which was likely fostered in previous lifetimes through the "bonds of love" as a former parent, grandparent, aunt, uncle, brother, or sister. Spirit guides rarely stay with a person for an entire lifetime, and often appear at times of stress or challenge and guide the person for periods as short as six months or as long as five years. According to the Master Teachers, there are some rare instances that the spirit guide directs and assists an individual for as long as fifty years—as long as there is cooperation and harmony with the I AM Presence. The spirit guide often prepares an individual to meet a Master Teacher.

The Mighty Witness

An aspect of the soul, which has seen, heard, and experienced firsthand all of the events, incidents, and encounters involved throughout numerous lifetimes, and this includes the timeframe that is said to exist in-between lifetimes.

Master Teacher

An ascended or unascended spiritual teacher who purposefully and intentionally chooses a student to mentor with their particular teachings, practices, and techniques. A Master Teacher differs from a spiritual practitioner in that they have close, personal experience with the various disciplines and spiritual practices that they teach and share. A Master Teacher has also received the vital energies of spiritual initiation directly from his guru, and can readily identify the *lineage of gurus* associated with the teaching, the authentic source of the knowledge. Because of this relationship, a Master Teacher will also personally know and have intimate knowledge of his or her own guru—Master Teacher.

An Ascended Master often works to relay their spiritual teachings through automatic writing, telepathic rapport, clairaudient, or full-body trance channeling, often a form of mediumship. Master Teachers have the ability to contact their students through the Astral Plane and often appear in visions and dreams. Ascended Masters, however, lower their energies from the Fifth Dimension (a Causal Plane of perfected mental thoughts) to the upper levels of the Fourth Dimension (the planes of beauty and Astral Light). The chela is encouraged to raise their energy and vibration to meet the Master Teacher. This is often referred to as "energy-for-energy."

It is claimed that once a chela has garnered a certain amount of Causal and Astral light through the I AM Presence, the appearance of a Master Teacher will not be denied. Saint Germain explains, "The student does not choose the Master Teacher, the Master Teacher chooses the student."

Holy Spirit

An individual manifestation of the light and spiritual energy of the I AM Presence. Collectively, this same energy is known as the "Holy Comforter." The Holy Spirit is also known as the Higher Self.

Holy Christ Self

Another name that identifies the presence of the I AM, or the great ambassador to the Oversoul. Esoteric teachings refer to the Christ Self as the higher, refined Astral Body.

1. Serrano, Ricardo. "Physical Death and Spiritual Liberation through Soul Realization." Accessed July 02, 2016. http://www.qigonghealer.com/soul.html.
2. "Jurisdiction." Wikipedia. Accessed July 02, 2016. https://en.wikipedia.org/wiki/Jurisdiction.
3. "Sacrifice." Wikipedia. Accessed July 02, 2016. https://en.wikipedia.org/wiki/Sacrifice.
4. Campbell, Joseph, and Bill D. Moyers. "Sacrifice and Bliss." In The Power of Myth. New York: Doubleday, 1988.
5. "To Plunge into the Ocean of Bliss." http://www.boldsky.com/yoga-spirituality/spiritual-masters/sri-ramakrishna/eternal-bliss-swami-vivekananda-160609.html.
6. "A Common Belief System Founded in 1844." 1844-Founding. Accessed July 02, 2016. http://www.oversoul1844.org/1844-Founding.html.
7. Osuji, Ozodi. "Can An Unhealed Healer Heal Igbos Tendency to See Themselves as Victims?" http://chatafrik.com/articles/us-affairs/can-an-unhealed-healer-heal-igbos-tendency-to-see-themselves-as-victims#.V3fzv6JCZII.

2

The Next Level
Saint Germain

Greetings, Dear chelas, in that mighty Violet Ray, I AM Saint Germain and I stream forth on that mighty Violet Ray of Mercy, Transmutation, Transformation, and ultimate Forgiveness. As usual, Dear chelas of my heart, I ask permission to come forward.

Response: *Please, Saint Germain, come forward.*

There is indeed much more work for us to accomplish together and this discourse will focus upon the work at hand. You see, Dear ones, there are many shifts that are now occurring within the dimensions of the Earth Plane itself. There have been many who have been worried about the alignment of the planets. Do we need to take a break?

(The telephone rings.)

Answer: *I don't know. Please hold.* (Pause) *Please continue.*

Little interruptions within the work at hand happen quite often among humanity. A focus comes forward within a moment and all is ready, all is prepared to bring it forward, and then come the little interruptions. These little interruptions are of the ego . . . interruptions of anger . . . interruptions of jealousy . . . interruptions of ultimate fear. And what do they interrupt but the flow of ultimate love that all is contained within. Dear ones, Dear hearts, let us not worry about the interruptions as they occur upon the Earth Plane and Planet but instead, let us focus on that work at hand. With that work at hand comes that most refreshing drink. There, the Cup is filled ever-present with the omni-essence of the Divine God source. When we keep upon that flow and keep upon the work, do we not always feel reinvigorated? Do we not feel always that great immortality of the Divine Self? So let us now proceed.

Yes, many have asked, "What about the alignment of the planets? What about this great shifting and rifting of the dimensions?" You see, Dear ones, the planets are servants of that Great Central Sun, arcing their Ray Forces forward to the Earth and indeed to other planets to bring forth a subsequent evolution of all life force and lifestreams. Dear ones, Dear hearts, many are worried about these dimensional shifts and yet, I say in the same way that many were concerned over mechanical failures at the year 2000. It is important to not worry about the dimensional shifts when the Rays bring forth their grandest service.

The dimensional shift that is about to occur within the hearts of men is indeed one that will bring forward that great choosing. And now we shall say: "How can choice exist when all is predetermined through this force of the Rays?" But I say unto you, there is indeed an element of choice. It is an element of perception within itself. It is indeed an element of attitude. It is that emotional coloring, shall we say, of the lesson that is learned.

When one is given that grand opportunity for the greatest of all lessons, they can always have their own attitude or perception of that lesson. Now, this great shifting will of course bring upheavals in the social and economic states. It may also bring forth several Earth Changes, but among the highest benefit that this shifting brings, is an opportunity to face the Inner Self, to unite with the true self and bring forth the Divine Purpose in the greatest cooperation and in complete and absolute harmony.

This great alignment has been brought forth in other times on the Earth Plane and Planet. It is an opportunity to shift and move the self towards the path of Ascension. It is an opportunity to detach more from the elements of illusion and bring forth true understanding. Yet, there will be those among humanity who see it as an opportunity to present the element of fear. But I say unto you, Dear ones, Dear hearts of mine, use it as an opportunity to love more; use it as an opportunity to understand at a greater level. In the great depths of the soul comes this understanding that all is presented, shall we say, for greater learning, greater contemplation, and to relinquish the ego state. Dear ones, Dear hearts, use this time to bring forth a greater integration of the soul, to move the soul forward, and understand the completion of a cycle.

In this great rifting that is about to occur, there will be many dreams of past lives that have been upon the Earth Plane and Planet. These past lives are being presented so that the soul may grow in its own eternal memory of itself and have the opportunity to come to the true foot of God. Now, when I say this, it is to begin to understand the true self uniting through the I AM Presence and into the consciousness of Unana, that of unity consciousness. These past-life dreams will bring up memories of traumas . . . memories of unfulfilled expectations . . . memories of unfulfilled desires. Transmute them immediately in this dimensional shift by calling forth the Alchemical knowledge of the Violet Flame. It is only in the soothing arms of the Violet Flame that then the soul will be able to view these circumstances and situations of the past with complete detachment.

Now, there are those who may view these past lives and then re-enact these same circumstance within their life; indeed this planetary alignment will bring such action. You see, Dear ones, Dear hearts, when such an alignment occurs, the energy affects the Kundalini at accelerated states and, therefore, the light and sound grid that composes the whole Human Aura. This light and sound grid also creates the many light bodies that you have brought into this lifetime for this, shall we say, individualized experience.

The memory is all contained, is omnipresent, as I have stated before, yet this memory is imperfect in the individualized experience. Now with such an alignment of the Ray Forces affecting the Kundalini, affecting each of the chakras, and ultimately affecting the human body through the spectrum of the light bodies, there are those who will begin to re-enact situations from the past. There will be many who will appear, shall we say, during this alignment, in each and every person's life; new faces, new experiences, each of these, a result of actions from a prior lifetime.

Now again, it is perception, how we perceive, act, and move, is it not? It is important to take a perception of detachment using the Violet Flame and from that deep wellspring within, reflect upon the current actions and activities, so it is understood completely within itself and no more action is then required. What I am speaking of is a complete detachment from action within itself, to view yourself only from the state of the Ever Present Soul who is now upon the path of liberation.

Liberation within itself is indeed a new path, is it not? When one decides to free themselves from the wheel of birth, death, rebirth, death, it is most important to understand first, the immortality of the soul, the immortality of consciousness. Now let us not focus too much upon the physical body, for when that is done, it brings about another harrowing escape from maya, or illusion. Let us focus upon the true essence of who you really are, the true energy of who you really are, the divinity, the God-ship, the true HU-man that you really are. Let us not get off into, as I have said before, side-line jeers and noise. Let us focus on who you are . . . the actions that you take. These actions, the result of other actions, thus lies the Law of Karma within itself.

Let us now focus upon the purpose of who and what you are. Let us focus on the forward movement and that healing release of the past. Now, when I speak of release of the past, I do not say, let us forget the past, but let us remember the past from that sense of detachment. You will remember in this alignment such embodiments that you had within the Animal Kingdom; such embodiments that you had even the first time you were born; when you took that first breath; when you were first held at your mother's breast. This is a grand opportunity for those who wish to go there, for those who wish to face the death of the soul. It is not for the faint at heart, for along with the memory comes also the emotional imprinting. That is why I have given you the doctrine and the continued education, or shall I say, better than doctrine, that mighty law in action, the Violet Flame.

The Violet Flame has been brought forth to allow all emotional imprinting to come, shall we say, to a balanced state. When the soul is able to view such experience with complete and total detachment, they are then ready to pursue the path of complete liberation. But you see, when the past is viewed with emotional attachment . . . with that feeling that one must get even . . . that one must fulfill another desire . . . that one must meet up again with that set of circumstances and situations, you see the soul is not ready yet for liberation. But kindly and gently, the Violet Flame leads the soul on its way.

Know this, Dear ones, Dear hearts, even if your liberation is not obtained in this embodiment, know that through the use of the Violet Flame that in your next embodiment, you will be firmly placed upon the path. All is based upon this inevitable Law of Attraction, for you see, as I have said so many times before, "things do not happen to a person and yet they happen with."

In this grand alignment that now comes about, one will see the many tragedies and pitfalls upon the Earth Plane and Planet. Yes indeed, that is one perception, is it not? And then one can see beyond and taking a new perception, a new attitude, a new lens to view each circumstance and situation through, will see the great reward and each lesson that the soul has learned step-by-step to lead it now to this point.

There is the perception that all things happen through random acts, but indeed do we not now know better? Through karma, we all understand that all actions are seeking their right cause; all actions are seeking, shall we say, a proper balance. Many scientists upon the Earth Plane and Planet understand this same mighty law and one way to sum this up is to understand the laws of gravitational pull. As an apple falls from a tree and touches the ground, in the force of its fall, even that, Dear ones, Dear hearts, is based upon that mighty Law of Attraction. All things are pulled to their own vibration; all things meet that which is indeed their equal. Now, there are those in the viewing of such situations, in this grand alignment of Ray Forces, who shall say, "This was done to me. I did not attract this. It was given to me." But know this: it was indeed given to you as a great test of who and what you are, who and what you are ready for, and what you now are ready to walk through.

Each test is given, shall we say, Dear ones, Dear hearts, as an open door for you to walk through, a new experience for you to cleanly, clearly wash your hands from. Now, when I say to wash your hands from, what does this clearly mean? To detach yourself from that prior experience so that you may move on to the next level of vibration; for you to say, "This experience now I bless. I have learned much from it and now I move on to my next set of experiences." But those who enter the next set of experiences without clean hands, are not yet ready then to obtain the full benefit of the next vibratory level. This is the use of the Violet Flame. It brings forth that great purification of the self. It brings forth the Alchemizing waters, where all transgressions that are held within the soul, transgressions of missed perception, shall I say, are then understood in the grandest of all laws, that of love. For indeed, Dear ones, you have been brought here by a force greater than yourself but it is indeed a force that dwells within you and when properly nourished and focused upon, will begin to emit its own grand Rays of light and sound.

This is indeed a wonderful opportunity. It is important not to focus upon a date but to focus upon the energies. Focus upon the experiences, for there indeed is the true seamless garment, the garment of experience that each and every one of you wears. Questions?

Question: *This alignment that you are referring to, is this an alignment of our axis or is it an alignment of our solar system?*

It is all, Dear one. It is an alignment within the solar system itself . . . it is an alignment that is astronomical . . . it is an alignment that is astral-logical . . . it is an alignment of the Ray Forces as they bring forth their grand interplay of light and sound . . . it is an alignment of the axis of the Earth itself . . . it is an alignment of your axis individually. It brings forth an alignment for the greater plan of humanity, to bring it forward in its own evolutions.

Question: *These astronomical bodies are so very large, they're aligned the moment that we are speaking, is this not so?*

This is so, Dear ones. That is why I say, focus not upon the date but focus indeed upon the energy. All have felt with the last lunar eclipse, a shifting of the dimensional forces. This was indeed the beginning, the advent, shall we say, of the interplay of the Rays of the Great Central Sun. Now this is an opportunity, it is an open door that humanity may walk through.

Question: *Are you saying that those that are ready can actually make the Ascension during this time?*

Now, let me not mislead you. Of course there will be those few who are now readied and will make that dimensional leap, but there will be those who will now move further upon the path and the greater plan. There will be those who will be now placed upon that path of liberation. But let us celebrate, for indeed, is it not wonderful to be handed the keys of complete and total liberation? As we have said before, there are always those who want to improve the food and the water within the prison, but it is rare indeed when the keys to complete and total freedom are given. This is an opportunity to accelerate along the path of liberation, to release, as I have said, with complete and total purification, the past and move forward to greet God. Now, when I say God, I speak of that mighty Source or Law of Love. More questions?

Question: *Yes, this is very interesting. Are you complete in your discourse on this dimensional shift?*

Yes, Dear one, proceed.

Question: *And do I have permission to ask personal questions for a friend?*

Proceed.

Question: *Can we go to Egyptian history? Is there any undiscovered royal tomb still existing in the country of Egypt or within the Egyptian empire as we speak?*

Of course, as all things are vibrational in nature, there are many discoveries waiting for humanity. We spoke at one time of the melting of the Northern slope of the Yukon and Alaska of the United States. There is contained another such civilization which will be understood when the right vibration and right time has come. Not only are there tombs of royalty, but tombs, shall we say, of a civilization within itself, the remnants of technologies that humanity is not ready or fit to understand. Technology was not then in the way that you would understand mechanical science today, but technology as it existed in evolution, technology that existed among the entire civilization, in terms of vibration and spiritual at-one-ment. The timing and intent, in terms of discovery, will only come about when the mass vibration of the Earth is ready to accept its full gift. You see, Dear ones, have you not noticed that when you listen to a discourse, after some time, that you hear it with a new set of ears, that you see experience with a new set of eyes?

Response: *This is very true.*

This is the same of all discovery upon the Earth Plane and Planet. Indeed there were civilizations that existed prior to the existence of this civilization and they were indeed grander in terms of evolution. They were descending, shall we say, from a point of higher vibration to, as you understand, this time of Kali Yuga. In the Ascension phase of the history of the Earth, which comes under that grand direction of the interplay of the Rays, a time shall come when vibration will seek like vibration and it should be understood at that time to the fullest of the vibration that is available. Do you understand?

Response: *I understand what you are saying about readiness and evolution.*

As I have always stated before, when the student is ready, the Master appears.

Question: *So you are saying that, in reference to my question, for undiscovered royal tombs still existing within the former empire of Egypt, that there are indeed those, but there are also other civilizations which you are saying were more advanced and you are giving that location in the Northern part of what is now Alaska?*

This is so, Dear ones. However, as you have understood, at the end of each epoch or mini-epoch, as a best way to understand the concept, comes about a changing of the guard. A new wave of collective souls enters and very often, in order for the new vibration to succeed within its Master Plan upon the Earth Plane and Planet, Earth Changes, or shall we say, catastrophic changes, then occur at some level. Sometimes these changes occur through nuclear destructions . . . through wars . . . through great famines . . . social and economic upheaval . . . grand epidemics. These are all planned with the timing and intent to bring forth a purification nature to the schoolroom so the new vibration then is fit to handle the work at hand.

Question: *I see. So even though it's never discussed, there was a war in Atlantis. Is this not so?*

Indeed there was. This, several of your historians have documented; however, as you look into the past from a vibration which is lower than what you are looking into, it is more difficult to understand the circumstances and the situation. Of course, it was not a war that existed from outside forces, it was a war among those who occupied the Earth Plane and Planet at that time among themselves. Do you understand?

Question: *So in a certain sense it was a civil war?*

A civil war, a disobedience, shall we say, to that mighty Law of Love; however, as you understand now, it was an absolute necessary step to bring about a clearing, so to speak, a purification of the darkness that was ensuing upon the Earth.

Question: *With regard to Egypt, the seeds of the Egyptian culture, where did they come from?*

That, Dear ones, is difficult to pinpoint. The culture, at one point in time, was primarily Atlantean but invasions of Nordic tribes and also invasions from other planetary systems also helped to bring the creation about. As you see, even with the United States itself, it is an ever-evolving melting pot and each great civilization becomes a melting pot of all cultures. This is that mighty Law of Brotherhood and Sisterhood, which mirrors the Law of Love in action. When there is a secular division brought about within a society, when there is intolerance towards those of different faiths . . . intolerance of those of different race . . . intolerance towards one sexual identity, that is when the consciousness falls, that is when the consciousness cannot be held towards bringing that society, that civilization, to a greater understanding and demonstration of that mighty Law of Love in action.

It is through the type of consciousness we have spoken of before, known as Unana, that brings the higher vibratory level. This too has been accomplished upon the Earth Plane and Planet, even in times of great, great darkness. When the focus is placed upon that mighty Law of Love in action, which is known as Unana, great miracles and leaps in consciousness can then occur. But when the focus of the consciousness is placed upon separation or, shall we say, secular action, it is almost impossible. Questions?

Question: *I understand. Also in regard to Egyptian history, the king who was known as the boy king, King Tutankhamen, was he murdered during his reign?*

Now, again let us explore the laws in action. Have we not learned in totality about like vibration? Have we not learned in totality that things do not happen to, but happen with? The question would be murder or would the question be karma? Would the question be action to vibration?

Question: *I understand what you are saying. Was there someone who was responsible for the fulfillment of that karma for that king's end of reign?*

During that time, many of the original laws of the first and second civilizations of Egypt had been lost and there had become a political warring, so to speak, among the people. This can be completely understood by looking at your own political systems and even the political systems that existed prior to the formation of the United States and the monarchies of England. This was all brought forward for a greater understanding and evolution. However, as it so often is, lessons are never learned.

Question: *I see. So there was political upheaval within the government?*

This is so.

Response: *Yes, so what you're saying is that it was a larger conspiracy than just one individual that was responsible.*

There is always conspiracy when true harmony and transformation is not present.

Response: *I see what you're saying; so we don't know exactly who carried out such an action.*

Proceed.

Question: *Yes, another question I have is really of a more personal nature and it deals with a friend and his wife, who would like to know an appropriate place for them to relocate from Houston?*

Are these two Ascended Master chelas?

Response: *Not at this point.*

Then it is important that they learn and begin with the Twelve Jurisdictions, so they may bring their focus into a proper alignment.

Response: *I see.*

Begin first, Dear ones, with this work and then a greater understanding will be brought forward. As you see, Dear ones, it is not ever the work of the Master Teacher to tell a student or chela what to do; however, the Master Teacher is always present to engender, help, and assist that mighty flame within the heart to continue in its growth and evolution. Focus upon the twelve spiritual laws and these answers will come from the heart within.

Question: *I see. Are you saying in that focusing, that assistance will come to them with their decision-making process?*

See for yourself, Dear chela of mine. Has it not brought forth assistance to you?

Response: *In all honesty, at all times it has, yes.*

This is that mighty law in action. Vibration seeks its own level. Vibration understands its own level.

Response: *I do see what you are saying. I think they were probably looking for a more tangible decision-making process but I understand what you are saying. You cannot interfere but you can only bring them to the law that empowers them to their own choice.*

This is so, Dear one, Dear heart, and yet these teachings are brought to bring eternal freedom. These teachings are brought to bring choice and cause, action within itself and alignment to that mighty Will. Now, there are those who will choose not to bring their will to an alignment, at least in this embodiment, but there are those, if properly prepared, who will begin to understand.

It is important to always go within. It is important to always listen to the longing and the urging of the heart. But for those who seek to bring their will into a greater alignment, study first the Twelve Jurisdictions and this will open again another door. This again, will open a new understanding of vibration.

Question: *Are there any areas in Texas which will remain safer than others that you could possibly recommend during the Time of Changes?*

Texas too will be affected by great floods and also great fires, fires brought about through the burning of oil floating upon water. There is also a problem with the water source itself in many of the towns that are near sea level or 500 feet above such elevation. However, again, the Golden City Vortices have been brought forward as that great Divine Intervention, to bring the chela or the student into greater understanding of the Divine Will in action. They are brought forward to bring, shall we say, that most refreshing drink, an understanding of that mighty Law of Love in action and an understanding of complete and total purification. Proceed.

Question: *I see. So, it is really only the Golden City Vortices that you can vouch for as being stable enough in these Times of Changes?*

Of course, safety is always a matter of the heart and if one feels directed to live in an area outside of a Golden City, they must go for who-knows-what experiences, then await them for their own awakening process.

Response: *I understand what you're saying.*

The Golden Cities have been brought forward to bring a level of spiritual initiation to the soul and ready it for the path of liberation; however, each case is always so individualized.

Response: *I understand completely what you're saying. That inner search is the greatest of all searches and with that, the external search is made very simple.*

To interfere with that process would impede the growth of the soul. Listen always to the heart, Dear ones, for there, all answers are complete.

Response: *That is truly the test, listening to the heart. I've noted that in my own self, for there was no one externally saying to me to help or to do what I'm doing, but only the internal urgings.*

Take my hand, Dear chela, and walk with me for a minute. Let us reflect for one moment upon the grand inner garden. Come and sit with me. In this inner garden, do we not hear the perfection of All That Is . . . soft birds singing . . . a waterfall within the background . . . sweet scents drift in the air? In this state of contemplation and complete reflection, the heart comes into balance, does it not?

Answer: *Yes it does. This is very true.*

All longing and desire within itself becomes satisfied, does it not?

Answer: *Yes it does.*

Remind your Dear friend of this experience, so peace may be found.

Response: *I will, as you have instructed.*

Proceed.

Question: *Many times we have wonders and questions about the world and sometimes I think that keeps us very trapped in the ongoing intrigues here. Could you comment on that?*

As I have always stated, there are those out upon that field, playing the game. Playing, shall we say, is working towards that goal of seeking their own victory in the light of Ascension, seeking their own victory in liberation in the dual form. Then there are those who stand out in the crowd. They are not participants; they are not playing that game. They do not feel the sweat on their brow; they do not feel the ball in their hand; they do not feel the pain when they are fallen or the victory when they achieve the goal. Instead, they stand by and are not participants. But yet, they cheer when the goal is achieved and pass their judgment with each fall. But they do not participate. They do not understand what it is like to seek that freedom. They stand by, watching in awe and wonderment of the achievements of that one who has the talent, who has the ability. They stand by, hoping and wishing that if only they could hold the ball within their hand, if only they could become that participant.

Dear ones, Dear hearts, do not become distracted by the crowd. Instead, invite them to come upon the playing field. Invite them to come and put the ball within their hand. Invite them to join, shall we say, in that game of the dual force. Then, they too can feel for once that mighty victory. Yes indeed, they shall have pain and suffering but is it not worth that price? Proceed.

Answer: *It is worth that price. I will invite them all, hopefully through this transmission and transcription, to see this as an invitation to join on that path of freedom. At this moment, I have no further questions.*

Then I shall take my leave and will be back at the appointed time. Om Manaya Pitaya Hitaka.

Response: *Hitaka, thank you.*

I AM Saint Germain.

Study Guide for The Next Level

Topics:
Interruption
Alignment of Planets and Dimensional Shifting
The Great Rift
Immortality of Consciousness
Law of Attraction and Repulsion
Dimensional Leaping
Descending and Ascending Cultures
The Melting Pot
The Playing Fields

Satellitium—A Grouping of Planets

When three or more planets occupy the same astrological sign, based upon a sidereal zodiac, the Spiritual Teachers refer to this as an "alignment." The faster moving planets, i.e., the Moon, Venus, and Mercury, create this configuration more frequently, and this is often referred to as a *stellium*. A stellium creates a focus and concentration of energy, and will stir events according to condition and circumstance. When the slower moving planets, particularly Jupiter and Saturn, align or group as a satellitium, life on Earth is even more affected, and it is claimed that the potential for spiritual growth and development is nourished.

Saint Germain's Teachings on Planetary Alignments

1. The planets are servants of the Great Central Sun, and dispense the Rays to Earth through its solar eminence. The Rays determine life's evolution on Earth, and influence other planets in our Solar System.
2. Dimensional Shifts brought about by Planetary Alignments activate the individual's will and affect the types of choices made.
3. Dimensional Shifts always create change, either for good or bad in societies, affecting economies. During these periods the Earth is susceptible to Earth Changes.

Jupiter and Saturn Conjunctions

♐ 3/30/2019 to 4/24/2019	
11/5/2019 to 6/29/2020	
♑ 3/30/2020 to 6/29/2020	
11/21/2020 to 4/5/2021	
9/15/2021 to 11/21/2021	
10/6/2029 to 1/25/2030	Saturn in ♈ Jupiter in ♎ Seventh House Aspect
12/27/2028 to 3/30/2029	
9/23/2030 to 2/18/2031	Saturn in ♉ Jupiter in ♏ Seventh House Aspect
6/15/2031 to 10/16/2031	
8/14/2032 to 10/24/2032	Saturn in ♊ Jupiter in ♐ Seventh House Aspect
♌ 10/8/2038 to 10/22/2038	
6/2/2039 to 7/13/2039	
♍ 11/5/2039 to 5/1/2040	
6/30/2040 to 12/4/2040	

FIGURE 1-B
Sidereal Conjunctions of Jupiter and Saturn to 2040

4. Planetary alignments bring Dimensional Shifts which help individuals to empower the I AM and unite with the wisdom and truth of the inner self. This integration brings harmony and a sense of cooperation (or peace) to individuals.
5. Inevitably, during these Times of Change, planetary alignments assist the Ascension Process through showing the individual what is truth and what is illusion. This helps one to experience detachment.
6. During alignment periods, the shifting between dimensions may be so intense that people can easily experience fear. Saint Germain claims the best way to thwart fear is to "Love more." This deep source of love, through contemplation, allows one to relinquish the ego and the soul to move forward in integration and growth.
7. Alignments help to create spiritual detachment which in turn can open the soul's memories of past lives. This wellspring of memory,

similar to what is found when one enters the Akashic Records, opens a plethora of information for the individual. This prepares the consciousness for what Saint Germain calls "facing the death of the soul."

8. Facing the "death of the soul" is far from death! Indeed, it is the death of the soul from the Earthly, karmic painful experiences in limitation of the Earth Plane. The soul is now initiated, through complete knowledge of itself, to gain entry into the dimensions and experiences beyond the physical plane entrance into the Ascension Process.

Dark Rift

A series of overlapping, nonluminous molecular dust clouds that dims our view from Earth of the Galactic Center, also known in Ascended Master Teaching as the Great Central Sun. The Dark Rift comprises both plasma and dust and, when viewed without a telescope, it appears as a dark lane that is flanked by the stars. This creates the illusion that our Milky Way is divided into two equal portions, above and below. Some Mayan scholars theorized that this Dark Rift aligned with our Solar Sun on December 21, 2012. Others contend that this alignment has occurred for many years since 1970 and will continue until 2110. This obvious darkening of the Ray Forces to Earth is a partial theory for the cause of many global changes, primarily the possibility for catastrophic Earth Changes. From this viewpoint, the Dark Rift instigates the shadow side of the Rays to manifest, which, according to the Master Teachers, waxes and wanes in potential and strength. [1,2]

Saint Germain's Teachings on the Great Rift

1. During phases of dimensional rifting (the process of the individual absorbing evolutionary Ray Forces from the Great Central Sun) the dream state opens the experiences of past lives to many individuals.
2. The experiences focus upon past traumas, unfulfilled desires, and painful unfulfilled expectations. This causes these experiences to emerge to conscious awareness for personal transmutation through the Violet Flame.
3. Sometimes the individual will re-enact the same circumstances and situations from the past life into this lifetime.

4. The Kundalini System (Chakra System) is also affected during times of rifting. This light and sound grid actually magnetizes to us many people whom we have known in past lives, all the result of past action.
5. "Rifting" allows one to complete and liberate from karmas, initiating the liberation process of the soul, known as Ascension.

Ever Present Soul

The soul who has purposefully and intentionally embarked upon the path of liberation and the attainment of Ascension. This embraces not only physical immortality but the immortality of the soul through the deathless stream of consciousness. The Ever Present Soul is analogous to the "witness."

Immortality of Consciousness

When the soul embarks on the journey of Ascension, it must first accept its birthless, deathless origin. The Ascended Masters refer to this as the "immortality of consciousness."

Saint Germain's Insights on Use of the Violet Flame for Spiritual Liberation

1. The Violet Flame balances the emotional imprinting and scarring that imprints upon the soul and is carried lifetime after lifetime.
2. Once balanced, the soul develops the necessary states of emotional detachment. This calms the creation of karmic desires and calmly yet gently prepares the soul for another level of spiritual development.
3. Use of the Violet Flame is carried from one lifetime to the next. Saint Germain assures his students that if the Ascension is not obtained in this lifetime, that the Violet Flame will place the chela "firmly on the path" of spiritual liberation in the following lifetime. He further claims that this process is calibrated by the Law of Attraction.

Law of Attraction

Based upon Hermetic Law, when an Ascended Master refers to the Law of Attraction, he or she is also referring to the Law of Repulsion and the Hermetic Law of Mentalism and the Law of Vibration.

This physical and spiritual truth serves as the foundation of the Law of Duality—the Yin and the Yang. In simple terms, like charges repel and unlike charges attract: the Law of Polarity. Under these circumstances, everything in nature follows one of two opposite paths, each with its own essence. Life exists on a spectrum, one that offers an infinite number of possibilities between its opposite ends: darkness is less light; fear is less courage. Of course, this notion applies to the intricacies of daily life when humans are faced with innumerable viewpoints or solutions to a problem. Indeed, opposites exist within each other.

Based upon the Law of Cause and Effect, the Master Teachers enjoin our karmic pasts and co-creative choice as the Creator of all circumstances and situations we are presently experiencing. From this esoteric viewpoint, events rarely occur randomly or by chance or mistake. The Ascended Masters simply describe this universal principle: "Things do not happen *to*, they happen *with*."

Prophecies of Change

1. During times of planetary alignments, Earthly events become susceptible to accidents and unforeseen tragedy; however, through honing our spiritual perception, random acts may be the grace of karmic balance.
2. Humanity may endure many tests, especially personal karmic tests that inevitably open new doors for spiritual growth and integrate new spiritual vibrations.
3. With each new level of spiritual growth comes a new energetic, spiritual vibration. This time leads to self-purification, alchemy, and personal understanding of the Law of Love.
4. There will be many who are not spiritually ready to absorb the full benefit of the new spiritual energies on Earth. For those who are awakened, it is suggested that one stay focused on personal, spiritual experience.

FIGURE 2-B
The Rapture: One in the Field
An etching by Jan Luyken illustrating Matthew 24:40 in the Bowyer Bible, Bolton, England.

5. Focusing on our own spiritual experience restrains pensive thoughts regarding the future and focuses our spiritual consciousness upon the *Now*. This process is prophesied to nourish the new Rays of Light and Sound within, and these energies grow in strength and power.
6. The alignment of planets influences the axis of the Earth. This creates yet another opportunity for humanity's spiritual growth and evolution.
7. Astrological events have the capacity to create "open doors" or potential for humanity's spiritual growth and evolution. This causes many to enter the path of liberation—the Ascension Process. Ascended Masters often refer to these opportunities as a "dimensional leap."

Dimensional Leap: A dimensional leap is a term Ascended Masters use to refer to a large amount of humans realizing the HU-man (God Man) within, and therefore obtaining a new spiritual viewpoint. This new viewpoint is so sudden and extraordinary that the large group who travel to this new stage of spiritual growth seem to literally hurdle into a totally different dimension altogether. Many occultists claim that as Earth enters a new vibration, a certain amount of humanity's population will surprisingly obtain this new spiritual directive. This, of course, is prophesied to change Earth's cultures and societies as she enters the beginning stages of a Golden Age. Some esoteric students claim that humanity's mass entrance into the New Dimensions will permanently alter the human physical bodies (DNA and RNA), and some resonate at the fourth and fifth dimensions as their gross, corporeal bodies will appear and then disappear on the Earth Plane. This bears some semblance to the Christian Rapture that in biblical texts alleges certain persons will be "caught up" or taken away to the heavens in a sudden event. [3]

Prophecies for the New Times

1. Under Alaska's ice are remnants of a lost civilization and their technologies.
2. This information will be discovered and understood as the Earth and humanity rise in vibration and enter the New Times. The metaphysical underpinning for this discovery is based on the esoteric understanding of Descending and Ascending cycles.
3. As we enter the New Times, the beginning of the Golden Age, many new souls incarnate on Earth. This new wave of souls assists the Earth to change and rise in vibration; it is also prophesied that as Earth rises in vibration there may be simultaneous catastrophic Earth Changes.
4. The Great Purification of Earth may include: nuclear wars, famine, social and economic upheaval, and mass epidemics. Even though these events are catastrophic, these events have some positive aspects as they assist the Earth to change and rise in spiritual vibration.
5. The ancient epochs of Earth saw many civilizations suffer horrific wars (Atlantis) which, inevitably resulted in the clearing of Earth's darkness at that time.
6. Through Unana (Unity Consciousness), great leaps in consciousness are achieved, accompanied by many miracles.

Descending and Ascending Civilizations

Since Galactic Light controls life spans, an individual's memory function and capacity, our spiritual development, and humanity's overall propensity for spiritual evolution, inevitably this energy controls and guides the growth and expansion of humanity's civilizations. Conversely, Galactic Light also controls the demise of outdated civilizations and prepares the Earth to nourish and sustain the birth of yet another new culture of humanity. Our ability to recognize and understand past cultures is also driven by the availability of Galactic Light expressed through our current spiritual knowledge, philosophic viewpoints, current archaeology, sciences, and technology. Dr. David Frawley explains this phenomenon regarding the cycles of humanity: "A culture cannot apprehend the existence of any culture higher than itself in the cycle of world-ages." He describes Bronze Age cultures of ancient Egypt, Babylonia, and Assyria in spiritual proximity to "our Greek cultural matrix." And even though we know that other cultures likely existed before 12,000 BCE, we have few records or awareness of their histories. Frawley clarifies, "These we cannot find because we do not understand the level on which they existed."[4]

Remnants of these ancient cultures were likely wiped out by Earth Changes: earthquakes, devastating floods, and climate change that shifted the cultures to the current age of humanity we are now experiencing. Most occultists and esoteric historians agree that ancient worldwide cataclysms often synchronize with changes in the world cycles that were esoterically calibrated by light and sound frequencies impacting Earth from the Galactic Center. The influence of the past cultures of humanity, i.e. Atlantis, Lemuria, and Mu, were completely eliminated before a new cycle or civilization began. As light frequencies build throughout the current Golden Age, we will discover and recognize older civilizations of Earth because our spiritual intelligence can recognize and identify their existence.

We are currently living in an Ascending Cycle, that is, Galactic Light frequencies are building in intensity, power, and concentration alongside the development of Earth's 51 Golden Cities. This is a joint effort of Babajeran (our Earth Mother) and the Divine Beings of Earth through their stewardship of the Golden Cities (the Western Shamballa Tradition). It is prophesied that these benefic energies will reach their summit around the years 7699 to 12,499 CE. After that, light energies begin to decrease, and a Descending

Cycle will prevail. Cultures birthed in descending cycles strive to protect their traditions and spiritual heritage. Ascending cultures are constantly moving towards the light of truth that is yet to be defined or fully realized.

Melting Pot

According to the Ascended Masters, many of Earth's civilizations contained combinations of different cultures, including those from other planets. This esoteric evolutionary concept is known as the "melting pot," and its common spiritual denominator is known as the Law of Brotherhood and Sisterhood. Mirroring the Law of Love, the Master Teachers encourage tolerance in these facets of culture and society: religion, race, and sexual orientation. This form of tolerance is the activity of the Law of Love, a vital spiritual component to achieve Unana—Unity Consciousness.

Saint Germain's Suggestions on how to Study the
I AM America Teachings

These suggestions were made by Saint Germain to a questioner about how to familiarize and gain knowledge of the I AM America Material

1. If you are not yet a chela (student) it is important to first study the Twelve Jurisdictions. These twelve spiritual precepts will hone and prepare your consciousness to work with a Master Teacher.
2. A Master Teacher will never tell you "what" to do; however, the guru's ever-present energies will engender and assist the growth of the Unfed Flame's qualities of love, wisdom, and power within the heart.
3. Your focus upon these twelve spiritual virtues will help you receive answers from within. Saint Germain refers to this metaphysical law as the "Mighty Law in Action," as "Vibrations seek their own level. Vibration understands its own level."
4. Master Teachings are designed to engender freedom, choice, and knowledge of one's will.

Vibration

In common English, vibration comes from the word vibrate, which means to move, swing, or oscillate. In Ascended Master teaching, vibration is associated with light's movement in both physical and spiritual presence.

The Theosophical viewpoint of the Law of Vibration is that every particle of the universe communicates its distinct vibration upon all other particles; therefore everything vibrates and nothing rests. This includes thoughts, ideas, beliefs, and attitudes; this notion is the metaphysical foundation of the "Law of Attraction."

Earth Changes Prophecies
1. During the Time of Change, Texas will be affected by both floods and fires. Saint Germain also specifically prophesies that burning oil will float on water. This may affect the water sources of towns and cities near sea level up to 500 feet in elevation on the Texas coast. [Editor's Note: An example of this type of catastrophe is the Deepwater Horizon Oil Spill, more commonly known as the BP oil disaster, where 4.9 million barrels of oil were dumped into the Gulf of Mexico, following an explosion on a drilling rig.]
2. Golden City Vortices can help to ameliorate or change all prophecies of destruction and adjust the Great Purification by facilitating humanity's Spiritual Awakening.
3. While the Golden Cities instigate spiritual initiation and the path of liberation, Saint Germain reiterates that every person's spiritual growth and evolutionary process is unique and individualized.
4. Safety is a matter of the heart! During the Time of Change if you are spiritually directed to not live in a Golden City you must follow your guidance. Saint Germain reminds one, "Who knows what experiences await (your) awakening process!"
5. Always listen to your heart as these answers contain spiritual answers and solution for *you*.

FIGURE 3-B
Arjuna and His Charioteer Krishna Confronts Karna

The Playing Field

The Master Teachers encourage their chelas and students to fully embrace the Co-creative experience with the I AM Presence and compare this important spiritual process to a playground or "playing-field." This analogy encourages a spiritual practice that embraces courage, passion, and the focus to achieve one's personal goals. In order to cultivate and fully realize the I AM, Master Teachers remind their students to ignore the spectators (metaphor for the ego) and those bystanders who do not fully experience life as the one playing upon the field. The spiritual ideal of embracing the fullness and true purpose of life is mirrored in the Bhagavad Gita, and the playing field becomes the allegorical field of human action or human dharma (purpose).[5]

1. "Great Rift (astronomy)." Wikipedia. Accessed July 09, 2016. https://en.wikipedia.org/wiki/Great_Rift_(astronomy).
2. Jenkins, John Major. "What Is the Galactic Alignment?" Accessed July 09, 2016. http://alignment2012.com/whatisga.htm.
3. "Rapture." Wikipedia. Accessed July 09, 2016. https://en.wikipedia.org/wiki/Rapture.
4. Frawley, David. "Cycles of Humanity; Ascending and Descending Cycles." In Astrology of the Seers: A Guide to Vedic/Hindu Astrology, 59-62. Salt Lake City, UT: Passage Press, 1990.
5. House, Jeanne M. The Bhagavad Gita: A Primer. Accessed July 09, 2016. http://www.reversespins.com/gita.html.

Illustrations:
1. Betz, Martha, and Keith Betz. Laytonville, CA: Production Werks, 2001.
2. Rapture, One in the Field. Digital image. Wikipedia. N.p., 13 Aug. 2009. Web. 1 Aug. 2012. An etching by Jan Luyken illustrating Matthew 24:40 in the Bowyer Bible, Bolton, England.
3. Arjuna and His Charioteer Krishna Confront Karna. Digital image. Wikimedia. N.p., 9 Oct. 2009. Web. 1 Aug. 2012. Artist/maker unknown, India, Himachal Pradesh or Jammu and Kashmir. Circa 1820.

3

Golden Ray, Stream Forth!
Saint Germain

Greetings Beloved chelas, in that mighty Violet Flame, I AM Saint Germain and I stream forth on that mighty Violet Ray of Mercy, Compassion, Forgiveness, and Transmutation. Dear hearts, Dear ones, I request permission to come forth.

Response: *Please, Saint Germain, you are most welcome. Come forward.*

There is much work upon the Earth Plane and Planet. Yes, work not only of education . . . work not only of compassion . . . work not only of forgiveness . . . work not only of transmutation and transformation, but also that mighty work of building consciousness. For you see, Dear ones, Dear hearts, at this time in the history of the Earth, the great flood of consciousness is scheduled to come forward. This has been spoken of by beloved Brother Kuthumi as the Golden Ray. Of course, what we are speaking of is that power from the Great Central Sun itself arcing to your solar system. It is this Golden Ray that will bring forth a dawning of a new consciousness. It is this Golden Ray that will bring that great leap in consciousness, which will bring enhanced spiritual understanding, enhanced spiritual knowledge, and enhanced spiritual wealth.

You see, Dear ones, Dear hearts, it is this growth in consciousness that will bring the New Times, the Golden Age, a Golden Crystal Age, shall I say. That time, or consciousness within man itself, will grow to a level that it has not known for many thousands of years. You see, Dear hearts, you have been bound into the darkness of Kali Yuga and have not known, shall we say, the light of the Great Central Sun falling upon the true face of knowledge, your true consciousness for some time. It is through this work of the Golden Ray that this consciousness is then opened up, or shall we say, bursts forth, as when there is a paradigm shift, or as you call it "pushing the envelope." It is now time for us to open this consciousness, for you to become aware of it and bring about its total and complete enhancement.

This consciousness that comes forward will bring about many new changes in your technology. Not only will it bring forth new plans in laser technology, new plans in the computer industry, and new plans in the growth of medical knowledge, but it will also bring about the complete and total awareness of the environment. There will be many businesses and focuses within social and economic climates that will understand the great importance of the environment and the need for it to be impacted in a more perfect way with any type of technology.

The time that you have entered out of, which is the Industrial Age, was a time of great pollution of Mother Earth, beloved Babajeran. Of course, now through the new knowledge and information, it is important to understand that much of this pollution needs to be cleaned up to pave a pure pathway of consciousness for the Age of Information.

This Age of Information shall also be guided and directed by this Ray of Consciousness known as the Golden Ray. The Golden Ray brings a complete and total understanding of the true HU-man, the true human who is indeed divine. It is as simple as accepting the divinity within, is it not? So, Dear hearts, Dear ones, know that this Golden Ray comes forward for the benefit of all. It does not come forward just for the benefit of the spiritual elite. Indeed, it is meant for all and is about a complete and total understanding that will pave the way for the New Times.

The Golden Cities themselves are also affected by the Golden Ray. Of course, their activation has a timing and intention with each Ray Force that it represents within itself, but the Golden Ray itself plays a role in their activation at higher levels. A portal of cleansing karma opened at the last lunar eclipse and with the Golden Ray working alongside it, will lift you into a stream of new consciousness. It is most important that we work towards bringing this new stream of consciousness forward, so that all may understand and utilize the work of the Golden Ray.

> Mighty Golden Ray stream forth now
> into the heart of the consciousness of humanity.

> Mighty Golden Ray bring forth new understanding.
> Bring forth a new Spiritual Awakening.
> Bring forth complete and total divinity
> in the name of I AM THAT I AM.
> So be it.

It is through this work of the Golden Ray that even the Spiritual Hierarchy has been able to access, shall we say, deeper levels of consciousness and obtain greater points of contact. In this time of duality upon the Earth Plane and Planet, where darkness seems to produce an all-time low, as I have stated before, it is also the opportunity for light. This light may now come forward in full measure, so that the darkness is also understood.

Since you have read and understood the cycles of the Yugas, when you understand a descending culture, then you can also understand an ascending culture. What is this information all based upon but that of vibration, vibration within itself and how vibration serves not only for all past memory but all present and, subsequently, future experience. Vibration serves within the complete and total cycles the Laws of Harmony. As we have always stated before in the Hermetic Laws, it is within these cycles, as you have understood through beloved Kuan Yin, that perfect harmony is then absolute.

In this dual experience, as you see a great deal of darkness, is there not then also that opportunity for a great deal of light? The middle way has been brought forward to understand both of these teachings simultaneously. To live and to walk in balance is to accept the work of the Golden Ray. The Golden Ray brings a higher form of consciousness which understands why your past has been what it is. One may understand this simply as understanding the dark side. But perhaps, there are those who do not reach at all into the dark side that is part of them. Instead, it remains suppressed and therefore its expression is out-of-control.

Of course, the work of the Spiritual Hierarchy is always to bring the emotions into complete and total understanding but one cannot bring such into control until they have had the complete and total experience of them. So, that is why you, the soul in the sojourn of the physical body, have come here and put on the physical body . . . the emotional body . . . the astral body . . . the mental body. Each of these bodies brings their own service of the Rays forward and their own unique set of experiences. These experiences build one to the next, one on top of the other. These experiences then allow one to feel . . . allow one to take action . . . allow one to have complete and total experience.

But do we randomly create, randomly experience, have these actions, these feelings, these thoughts? No. Dear ones, Dear hearts, that is why you have been given the vehicle of choice, or the will. The chela who travels along the spiritual path then begins that spiritual tutelage of aligning that will to the Divine Will. In that greater alignment of that will comes the Golden Ray of Consciousness. This is most important, for the Golden Ray enters through the seventh chakra and runs along the Golden Thread Axis. It is most important to understand that the Golden Ray is in alignment to the Divine Will. It is that greater understanding that all experiences, good and bad, come together into a greater understanding, that of divinity.

All things work together for ONE, which is indeed, Unana or Unity Consciousness. Therefore, the Golden Ray is also identified with Unity Consciousness and those who call upon and use the Golden Ray will notice this affect immediately. They herald in a new consciousness even through the invocation of its presence. This great new consciousness allows for a greater acceptance and tolerance of one another. Brotherhood and Sisterhood reign supreme and you shall face that New Day cloaked in the glory of the Sun. Dear ones, Dear hearts, please consider this short lesson upon the Golden Ray. And now, I shall open the floor for your questions.

Question: *The Golden Ray is now making its appearance in our plane?*

This is so, Dear ones, Dear hearts. Its presence has been here from time immemorial; however, at times its pulsation, or shall we say, vibrational effect, is felt at greater levels. As you have been experiencing Kali Yuga, or a time of lesser light, it has been hard to identify and therefore utilize. But, Dear ones, Dear hearts, as I have explained in my last discourse on the opening of this time period, which is a portal for the cleansing of all past karma, as the Golden Ray comes forward, simultaneously, one faces the dark side of their soul. It is also in the dual expression that one finds the light side of eternity.

Question: *So, what you are saying is that no matter how much darkness is present, the Law of Balance will prevail?*

The Law of Balance is the Law Eternal.

Question: *I see. So, the Collective Consciousness, does it have only one heart?*

There is one consciousness and ideally one heart of consciousness; however, in the dual expression, there are many individuals with their individual expressions . . . their individual lives . . . their individual matrix of light and sound . . . which comprises a greater global matrix of light and sound. In the same way, in the physical body, there are cells that exist within the skin itself; however, upon the skin exist nails or hair, even different colors, freckles, moles. You see, Dear one, it is the same as understanding a microcosm within a macrocosm.

Question: *So all the souls present on this planet and in this plane are of one Collective Consciousness?*

There is one Collective Consciousness indeed and that Collective Consciousness is guided and led through the Laws of Vibration, so that a series of souls can attract a lesson unto themselves. Let me explain. You see, at this time upon the Earth Plane and Planet, those souls have attracted unto themselves those life experiences for the timing and intent of this present hour; but individually, there are many different paths of life, many different choices that have been made. There is, however, when one attunes to it, that greater alignment to that greater Divine Will and Divine Plan. That is the consciousness of Unana. That consciousness of Unana comes under the Jurisdiction of the Golden Ray.

Response: *So, now we are in this time period where the Golden Ray is expressing at a greater degree.*

It is so. Dear ones, Dear hearts. However, the proper preparation is the use of the Violet Ray of Mercy, Transmutation, and Forgiveness. This is how you can bring a greater alignment and preparation for the assimilation of this new Ray Force. As I have stated before, this Ray Force settles itself not only along the Golden Thread Axis but what you would know as the Kundalini current of the body. Therefore, it affects all cells of the body and performs, shall we say, a great acceleration. However, it is most difficult to feel until you can bring about that greater understanding of the Violet Ray.

> Mighty Violet Ray, come forth in all transmuting action.
> Mighty Violet Ray, come forth now and dissolve all discord
> and the cause and effect of all that is holding me
> from understanding and moving forward into the new Golden Age.
> I call this forth in the name of that mighty Christ I AM.
> So be it.

Response: *So be it.*

Call forth that mighty Violet Ray in action . . . call it forth within your voice . . . call it forth within your emotional body . . . call it forth within your mental body . . . call it forth in your daily action.

Question: *Does the Golden Ray affect those who are visiting our planet?*

The Golden Ray is brought forward at a vibrational level for those who are ready to receive its gift. You see, Dear ones, Dear hearts, those who are visiting the planet, some are of a higher vibration, some are of a lower vibration, so your question would be contingent then on those who are ready to receive.

Question: *I see. So when we refer to the alien influences that are not necessarily for the evolution of humanity, the Golden Ray will not affect them?*

Nor would there even be an awareness of it. In the same way, in your many lifetimes in the lesser light years of Kali Yuga, you were not even aware of that mighty Violet Ray in action. Mercy, Compassion, Forgiveness, and Transmutation were not any of the qualities that you carried forth in those embodiments. But subsequently, through application and Divine

Intervention, this Violet Ray has been brought forward. It can now be used to serve and assist humanity at this most wondrous time.

Question: *What about those who are being influenced by this alien force?*

They would not be affected at all by this mighty Golden Ray. You see, Dear ones, Dear hearts, it is brought forward for the evolution of humanity. Even though those of higher vibration would know of its influence, humanity within itself has its own scheme of evolution, which moves forward with its own Divine Timing and Intent.

Question: *Is this scheme of evolution also in the genetic code and structure of our physiology?*

It is not only carried within that genetic code but let us go one level deeper, to the choice of the soul. In the choice of the soul is engendered that Golden Thread Axis, which then aligns itself to a greater Plan Divine. The soul existed long before the physical body; however, it has been attracted not only through karma and purposes but is also attracted through mental activity and the thoughts that are held. These thoughts manifest themselves through choices. Choice manifests itself as a will, as a current of electricity that aligns itself then to a greater Plan Divine.

To understand this most simply, know that the soul itself has charted the course that it will now travel through in the world of duality, known as time. The soul moves forward in its sojourn in duality, putting on body after body, as one would change a set of clothes and yet at times, feels a discontent in some activities and a conclusion in others. But it is most important to understand that there is a plan that is moving forward and being fulfilled. Growth and evolution of this human soul is then achieved. This comes under a timing, a planning, and an intention. The Rays bring forth their service to bring this evolution and this essential schooling forward. So, understand, Dear ones, Dear hearts, that the Golden Ray then comes forward to bring this greater understanding and evolution. Questions?

Response: *I see. So the Golden Ray will really only affect a certain group of people on the planet.*

Again, it is at that level of vibration that it brings its affect. Understand it as simply, when you enter school as a young one, you understand only the rules of kindergarten. You understand how to make objects from clay; how to paint; how to draw; a time to rest; a time for a snack. These are the things, are they not, that are contained within a kindergarten schedule?

Response: *True.*

But as one proceeds through the grades, one moves upward and soon that schedule as a small or younger child is not suitable for the older child. Again vibration, shall we say, changes as the soul moves, grows, and learns. This of course is very simplistic and is only a model to grasp and to understand this concept. Questions?

Question: *Many. So in essence, the Golden Ray is a blessing coming forth to aid and assist the evolution of humanity?*

Indeed, it brings a greater blessing forward, for it allows an understanding of a greater reality . . . a greater reality that exists in the consciousness of Unana . . . a greater reality that exists beyond a dual consciousness. It is the next step that lies within the Violet Flame. Now, you will notice those who apply and use the Violet Flame on a regular basis will begin to have a gold tinge to the outside of their aura. This is the activation of the Golden Ray. However, it has been decided that in the next opening, this portal of entry that we have spoken of, that the Golden Ray will be flooded forth from our consciousness in complete and total harmony with beloved Babajeran, to bring an assistance for the evolution of humanity.

Now of course, if there are those who have not utilized the Violet Ray in their daily applications, it will be more difficult for them to recognize and understand this higher consciousness. But there are those who apply and use the Violet Flame on a daily basis and they will begin to notice a higher vibration. Some of these signs will be a high-pitched frequency, which at this moment you too can hear. There will be the sensation of music upon awakening from sleep or falling into sleep. This calls forth the greater harmony of the spheres; for you see, you have entered into a new dimension of sound frequency and a new level of understanding. Hence, it has its own light and its own sound vibration. Do you understand?

Question: *Yes I do. May we proceed with questions?*

Proceed.

Question: *I have some health questions to ask you with regard to a former secretary and her husband. Would you be able to do a scan and give us a course of action?*

[Saint Germain offers specific dietary suggestions for the individual's medical problems. This is followed by a spiritual cause discussion with general applications.]

Let us talk about the spiritual cause, for perhaps if we approach that first, the physical body will take suit, will it not?

Response: *Usually it does.*

The spiritual lesson is one of forgiveness, to completely forgive others for the way that they have behaved in the past and to not see that it was any result of this individual. This individual has harbored long-term resentments, which are deep-seated in the subconscious. This resentment has gone towards the self and has been seen within a mirror of self-hate and self-loathing. Dear one, Dear heart, understand that you attracted that lesson to learn complete and absolute forgiveness and compassion and now it is time to move forward and face the New Day. This lesson has brought forward great strengths and greater harmony within the soul, which are now achieved. These lessons now must be released for they are learned and completed. Questions?

Question: *I see. So, when following these suggestions, there will be great changes to the physiology and to the spiritual outlook of each chela?*

And as I always suggest, calling upon that mighty Violet Ray of Mercy, Compassion, and Forgiveness always brings about a most refreshing drink, a most high vibration, and a greater understanding of that mighty will in Divine Alignment.

Response: *I completely understand.*

Questions?

Response: *At this time I do not have any further questions.*

I shall take my leave now from your frequency and shall return at the given time.

Response: *One other question . . .*

Proceed.

Question: *Next week, we may not be available at the specific time. May we set this back one day?*

This shall work; however, I caution you, for you see, Dear ones, Dear hearts, we work always upon that ideal of rhythm. However, we shall return at the given time that you select.

Response: *I understand. Thank you.*

Om Manaya Pitaya Hitaka.

Hitaka.

Study Guide for Golden Ray, Stream Forth!

Topics:
The Gold Ray
New Consciousness
Age of Information
Absolute Harmony
Industrial Age

Gold Ray (expanded definition)
  The Ascended Masters Kuthumi and Saint Germain both prophesy that perhaps the Gold Ray is the most important energy force currently present on Earth. While its presence catalyzes the spiritual growth of the HU-man, it is also associated with Karmic Justice and will instigate change at all levels: Earth Changes, economic and social change.
  The Master Teachers prophesy that its appearance fosters the dawn of a New Consciousness for humanity, which ends the turbulence of Kali Yuga and ushers in a 10,000-year time of spiritual potential and opportunity for all—the Golden Age of Kali Yuga.

Prophecies of Change
1. The New Consciousness on Earth will assist the development of new technology, primarily in the information and medical arenas.
2. The information and medical industries gain new language through the development and use of laser technology. This new science helps to raise awareness regarding our fragile environments.
3. Awareness of the fragility of Earth's environments increases, and technology and science develop new business endeavors which are sensitive to Earth's ecosystems.

Information Age, or Age of Information
  The Information Age is characterized as the time of the computer, or Digital Age; however, according to the Master Teachers, the Age of Informa-

tion is a tenuous time in Earth's history when threshold decisions regarding the Earth and her natural environments will be made. The crux is the physical and psychic pollution that remains from the once expansive vision of the Industrial Revolution, and the new growth of spiritual consciousness beyond corruption, exploitation, and corporate greed.

As humanity's social and cultural vistas grow and evolve into the New Times, a "pathway of pure consciousness" is paved as we abandon the old paradigms of industry and embrace the Science of Divinity. The Age of Information plays a significant role as humanity redefines its individuality. Saint Germain suggests that the Age of Information breaks the barriers of elitist thinking, and is led by the Gold Ray of Brotherhood, Cooperation, and Peace through recognition of the innate Divine HU-man. This is a dichotomy to the technologically driven ideal of the Digital Age; in fact, Information Age is really a time period where hidden information is revealed and the perceptive truths of life are actualized. This marks the end of gross industrial and technological archetypes, and reveals a vision imbued with rich, yet complex discernment.

In fact, we currently are likely in the nascent, beginning stages of the Information Age. According to Harvard professor and librarian Robert Darton, several misconceptions and their counter realities stand out about this time:

- The paperback book is far from dead. The facts state that every year more paperback books are published, and this does not include nontraditional books.
- Everything is not available online and only twelve percent of the world's books have been digitized. Today, the average shelf-life of online information is only 44 days.
- Libraries are not outdated; in fact, many suffer from overuse and continue to serve as community centers of information.
- Printed material will not cease to be vital and important. But the market has shifted to a type of reading that may include both e-book, print versions, and audio versions enriching the ecology of information.[1]

Most importantly, Darton sees our culture shifting to consumption of more information that is not controlled by the traditional publishing industry, "Books used to be written for the general reader; now they are written *by* the general reader. The Internet certainly has stimulated self-

FIGURE 1-C
Starry Night by Vincent van Gogh
Impressionism during the Industrial Age often depicts the struggle between the working class and capitalists. Art historians claim that van Gogh believed that humanity needed to move towards nature in order to find a place in the modern world, away from urban environments. In contrast is Umberto Boccioni's vision in *The City Rises*, illustrates the utopian industrial ideal of machines, swift trains, and electricity transforming modern cities, states, and nations.

publishing, but why should that be deplored? Many writers with important things to say had not been able to break into print, and anyone who finds little value in their work can ignore it."[2]

Saint Germain's Teachings on the Gold Ray

1. The Golden Cities are affected by the Gold Ray, and the Ray's energies ramp up the energies of the Golden City Vortices. The Gold Ray also increases the energies of Golden City Vortices through subtle activation of the individual Ray that each Golden City serves.
2. Certain planetary configurations, especially lunar eclipse, affect the planetary energies and Golden City energies. According to Saint

FIGURE 2-C
The City Rises by Umberto Boccioni

Germain, lunar eclipses assist the process of shedding and cleansing individual karmas. These celestial placements work alongside the Gold Ray to initiate individuals into the New Consciousness.

3. Saint Germain gives this decree to initiate the stream of the New Consciousness within:

> Mighty Golden Ray, stream forth now,
> into the heart of the consciousness of humanity.
> Mighty Golden Ray, bring forth new understanding.
> Bring forth a new Spiritual Awakening.
> Bring forth complete and total divinity
> In the name of I AM THAT I AM.
> So be it.

This decree allows the Brotherhood to give further aid and contact to individuals who desire the Masters' help and assistance for spiritual development.

4. The Gold Ray initiates and transforms through the spiritual principles of balance and harmony. Working through the Hermetic Principle of vibration, Saint Germain claims that the Gold Ray creates, "Absolute Harmony."

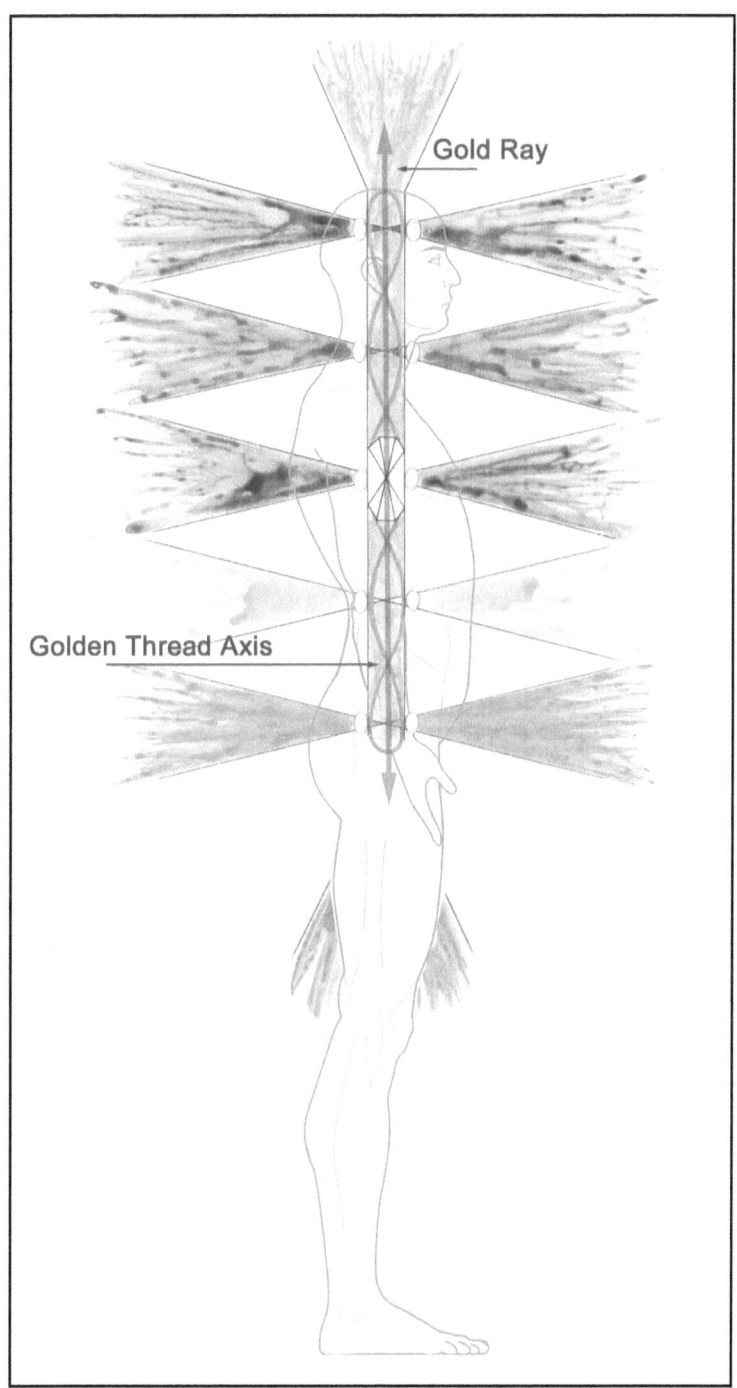

FIGURE 3-C
The Gold Ray and the Human Energy System

5. The Gold Ray balances and harmonizes the great spiritual darkness that today covers the Earth by introducing enough light to balance personal perceptions of duality.
6. The Middle Way, which is the spiritual notion that best describes the work of the Gold Ray, accepts the presence of both light and dark forces. This acceptance helps to heal our own individual dark side, which we may personally suppress—which can lead to the expression of uncontainable emotion. Saint Germain explains that "one cannot control" emotion until one experiences the full spectrum of emotion's anatomy. Each level of emotional experience and development expresses the presence and fluidity of varying Ray Forces through the unique experiences of each individual:
    a. Physical emotion is experienced or revealed through facial expression and body language.
    b. Feeling is the lower emotional body and expressed through instinct.
    c. Astral emotion is the higher emotional body, and manifests through dreams, goals, and desires.
    d. Mental/Emotional body contains the self-conscious emotions (guilt, shame, embarrassment, pride), and the higher emotions such as kindness, love, empathy, trust, respect, courage, and hope. [3]
7. The degree of emotion will determine the type and intensity of action because of the philosophic idea that nothing in life is random.
8. The Gold Ray of Consciousness helps the chela to shape and form the will and align our emotions and inevitably our actions to the Divine Will. The Gold Ray enters into the Seventh Chakra and its current flows alongside the Golden Thread Axis (Medullar Shushumna).
9. "All things work together for the ONE!" This principle of Unity Consciousness is the key to understand the activity of the Gold Ray. All experiences, good and bad, work together for the Divine Will.
10. Call upon the Gold Ray for acceptance of the unacceptable—tolerance for the intolerable. The Gold Ray helps one to structure the New Consciousness into a personal psychological framework

through the spiritual precept of Brotherhood and Sisterhood. Saint Germain explains, "You shall face that New Day cloaked in the glory of the Sun!"

Prophecies of Change
1. The Gold Ray has always been present on Earth in one form or another; however, at this time, humanity will be able to sense and experience its energies. Currently the Gold Ray is able to circumvent the prior darkness of Kali Yuga. [See *Divine Destiny*, "The Cycles of Human Perception and Consciousness."]
2. The presence of the Gold Ray assists the transformational cleansing of past karmas.
3. The ideal of Unana—the ONE—is initiated and inevitably created through the presence of the Gold Ray. Saint Germain suggests this decree for the Violet Flame to prepare spiritual consciousness to receive and apply the influence of the Gold Ray.

> Mighty Violet Ray, come forth in all transmuting action.
> Mighty Violet Ray, come forth now and dissolve all discord
> and the cause and effect of all that is holding me
> from understanding and moving forward into the new
> Golden Age.
> I call this forth in the name of that mighty Christ I AM.
> So be it.

4. The Gold Ray assists humanity's evolution at this important time. This process is calibrated by the premise of vibration and is a developmental step associated with the use of the Violet Flame. Those who apply this teaching may notice a golden tinge in their light bodies, hear a high-pitch sound, or celestial music (the Harmony of the Spheres) before falling asleep or upon awakening.
5. The Gold Ray floods the Earth with energies to evolve human consciousness. This energy is controlled by both the Galactic Center and further calibrated by the Spiritual Hierarchy to humanity.

Om Manaya Pitaya Hitaka

This statement, often made by Saint Germain at the close of a channeling, is spoken in the language of Owaspee—the secret language of the Angels that is often used by the Ascended Masters. [Editor's Note: During a ceremonial Nava Graha—a Vedic ceremony for the Seven Rays and Seven Planets—my Vedic priest clearly pronounced "Om Manaya Pitaya," with the exact enunciation used by Saint Germain and other Master Teachers. He repeated this statement several times as a benediction. After the puja I anxiously asked him its meaning. He replied, "I AM the Seer of the Lord." It breaks down like this:

> OM—I AM
> Manaya—the Seer
> Pitaya—of the Lord
> Hitaka—So be it!]

---

1. Darton, Robert. "5 Myths about the Information Age." Lecture, Council of Independent Colleges' Symposium on the Future of the Humanities, Washington D. C.
2. Ibid.
3. Simmons, Ilana. "The Four Moral [Emotions]." Psychology Today. November 15, 2009. Accessed July 20, 2016. https://www.psychologytoday.com/blog/the-literary-mind/200911/the-four-moral-emotions.

Illustrations:
1. van Gogh, Vincent. Starry Night. Digital image. Wikimedia Commons. December 4, 2004. Accessed July 20, 2016. https://commons.wikimedia.org/wiki/File:Van_Gogh_-_Starry_Night_-_Google_Art_Project.jpg. 1889.
2. Boccioni, Umberto. The City Rises. Digital image. Wikimedia Commons. May 19, 2005. Accessed July 20, 2016. https://commons.wikimedia.org/wiki/File:Umberto_Boccioni_001.jpg. 1910.

4

For Everything There is a Time
Saint Germain

Greetings, Beloved chelas, in that mighty Christ I AM, and I stream forth on that mighty Ray of Mercy, Compassion, and ultimate Forgiveness. As usual, Dear ones, Dear hearts, I request permission to come forward.

Response: *Please come forward, Saint Germain.*

There is much work to be done upon the Earth Plane and Planet and I ask you, Dear ones, to not tarry at all with this work. There is much to be accomplished and much to be achieved. As it has often been said before in those Christian scripts and hymns, to keep your eye upon the prize. Stay focused upon the goal, Dear hearts, Dear ones. We understand completely that you are within this time of great testing . . . a time of turmoil . . . a time of cleansing and purification. But the end result of this, is it not indeed transformation? It is not only a transformation that, yes, leads you to a new perspective and understanding but a transformation of the self, a transformation of the soul.

The old Alchemist often looked for those formulas that would turn lead into gold but what is more important? It is the movement of the soul in its growth and evolution towards the Divine God-ship, towards that great understanding of Unity Consciousness. This entry into a new level and understanding is of course all related to consciousness itself.

The expansion of consciousness has always been our work at hand, to help those who do not understand . . . to lend that helping hand to a friend who has stumbled along the path . . . to always be there with a smile and that friendly handshake of Brotherhood and Sisterhood. This is the true movement into collective light; this is the true movement into the Collective Consciousness. To help another is indeed a very good thing but good works, as it has always been said, are sometimes just not enough. What is meant by this, Dear ones, Dear hearts, is that experience above all things is the greatest of all teachers.

Experience is often the guide, as I have often said. It is not belief, or setting your goal upon something that you do not yet understand; it is achieving that experience through the ultimate of desires. Desire, as you know, Dear ones, Dear hearts, has always been that energy, a momentum within itself, that leads you forward from one experience to the other. There are, of course, the belief systems that state that we must drop all desire, but desire within itself, pure desire of that Source, of that mighty Light of God that Never Faileth, is the desire that I speak of today, Dear ones. It is a desire that leads us onward to that most refreshing drink. It is that desire that leads us onward to know our Brothers and our Sisters of Light and Sound. It is desire that leads us into the rainbow bridge and into a greater understanding and momentum of light and sound.

Desire within itself is always within the human who knows that it is much, much more than this one experience. There are many of those who know this and are always searching, are always upon that quest. That is the desire of which I speak. It is not the desire of greed; it is not the desire to attain more material wealth; it is not the desire to obtain fame and recognition. Instead, it is the desire to be united with the true self, that mighty I AM Presence. Through this uniting with the true self, the awakening is at hand.

> I AM the presence of life.
> I AM the presence of the Christ.
> I AM life eternal.
> I AM, I AM, I AM.

Know, Dear ones and Dear hearts, that through this decree comes the uniting with the true self, with the mighty I AM Presence. Know that through that mighty desire within you, you are linked as ONE to that true Source. In consciousness itself, all is linked eternally as ONE. To understand this, look at a body of water and see the glass reflection of clouds, buildings, and birds upon what appears to be the mirror of that lake. When you reach deep within, there are the waters of eternal truth and another world that lies beyond, even to the bottom of the lake. There, we see the plants, the fishes, and even another life that exists. Even beyond that, if you were to microscopically explore the surface tension of this water, you will find worlds within worlds within worlds. This is how consciousness is linked.

At times, one may ponder consciousness and only find such a small segment of it. One will see in looking into that, just a small perception. Maybe in that minute, they are only seeing that clear reflection that lies only at the surface. But within that water, there is a much more majestic world. In consciousness, that is ever encompassing and all understanding, lie the records of all that has been and all that ever will be. It is a difficult thing for the human to understand, for the human bases its world upon duality and linear timeframes. But when one moves into a new understanding, all experience is happening simultaneously; therefore, all consciousness is existing simultaneously and time, or the concept of time from a human perspective, is erased in its entirety.

When one encounters the mighty I AM Presence, they then begin to encounter this omnipresent consciousness, Unity Consciousness, Unana, as we have called it in many of our past discourses. Unana is a very important principle, for you see, Dear ones, all are linked as ONE. As beloved Kuan Yin has often said, "We are all indeed a Oneship." How true this is, Dear ones, Dear hearts, and it is through the focus upon this Oneship that then we are able to be of assistance. Once consciousness has entered into this Oneship, into the unity of All That Is of the great I AM THAT I AM, it cannot turn back. Instead, it must continue to expand and move even again beyond. It is that simple, that once you have dipped your hand beyond that mirror of illusion of the first level of the waters of time and you understand the worlds that lie within, you seek and want to swim.

Swimming in the sea of consciousness has always been a great trial for humanity, for it is almost impossible to swim within the sea of consciousness without conquering the concepts of duality. In duality, the birth of all the senses . . . the sense of taste . . . the sense of hearing . . . the sense of seeing . . . the sense of smelling, all of these senses interlace into deciphering and understanding the language of material reality. But let us move beyond that somewhat illusive reality and move into the super senses of clairvoyance, clairaudience, telepathy, and the development of these senses to bring one to another understanding of duality. The birth of the Christ within unites the dual forces. The uniting of the dual forces is understanding the masculine and feminine qualities that exist within one at all times.

You have known that you have had many different embodiments: man, woman, rich, poor, ruler, and peasant. You see, Dear ones, these experiences lead the soul into that great growth of which I have spoken of before. The growth of the soul is absolutely necessary. When the soul is complete, having its play in the field of experiences, then it begs to swim into the waters of consciousness, where it finds relief from the many questions of the first levels of desires. Now, these again, are the desires to attain materiality and to know more of the world.

To know the Source, to move forward to this God that Never, Never Faileth, one must always practice the principle of tolerance and nonjudgment; for you see, acceptance of All That Is is one of the most important psychological aspects that must be understood. Acceptance of All That Is embraces all ways of thinking; embraces all races of people, all colors, and specifically, embraces the genders. The enlightened soul, who has delved into the records of Akasha, knows that at all times, simultaneously, are the experiences of what is known to that soul as the past. However, experience within itself, when known in the greater reality of consciousness, is experienced more as a circular field of time in simultaneous reality rather than in a linear way.

To understand simultaneous reality, use that principle of sound. Now, in your time field and expanse of understanding, all it takes is to turn on a radio and listen to a song that had been heard before and constantly and instantly, that consciousness is taken back to that exact time and place. Has this not been so?

Answer: *Very true, yes.*

This is a programming, you see, for consciousness within itself is ever expanding and ever growing. These records of time, which are impressed upon the consciousness, are always impressed through experience. Experience is always the teacher and experience is indeed the programmer. Now, of course, there are those who have had experiences, which would be deemed forgettable or more negative in nature. That is why that mighty

Violet Ray has been brought forth. It is brought forth to reprogram the consciousness, to reprogram experience, so one may then begin to see the growth and the evolution of those experiences. But let us not get sidetracked in this instant and moment. Let us continue now with our discourse on understanding time and how it works.

When you begin to understand time systems—I will use in this case, light and its expansion upon the Earth Plane and Planet—one begins to see that there are times where light is ever expanding and times when light is indeed contracting. The Earth itself and the timeframe that you are experiencing in duality, is indeed a wave of consciousness. Of course, you may understand and say, how could a wave of consciousness create this body, create a body that ages under the impact of time? My hair, once filled with color, is now peppered with gray; my skin once youthened, is now falling into the wrinkles of time. You see, Dear ones, it is indeed consciousness within itself, a programming that you have accepted, that time can ravage eternal youth. Know this is a concept that must be understood, the programming of consciousness. Know, Dear ones, Dear hearts, that by embracing the idea of age, by embracing the idea of disease, one comes to an experience of having that. As I have always said:

> Down with death, immortal consciousness arise!
> Come forward now into the Truth of All Ages.
> Down with death, beloved mighty I AM,
> arise in all eternal glory.

Dear ones, these statements are statements to reprogram the consciousness, statements that are brought to bring about again that most refreshing, reinvigorating energy. When the soul has decided, unto itself, in its own evolutions, that it has had enough of the experience of death . . . enough of the experiences of decay . . . enough of the experiences of disease . . . it begins to seek and wonder beyond that illusive mirror of the lake.

Swimming into the waters again of experience, it seeks to know more, to understand more deeply. But yet, how can it dive into those deeper waters of understanding while staying on the surface tension? Of course, it must hold its breath and embrace with the greatest of courage, to travel to the depth that it does not know yet or understand. This is the ultimate in the release of fears . . . fears of the unknown . . . fears of betrayal . . . fears of the true suicide of the ego.

Dear ones, Dear hearts, I encourage you to continue with your work. Embrace each day, the work of the mighty Violet Ray and know that through its Divine Intervention, you may travel into a greater understanding of Unity Consciousness. You will also travel into a greater understanding of Brotherhood and Sisterhood. Embrace each day that you are all united as ONE and in that unity is the true love that embraces all. Work to obtain tolerance of all beliefs; work to accept all who come across your path in the work that you do. This does not mean that you are to embrace them at a vibrational level but embrace them in the unity, in the heart of God, that mighty Love That Never Fails, never wants. Questions?

Response: *The concept of time, in our perception, is linear. Your discourse is that time is not linear; it is simultaneous.*

It is a simultaneous spiral, which contains an energy unto itself. The concept of bending time is the overlapping of spirals. It is based upon a knowledge and an alchemy of the cycles.

Question: *So, since everything is made of light and sound, those spirals can be bent also?*

In their time and in their place; as it has been said, "for everything, there is a time." Everything has a Divine Order within the universe. This is difficult to understand when questions are asked with the seeming chaos of the mind; but, it is important to understand, Dear ones, Dear hearts, that there is an order and a rhythm to all things, even within the higher realms of consciousness. All contain this order because of ordered thought.

It is through thought, that which is known as Divine Mind and through the Heart of God, Divine Love in alignment to Divine Will, that mighty power, that all then comes into its field of action. All comes with a purpose and an intent. In the higher realms of consciousness, ideas that are related to material forces are then released and understood, shall we say, at their greatest of intention. Time within itself is not bent but rather, shall we say, activated upon its own time and arrival.

Question: *Activated upon its own time and arrival—are you saying then that there is a cycle to it?*

There is always a cycle. Remember, Dear ones, when I taught you about cosmic wave belts? An oceanic tidal system, so to speak, that exists within the universe. These waves of consciousness, as the best way to understand them, create a cycle of events that then happen and occur. Of course, these cycles of events are later recorded in history as the Bronze Age, or as the Industrial Age, or as the Information Age. Then they are recorded and deciphered into the hands of man and known within that timeframe and timeline. But all is cycling, if you will; all is happening with a great Divine Order. The oceanic tumblers come into their own effect, into their own time and intention. Now, when I say time, I speak of order. It is the only way to understand such a concept. But beyond time, beyond that Divine Order, is the unity of all things, that interlacing and interlocking consciousness that links all together as ONE.

Cycles are all interconnected. You cannot separate winter from spring or summer from fall. They are all interconnected and need and assist one another in the states of dual forces and such is so even within the higher realms; however, cycles are understood in their entirety and the birth of the Christ within allows one to understand how all is dependent and interdependent upon the other. Do you understand?

Question: *Partly. Are you saying that for the sake of experience, these waves exist from the source of Creation, yet unity still exists so that the soul may return home?*

As we have always stated before, choice always exists simultaneously with the order that is contained within. It is through that choice that activated will, when brought to a higher order and understanding, aligns itself to a greater plan and greater glory. This pivots and moves consciousness forward. Then all is related in a greater unification of time, if you will. Time is then understood only as experience, instead of a "date." It is understood for the programming of consciousness, of what it is, or the deprogramming of consciousness, of what it is. Time therefore becomes a grand selection, a choice, if you will, of experience. Do you understand?

Answer: *Yes, so when a person is recalling something that occurred to them, say for example in June of 1942, the June of 1942 date is only a numerical catalogue for the recollection of the experience.*

And then the past, does it not then become the present and intertwine itself in creating the future? This is how time, within itself, brings that all-encompassing menu of experience through which consciousness is programmed. Consciousness then has its own experience, if you will. However, the mind and the memory of humanity is not as developed as it has been in other "times" throughout experience of consciousness. Why is this so? We have spoken of this before, through understanding Rays of light and sound.

Earth, in its own evolution, in its own cosmic wave belt, is encountering a time of less light actually impacting the planet itself. Now, when we speak of this light, we talk about the light of consciousness. So, it would seem that the Earth itself is in a cycle of decay, but is it in a cycle of decay or in a cycle of purification? It is in this cycle of purification that the old and the useless can then be discarded and the new can be put on. This is that true seamless garment of experience; for the soul within itself and its desire to know God, to swim within the true waters of experience beyond the mirror of illusion, begins to desire to know the true self . . . the mighty I AM THAT I AM.

Response: *So what you are saying is that experience is indeed the seamless garment.*

It is indeed and that seamless garment is taken ideally through the will, through the choice. However, we have known that within illusion or maya, one forgets cause and effect, of which desires are the playful pet.

Question: *So, going back to your decree, "down with death," are you saying that this is a programming which exists collectively here, that when a physical body reaches the age of 20, it has a certain appearance, then at 40, 50, and 60, it has another appearance and that is from our programming?*

Believe it or not, Dear one, that is so.

Question: *And so when one chooses to take the time factor out, by recognizing that experience is continuous and timeless, containing all the experiences of every embodiment here, and always relating to the Source, that is indeed the pathway to overcome these perceptions?*

As it has often been said, let your life be sweet like the fragrance of a rose. What is meant by this? Take the experiences that you see as good, related to your Source in duality as positive and moving you forward, and let those be the programming of your consciousness. The work of the mighty Violet Ray has come forward to assist those who have brought into their level of consciousness an understanding of negative experience, so it can be removed.

You can always tell the spiritual seeker. The spiritual seeker is one who has carefully examined and knows of negative experience. Now, in a humorous model, one may see this as a constant and chronic complainer but yet, see it from this understanding: The one who complains all the time is now seeking to know the opposite, are they not? They seek then to make their life as fragrant as that rose.

The pain that they feel within is only their true desire, bringing them closer to the source of their own unity, their own Oneship, their own consciousness of Unana. That is why I have repeated: try to be helpful to one another. Help your Brother or Sister when they fall. Do not join in when they begin in their negative dialects and dialogues of what they see, of what they experience, of what has been the past programming of their consciousness.

Instead, remind them of the Law Eternal, for that law is written on the heart. It is indeed the Law of Love and through that mighty Law of Love is the Divine Intervention of the mighty Violet Flame of Mercy, Compassion, and Forgiveness. Teach them that they may choose the reality that they experience in dual forces and beyond that lies the birth of the true Christ, the true rising of the soul from lead into gold. It is only in this golden understanding that then consciousness embraces and understands and accepts. Questions?

Response: *It seems in the duality here, however, we learn at a much more rapid rate if something is distasteful or painful.*

It is often that the soul learns through what it does not want versus what it does. Again, it is always a matter of choice and programming the consciousness for the positive influences that one may choose. Of course, the soul does not say unto itself, "Oh, I desire again to have only negative influences. I desire again to only have negative experiences." When one wants God, wants to know the Source, it comes to seek the riches and the expansion of consciousness. It wants to have only joyful experiences; it wants to have only that goodness. But you see, Dear ones, Dear hearts, that is the trap of duality. It is important to understand that left and right are united, good and bad are united, negative and positive are united. These things in their Unity of Consciousness are indeed that birth of the Christ within. Then, contact with the mighty I AM Presence begins to unfold in its fullness.

Question: *Duality is united and its unification is at a point of neutrality isn't it?*

And that point of neutrality is the entry into Unana, is the entry into Unity Consciousness, where all opposites become reconciled unto the ONE. All is accepted and tolerated. Now, this is a difficult consciousness at times to sustain in duality itself but yet, it is essential for the growth of the soul. As I have said before, is it not so difficult to turn back once you have had the experience.

Response: *That's true. You can change your mind.*

As I have stated before, once you have had the experience, it is very different than having belief. Questions, Dear heart?

Response: *So now that we know that everything is simultaneously occurring, if we take that as a perception or a point of view of life, that gives us different tools to work with than seeing things as good or bad, or up and down, or dualistic in nature.*

It is then brought into an understanding of that aggregate body of light, where all experience is gathered unto itself and used then as a pinnacle, as a point of perception in consciousness.

Response: *I see. So, it is that point of perception that puts you in the middle of the duality and then allows you to see, perceive, and even experience All That Is.*

The aggregate body of light is the gathering of all lighted experiences that the consciousness chooses to move forward in its own evolution. That aggregate body of light would be seen from a dualistic perspective as all positive influences versus all negative influences; however, if understood from, shall we say, that point of unity, it contains all experience.

Duality is a system that is dependent upon itself; however, beyond that is a greater understanding of that system, the why and how of its existence. Beyond that is an acceptance of the All That Is, the I AM THAT I AM. From that point of entry lies the Mastery of duality. That is where death, disease, and decay can be overcome. That is the point of this discourse, Beloved.

Response: *So the point is the neutral point, the unity point.*

Indeed it is. Dear ones. So give your helping hand in true love, for the miseries of duality do indeed exist for those who accept them as such but remind them that beyond this duality, beyond this illusion, lies the truth, lies the mighty I AM, the God Source that exists beyond suffering, that exists beyond pain. There lies the true heart and the true Love of God that Never, Never Fails.

Peace within itself is found when one understands that all is existing within a balance. Peace comes from that plane of understanding that accepts and acknowledges true experience. These experiences of light and dark . . . of hatred . . . of love . . . of good versus bad . . . that tension . . . that plan, does it not give you the great experience? The great experience is where, exhausted and tired, the soul lies down upon a field of action and says to itself:

> Now I shall rest within the true Plan of God.
> Now I desire to only know that.

Again, as I have said before today, once you touch and know that essence, that energy of Unity, you can not turn back. Instead, consciousness must move forward in its complete and total evolution. Like a moth is drawn to a flame, it is the same principle. Once seeing that light that exists at the end of the long tunnel of duality, you reach your hands towards that understanding and move down that tunnel to know the true light, the truth of God, the truth of Source. There you meet the I AM THAT I AM and your perspective becomes much, much more time-bending . . . much, much more duality shaking. Do you see, Dear one? Experience within itself becomes the grand teacher.

Answer: *Yes I see that. What I have found is in our world, when we perceive that our body has a disease or we have a conflict or something, our first reaction or interaction is always to fight it and yet with this perception, fighting it is pointless.*

It may be given for experience; then again, it may be given to that soul to learn how to fight. There are always varying degrees of what a soul is learning and where the soul is moving towards. But understand this: in the higher reality of Unity, there is no right, nor wrong. All is accepted and all is tolerated within, as it is without.

Question: *There has been some recent concern about what has been popularly termed as "chemtrails," that the spraying of our populated areas is detrimental to our long-term health and even our genetic structure. Can you shed some light on this?*

Of course, there never is any end to illusion, secret upon secret upon secret, and darkness within layers of darkness, within more layers of darkness. But the body itself has been given to humanity as a great gift to have experience. In this time, or experience of lesser light, these are the end results of not understanding, of not having a truer or purer consciousness. Indeed, Dear ones, Dear hearts, much, much has happened upon the Earth Plane and Planet, has it not? Much happens when one takes on a physical body, does it not? We have many experiences that are related to the growth of the soul.

Again, that consciousness of disease, death, and decay, if you allow one of these to affect you, does it not then affect you? Have you not then entered into the agreement, the contractual basis, so to speak, to understand it with a legal mind? Disease within itself, do you not have the agreement to accept this then within your body? Disease within itself, does it not come from the mind within?

Mind has always been the builder, is it not? But let me say, Dear one, Dear hearts, all comes within that cycle of Divine Order and Timing. The body is not based, as I have said before, upon genetics. The body is built through light and sound. Beyond that is the understanding of true mind, the true ultimate builder of all reality and beyond that, the Hand of God, the true breath of all that unites us as ONE.

Study Guide For Everything There is a Time

Topics:
Time of Testing
Alchemy
Teachings on Desire
The Rainbow Bridge
Sea of Consciousness
Duality
Divine Mind, Divine Love, and Divine Will
The Rose
Point of Neutrality

Time of Testing

The Time of Testing is a period of seven to twenty years which began around the turn of the twenty-first century, following the time period known as the *Time of Transition.* According to Saint Germain and other Ascended Masters, the Time of Testing is perhaps one of the most turbulent periods mankind will experience and its first seven years is prophesied as a period of change and strife for many. As its title suggests, the Master Teachers claim this timeframe may challenge students by testing their spiritual acumen and inner strength. [Editor's Note: Other prophecies indicate this timeframe may be seven to twenty years.]

This period is also known as the great trial. Students will realize forceful contrast through adversity, while remembering the softer predecessor to this period: the benefic Time of Transition. This favorable twelve-year period began in the mid to late eighties of the twentieth century and ushered in tremendous spiritual exposure and growth through a proliferation of alternative self-help and healing groups, spawning a renewed zeal for other forms of faith. Beginning in 1988 and ending in the year 2000, (some I AM America prophecies suggest a longer duration), the beloved Ascended Masters, Archangels and Elohim flood the Earth with light (the Rays) to restore mankind's spiritual growth and acuity. Spiritual development achieved in this period proves essential because of the events which mark the end of its benevolence and introduce the Time of Testing. These events try humanity's resilience and challenge our grasp of Forgiveness, Tolerance, and Compassion amidst the violence of the 9-11 tragedy, war in the Middle East, and increased natural calamities.

Through the backdrop of world instability and global fragility, Ascended Master chelas and students hone the spiritual skills of transmutation and transformation. Humanity's ability to alchemize geophysical, social, economic, and environmental events may forecast mankind's ability to survive the catalytic and polarizing threshold of change we are now entering. Once we leave the *Time of Testing*, the Ascended Masters prophesy the Time of Change is upon us. This is a time of worldwide change, with possible Earth Changes which inevitably leads to global transformation prophesied by the Ascended Masters, religious Prophets, sages, and indigenous tribal leaders. *The Time of Change* ushers in the Golden Age of Kali-Yuga.

Alchemy

The ancient art of alchemy, which allegedly originated from the Land of Khem (Ancient Egypt), is secretly embedded in the texts of the Kabbalah, the Tarot, and the Emerald Tablet of Hermes. It is a hidden yet sacred science which bridges the world of chemistry and metallurgy with the spiritual worlds of Mastery and the Ascension Process. Many of its subtle and profound mysteries are lost to the worlds of the ancients, however the Master Teachers often refer to this word as the process of inner transformation, which builds and refines, and ultimately helps one to release Earthly bondage and to enter into the freedom of spiritual experience and knowledge. The alchemic spiritual process is often referred to by esoteric practitioners as transforming base metal into gold, a practical metaphor for the spiritual aspirant.

The science of alchemy is also known in Ascended Master circles as the "Sacred Fire," which is the seminal spark of the magnificent Violet Flame. Manly Hall writes: "The Great Arcanum (Knowledge) was the most prized of the secrets of the Atlantean priestcraft. When the lands of Atlas sank, hierophants of the Fire Mystery brought the formula to Egypt, where it remained in the possession of the sages and philosophers." [1]

Saint Germain's Teachings on Desire

1. Desire plays a pivotal role in setting the stage for the soul to gain the ultimate spiritual guide: personal experience.
2. Desire carries a momentum, and leads the aspirant forward in spiritual quest, from "One experience to the other . . ."
3. Some spiritual belief systems and teachings discourage desire; however, Saint Germain encourages the cultivation and identification of desire that springs from the source within. Desires that originate from the Co-creative light within help to groom and invigorate our spiritual growth.
4. "Purity of Desire" can help us to identify our spiritual community and initiate our understanding of self, which is critical to initiate our tactile experience with light and sound (the Rays).
5. The spiritual quest is initiated with perhaps one of the purest forms of human desire: the desire to unite with the true self, the I AM Presence.
6. This decree evokes the awakening to the true self, the I AM, and incites this desire to manifest into experience:

> I AM the Presence of Life.
> I AM the Presence of the Christ.
> I AM Life Eternal.
> I AM. I AM. I AM.

Rainbow Bridge

The esoteric term that describes the Human Aura, which contains a spectrum of light bodies, similar to a rainbow.

Teachings on Consciousness and Time

1. Through desire we are linked to the Source of Creation and the Source is linked by consciousness to the ONE.
2. Consciousness connects all worlds, seen and unseen, explored and unexplored. Since we only experience just a small amount of Creation at any given moment, our challenge is to know, understand, and experience what we cannot comprehend through duality and linear time.

3. Consider that both consciousness and experience exist simultaneously. This idea erases the notion of a linear timeframe.
4. Encounters with the I AM Presence are Omnipresent, or beyond the perception of linear time. Omnipresence moves our consciousness into Unana and the experience of the ONE.
5. The community of ONE—Unana—is a Oneship. Individuals who enter into this experience of consciousness and timelessness cannot turn back. That is, you will always seek to re-enter the reality beyond Earthly illusion and entrance into the unseen worlds. This encounter is referenced by Saint Germain as "Swimming in the Sea of Consciousness."
6. The practice of acceptance, tolerance, and nonjudgment is key to developing the Christ Consciousness. This critical development leads the soul beyond duality and the five lower senses through the development of the super-senses: clairaudience, hearing; clairvoyance, vision; clairsentience, feeling; clairalience, scent; and clairgustance, taste. The enlightened soul knows, through accessing Akashic Records, that in our Earthly experiences the soul has had many lifetimes as both sexes, as all races, and in numerous contrasting situations and circumstances.
7. The enlightened soul experiences time as a circular field of simultaneous realities. That is, all lifetimes—past, present, and future—are interconnected to the Ever Present Now.
8. Consciousness can be programmed, and it is always growing and expanding. The Violet Flame is one of the quickest methods to reprogram our consciousness. To reprogram our consciousness and the collective idea of age, decay, disease, and death, repeat this decree to release fear:

> "Down with death, immortal consciousness arise!
> Come forward now into the Truth of All Ages.
> Down with death, beloved mighty I AM,
> Arise in all eternal glory."

Perspective of Time	Linear Time Experience	Timeless or Peak Experience
FELT EXTENSION OF TIME	Time is linear, extending continuously from past to present to future; we experience time duration (how long things last).	Time is not felt to extend or is linear; there is timelessness, duration is not sensed.
FLOW OF TIME	Time is a series of transactions felt to pass or flow constantly and continuously.	There is an abiding Presence (the I AM) admist movement. No experience of flow, however events still occur.

FIGURE 1-D
Experience of Time

9. According to Saint Germain, time is akin to a spiral that can be bent to create an overlapping series of spirals. This esoteric process controls the cycles of time. "Everything has a Divine Order within the Universe."
10. Consciousness manifests itself like the *Cosmic Wave Belts* of the galaxy. As organized waves of energy, consciousness will predicate the Ages of Time, and the events humanity will encounter. The creation of time through waves of consciousness is also known as "oceanic tumblers," which creates interconnected cycles of time.
11. Within the ordered cycles of time, the activated Will (the collective of all individual wills) aligns to the Divine Will. This alters the perception of time as linear into *experience*. Again, through experience, time is programmed or deprogrammed, and through choice simultaneous realities appear.
12. Through conscious choice, the duality of time is swept from negative to positive experience. The Master Teacher advises: "Let your life be sweet, like the fragrance of a rose." This statement, claimed to be a teaching from the Avatar Babaji, is an esoteric statement that reiterates the cultivation of the Christ Consciousness.

FIGURE 2-D
Buddha meditating under the bodhi tree.

Linear Time

The notion that time exists from one viewpoint: the past, the present, and the future. In Ascended Master teachings, this perspective is known as linear time. The complexity of time is best understood by our own experience and the experience of linear time can only be held in the pres-

FIGURE 3-D
The Indian mystic Ramakrishna in trance.
Ramakrishna in samadhi supported by his nephew Hriday and surrounded by Brahmo devotees. Photograph taken on Sunday, September 21, 1879 at the house of Keshab Chandra Sen, Calcutta.[2]

ent moment. The Western cultural worldview of time is that its passage is independent of consciousness.[2] However, time is perception that comprises our present feelings, emotions, or intuition and can alter or change the conventional idea of a linear timeframe. Meditation instructor Stephen Randall compares the two perceptions of time in the "Experience of Time."[3]

Sea of Consciousness

A refined state of higher consciousness, developed through the individual practice and application of the Twelve Jurisdictions, which allows one to enter into a state of Unity Consciousness, or the ONE. This entrance marks the development of faculties that in the ordinary human are dormant, and this awakening hones the mind, its perceptions, and development of the Will and the ability to make effective choices and decisions. This mindful discernment parallels the development of the Super Senses, and the transcendent reunion with the I AM Presence. The entrance into the state of universal consciousness results in personal tranquility and peace, and produces a sharpened and attentive awareness that pierces illusion and the mental phenomenon of both the Physical and Astral Planes. It is the acclaimed level of consciousness attained by Buddha and the frequent domain of mystics, enlightened spiritual teachers, and those on the Path of Ascension.

Duality

The metaphysical and philosophical premise that creation manifests in twin opposites is the common underlying notion of duality. Ascended Masters claim that the five senses are birthed in the dual planes of causation: taste, sight, hearing, touch, and smell. The higher senses of telepathy, clairaudience, and clairvoyance function beyond the duality, and rely on the development of the Christ Consciousness—also known in religious and theosophical circles as the Unfed Flame—in order to fully develop and function. The following table illustrates how the principle of dualism encompasses both the moral and philosophical dilemmas of religion.

RELIGION	DUAL FORCE ONE	DUAL FORCE TWO
Christianity	God (Good)	Satan (Evil)
Taoism	Yang (Male)	Yin (Female)
Hinduism	Vishnu (Supreme God, absolute truth)	Jiva (Individual soul, separate reality)
Eastern Philosophy	Consciousness	Physical atoms
Western Philosophy	Mind	Brain

The pairs of opposites are endless in their subtleties and nuances and are best understood through the study of Hermetic Law. [Editor's Note: For more information regarding Hermetic Law see *Points of Perception*.]

Simultaneous Realities or Experiences

A transmigratory experience based on a nonlinear perspective of time. It holds all the possibilities of past, present, and future events. Simultaneous realities maintain the capacity for multiple experiences and outcomes. Each reality exists side by side. A person could consciously open himself or herself to these scenarios to gain insight and self-knowledge.

Prophecies of Change

The current time we are experiencing individually and collectively is predicated by a "wave of consciousness." This wave is co-created by both the Galactic Center, and collectively and individually by "us" (on Earth) as the witness.

Divine Mind

Divine Mind is the principle or idea that a universal mind or soul creates a rational order in the cosmos. According to Ascended Master Teaching, Divine Mind is "ordered thought" which in turn is responsible for the rhythm and timing of all events from small cycles of time to million-year epochs.

Divine Love

Divine Love is defined as the Heart of God, or the heart of the Creator of all things seen and unseen, created and uncreated.

Divine Will

The idea of God's plan for humanity; however, from the perspective of the HU-man, the Divine Will is choice. Ascended Masters often refer to the Divine Will as the power through which all things created manifest form on the field of action—the physical plane.

Cosmic Wave Belts

An interstellar band of energy comprising cosmic waves that creates a significant force in the universe, especially during the Time of Change on Earth. The cosmic wave belts resemble the ebb and flow of tides. Originating from the Sun, cosmic waves drift to certain points in the universe, then recede. And just as the momentum of shoreline ripples collide with the ingoing and outgoing surf, the undulations of the cosmos assume a similar motion, creating an infinite and dynamic flooding of the universe. Cosmic wave motions affect the Earth's inhabitants, particularly the human and animal nervous systems. But, these waves produce positive results, too. They trigger an evolution in consciousness, and initiate a great understanding of unity and compassion.

According to the I AM America prophecies, the movement of the empyreal swells influences the planets of the solar system, controls time, and subsequently governs evolution. During the Time of Change on Earth, the "jumbling and tumbling" of cosmic wave belts causes the deceleration or compaction of time. Saturn and Neptune, however, toss a lifesaver to Earth, helping our planet and ultimately humanity, to adjust to the tempestuous eddies.

Christ, the Rose of Sharon

The Christ Consciousness is known in esoteric circles as the "Rose of Sharon," which takes its name and definition from the Old Testament: "I am the rose of Sharon, and the lily of the valleys." This passage from the Song of Solomon is a metaphysical premise that holds the emblematic Rose Croix (Rose Cross) through two symbols: the rose of the Christ Consciousness, and the lily as immortal life. This allegory concludes that the "secret of immortality is revealed and through his (Christ's) death an immortal life of purity and happiness is made available."[4]

Spiritual Teachings of the Rose

1. Work to see the positive side of a situation as much as possible. This helps your spiritual development to move quickly.
2. Pain is the desire which draws one closer to the source of Unity, Oneship, and the consciousness of Unana.
3. Be helpful to one another and help your brother or sister when they fall.
4. Forget the old negative dialects and dialogues of the past. Remember and practice the Law of Love, and the Divine Intervention of the Violet Flame of Mercy, Compassion, and Forgiveness.
5. We choose and create our reality and experiences within and beyond duality.

FIGURE 4-D
Rosicrucian Rose
According to Manly P. Hall's *Secret Teachings of All Ages*, this is from the 18th-century work Geheime Figuren der Rosenkreuzer. The rose is a yonic symbol associated with generation, fecundity, and purity. The fact that flowers blossom by unfolding has caused them to be chosen as symbolic of spiritual unfoldment.

6. The Christ Consciousness is the true alchemy of the soul and the birth of Christ is within. Through this essential naissance, contact with the I AM Presence develops and unfolds.
7. The spiritual consciousness of I AM THAT I AM lies beyond duality, where death, disease, and decay are overcome.
8. Once you achieve contact with the energy of Unity and know its essence, you cannot turn back. Your consciousness will move toward this light, to experience the truth of God—I AM THAT I AM.
9. Above all, experience is the grand teacher.

Point of Neutrality
The ability to see or describe duality, but not engage in it. This is also the philosophical viewpoint described as the metaphysical term "Zero Point." Since zero marks a neutral point in mathematics, its metaphor invites human consciousness to enter a new philosophical and spiritual plane beyond dualistic thinking.

1. Hall, Manly P. "The Theory and Practice of Alchemy." In The Secret Teachings of All Ages, 203. Los Angeles: Philosophical Research Society, 1988.
2. Randall, Stephen. "Mastering Linear Time." A New Vision of Reality: Time, Space, and Knowledge. Accessed August 12, 2016. http://www.tskassociation.org/mastering-linear-time.html.
3. Randall, Stephen. "Linear vs. Timeless Views." Accessed August 5, 2012. http://www.manage-time.com.
4. "Masonic Compendium." Rose of Sharon. Accessed August 12, 2016. http://masonic.wikidot.com/rose-of-sharon.

Illustrations:
1. Buddha Meditating Under the Bodhi Tree. Digital image. Wikimedia Commons. December 14, 2009. Accessed August 12, 2016. https://commons.wikimedia.org/wiki/File:WLA_brooklynmuseum_Buddha_Meditating_Under_the_Bodhi_Tree.jpg.
2. "Ramakrishna Trance." Digital image. Wikimedia Commons. September 5, 2008. Accessed August 12, 2016. https://commons.wikimedia.org/wiki/File:Ramakrishna_trance_1879.jpg
3. "Rosicrucian Rose." Digital image. Wikimedia Commons. June 10, 2009. Accessed August 12, 2016. https://commons.wikimedia.org/wiki/File:Rosicrucian_Rose.jpg. Rosicrucian Rose—circular diagram of alchemical symbolism with seven planets at top and Latin "VITRIOL" acronym around the circumference. Circa 1710s.

5

Secret Teachings on the Map of Rings
Saint Germain and Sanat Kumara

Greetings, Beloved, on that mighty Violet Ray, I AM Saint Germain and I stream forth on that mighty Violet Ray of Mercy, Compassion, and Forgiveness. As usual, Dear heart, I ask permission to come forward.

Response: *You have permission, Saint Germain. You are most welcome.*

There is much work that we will proceed with. The work of prophecy has been brought forward to lighten hearts . . . to shed, shall we say, understanding on this time upon the Earth Plane and Planet . . . and to give to humanity that most refreshing drink in a time of great trial and tribulation that is known as a Time of great Testing. But yet, Dear one, Dear heart, there is other work that is of great import, other work that needs to come forward from the Great White Brotherhood and Hierarchy of Brotherhoods and Sisterhoods of Light and Sound. This work comes forward on that mighty Green Ray of Scientific Understanding and Development. It comes forward to bring a greater understanding of the true Laws of Forgiveness, the true laws behind healing and the change of one age into another.

You see, Dear ones, when one door closes, does not another one open? When there is a consciousness that is ready to close down its Ray of understanding, a new Ray of Light then appears to grant an opening and an entry into a new consciousness and another way of understanding. The work that is brought through on this stream of consciousness has been sponsored by beloved Brother Sananda. Beyond this great Lord of the Transition is another Lord who oversees this project, whom you have known as the "Ancient of Days," or our beloved grandfather, Sanat Kumara. He is the Keeper of Ancient Wisdom. He has been a teacher, not only of mine, but a teacher also of yours, a teacher who is now coming forward to lend insight and understanding. Do we have your permission now to bring this energy forward?

Response: *Yes, most certainly.*

Greetings, children, I work upon that Ray of Wisdom and I carry with me, shall I say, archetypes of all forms of wisdom that have come forward to lead humanity in its evolution . . . lead humanity forward at times of great darkness . . . lead humanity forward into enlightenment also. At great times of light, I AM ever present . . . I AM always available . . . I AM always here . . . I AM truly as ONE in that I AM THAT I AM.

There is much work to be done and it is important now to open your consciousness to a new wavelength of understanding. I have been present in your history of the Earth in many different times, brought forth at times of import to bring understanding and insight into topics that will lead humanity forward, shall we say, beyond Time Compaction and into a great leap in evolution and understanding. It is important, Dear ones, Dear hearts, that my consciousness speaks to you . . . speaks to you in the most ancient of ways . . . speaks to you in the most current of ways . . . speaks to you of the future that comes.

We have spoken to you before of what is known as the Map of Rings. It is a map of Elemental Life Force . . . a map that was kept quite guarded . . . kept, shall we say, in a secret chamber, even in the heart of the Hierarchy itself. Its purpose is to grant a better understanding of the process of Ascension and also of the cooperative forces of Mother Nature, the planet itself, beloved Babajeran. The complete harmony and intention of her energy bodies bring forth a Divine Intervention, a Divine Intervention from the catastrophes and calamities that could possibly await humanity as outlined in the many Earth Changes Prophecies.

This wisdom was given to the many different tribes of the Native Americans that you know now in your time period; however, this wisdom was also dispensed in an earlier form to many other cultures and societies. Indeed, it is not a new understanding but yet, it is an important understanding if one is to glean the most important aspect and understanding of the Golden City Vortices. While the Golden City Vortices do not comprise a many-ringed map, all things are connected to the ONE; this universal grid of energies that enfolds the Earth, it too is contained as ONE.

Through the Many-Ringed Map that covers the Earth Planet, the waters flow, the winds blow, and mountains are formed. It is important to understand that it holds the grid itself of the physical manifestation of the Earth. When it is understood how it works in its energy and electromagnetic context, you will then be able to gain a greater understanding of the Golden City Vortices and how they bring forth their Divine Intervention. The Golden City Vortices work, of course, on that dimension of the mighty Angels and Archangels of service. So you see, beloveds, Dear children, this is also a map.

When we speak of the Golden City Maps of Divine Intervention, brought through the Holies of the Holies . . . brought forth to bring you into your Divine Awareness and destiny . . . brought here to bring you healing at many levels of body, mind, and spirit, it is all designed to bring you into that greater understanding and majesty of Oneship. The Many-Ringed Map has always existed upon the Earth Plane and Planet and through its understanding, many have, shall we say, gained in Mastery of the Alchemical knowledge that exists within the Earth itself, unfolding the mystery of Creation.

The Many-Ringed Map is a foundation through which the Crystalline Cities can exist and build upon. It is a foundation, shall we say, a building block that is most important, comprising not only the Devas, but also the Elemental Kingdoms and contained within that, the Gnomes, the Sylphs, the Salamanders, and the Undines. All of these beings, representative of earth, air, fire, and water, bring a total unity, a comprehensive understanding that life is contained within and beyond consciousness always and beyond the consciousness of your own understanding.

Other cultures have understood the existence of such an energy and this power has always been one that was accessed by those who were ready to dwell within, to the great mysteries and beyond. It is, however, a map of forces and these Earth Forces are bound to certain planes of understanding and reality. It has a limitation in this respect, Dear children, in that it is dual in its nature and force; however, it is most essential for an understanding of the dual forces. One is then prepared to understand the forces of the Trinity and the birth of the child, the Christ that exists in Unity Consciousness beyond all duality. There you find the birth of the Crystal Age, the Crystalline Cities.

Through the process of Ascension, the consciousness is lifted beyond that of duality and brought to the apex of understanding, that within itself is the Divine Man. From lead, it is Alchemized to gold. These are the teachings that are brought forward, of course, in the Golden City Vortices but it is important to understand the Many-Ringed Map and its implication.

In the past, there have been many great battles that have been fought upon the Earth Plane and Planet. Always these battles are fought with swords of righteousness, one side believing unto itself that its beliefs are of the purer and the greater understanding. Standing up to one another, they turned their back on the consciousness of understanding. But know this: within that dualistic understanding of good versus evil, there is another understanding that rises above that dualistic understanding and therein lies the birth of greater enlightenment, the Unity Consciousness of the Christ. Within this Unity Consciousness of the Christ is where all healing forces lie. Within this Unity Consciousness of the Christ is where the Ascension is met.

When the soul is questing, or as Saint Germain would say, thirsting for that most refreshing drink and dives into the true waters of clear, perpetual understanding, upon this Wisdom Ray is this great grid which covers your Earth. The Rays of Understanding that guard within them the evolution and the nourishment of humanity are under the direction of the Galactic Center of the Great Central Sun. This mighty Sun of Consciousness arcs its Rays throughout your solar system and there, they land with grace upon many planets. The Earth itself is brought forward into its own evolution through the timing and intent, even along that the same vibration rate that is understood through a different filter in that of Venus, Mars, Jupiter, or Saturn.

This alignment of energies comes forth, shall we say, as sympathetic harmony, the Law of Total Sympathetic Harmony. Sympathetic harmonies bring one unto the other. One is attracted then to another person for the purposes of understanding something that is harmonious within himself. A North Pole, for instance, is not attracted to a South Pole. Instead, they are separated, in this case on your Earth, by earth itself, with massive amount or quantity, density, space, or time. But those who are attracted to one another, come unto themselves through sympathetic harmony.

There is a harmonization at many levels, through thought, feelings, and actions, as you have been taught. All of these many forms of consciousness find and arrest themselves in a resonance and vibration of sympathetic harmonies. This is the understanding that is brought forth in the Harmony of Spheres, that greater music that exists beyond the dimensions that you now experience, even beyond that of Unity Consciousness. The Harmony of Spheres is very important to understand even in your own day-to-day life and day-to-day relationships. This is a mighty law that is in action at all times and is brought forth, shall we say, to bring you into a greater understanding of your purpose and your nature.

The planets are all in sympathetic harmony to one another, for how could they not be, all revolving around one Sun? They work in a harmony and a resonance . . . each serving and assisting each other . . . each carrying, as you well know, their own civilizations. Each exists in a sympathetic resonance and vibration to their own planetary life force and stream but yet indeed they are all related to one another. All then come under that same vibration, as they are all engaging at some levels in a Unity of Consciousness.

Now let me return to the Many-Ringed Map and then you will begin to understand how sympathetic harmonies and dualities do indeed work together. The Many-Ringed Map circulates first in the apex of each Golden City. The apexes were given as very important locations. Apexes were given, shall we say, as centers of great electromagnetic force, radiating in what you would know as the great circle of life. This grid of life springs from the center of the Earth and extends itself on to the Great Central Sun. Through this Many-Ringed Map, a system of circles then envelopes the entire area. From this form again many small vortices upon vortices. This concept has long been understood.

Different magnetic and electromagnetic anomalies do appear and other cultures have understood and utilized these forces. Some of them contain, shall we say, negative energies. When I speak of a negative energy, I speak of a polarized feminine force. Some contain within in them positive energies and again, I speak of a polarized positive masculine force. Each of them works through that duality of consciousness. Of course, as these Many-Ringed Maps separate themselves from one another, it is only at the central point where the rings do come together that the Christ is born. The child of that unity becomes yet a new dimension and a new understanding.

This Many-Ringed Map extends itself even beyond your Earth and there is indeed an inner connectivity to other planets, as again, I have explained in sympathetic resonance. Through this principle of sympathetic resonance, there have been those of the past who, entering into the deeper states of consciousness, transcend time and duality and travel beyond this Earth and are able to view the Earth as it is in its own sphere of influence, in its revolutions about your own Sun. Through this, that language and universal bank of knowledge from what you would call the Akasha, has been achieved and understood. Within this great library of light and sound, there are the records of all of the planets that are held within this sympathetic resonance, held of course through vibrations of light and sound and impregnating the entire solar force with its child of consciousness. There, one is able then to transcend the idea that time is dual in understanding, as one is able to view past, present, and future as one continuous stream or thread of consciousness.

There have been those who existed in other cultures before you, who have viewed this time and knew that there would be three great wars that would come upon the planet. Of course, now you may ask yourself, because we have only had but two, where is that third war yet to come? That of course is always one of those questions. Will it be fought in the same manner that the physical wars were fought? Or is it that third and lasting battle, which is the battle within, where the soul seeks its unity and great victory over duality. Of course in Akasha, this has always been the reason for any war, within itself. But now, let us not get sidelined with things that may only tantalize the consciousness and keep it from, again, its ultimate victory in the Ascension.

I have schooled my Brothers and Sisters upon this thought of ultimate victory. This is where we must always keep our consciousness, in its purity, consciousness in its intention. When you begin to understand the forces of the Many-Ringed Map, it is a wisdom supreme and divine. As you have been told before, when you are given true wisdom, there is indeed no greater test.

The Time of Testing is also a time where the floodgates of Akasha come forward to bless those who, we have always said, "have the eyes to see and the ears to hear." Once you have been given this greater information, which is every "A-Ha!" you have ever felt or understood, there is indeed no greater test. Now it is time to bring that will and bring these teachings and put them into action, is it not?

Answer: *Yes it is.*

Let us now continue in the understanding of the Many-Ringed Map. It contains within it the vibrating resonance of Mother Earth herself. It is that drumbeat that is heard from every Shamans drum. It is that great understanding that has been brought through every single cultural understanding that is the absolute sound of Babajeran herself and the Ray Force that is contained within her.

As you know, Babajeran has been called by many names, by many different cultures; however, it is most important that we focus upon her purpose and what she provides for those within this universe. In sympathetic resonance, she allows an opportunity for the body to be put on in its entirety, clothed, shall we say, in the rainbow bridges of the senses, the emotions, or the feelings. This coat of many colors that one puts on is also discarded in a blink, or shall we say, a blink of consciousness that is known as a lifetime. Yet it is simply that change of clothes, as we have always taught you, Dear ones.

One lifetime is that simple but just that one change of clothes of course is something to consider, is it not? Especially when one is concerned about the appearance of that set of clothes as it is harmed through the consciousness of age. Again, let me remind you that death is but a consciousness; disease is but a consciousness; the aging process is but a consciousness. These are the limitations of duality; the limitations when the consciousness is not allowed unity.

The foundation of duality is only brought to show the magnificence of Creation, that there are indeed many different varieties of light and sound that exist under one Sun. As you yourself have said, Dear one, Dear child, are there not many flowers within the garden of Creation? Tulips, daisies, pansies, roses, lilacs, all containing within themselves that one sweet fragrance but imbued with different colors. We differentiate because of duality. It creates that field of sympathetic resonance which allows like vibration to provide a greater field of understanding and experience. This, in turn, allows the consciousness to develop one aspect at a time and keep its focus upon the lesson of that particular soul's sojourn, or shall I say, that multicolored robe that is put on for that one experience.

To understand that all of these flowers come from the same life force is the birth of a new understanding of the flowers. The flower then becomes plural in essence and the soul itself becomes plural in essence. It understands that the individualized experience is united in harmony and a greater sympathetic resonance . . . its purpose is greater . . . its cosmology is deeper.

The Many-Ringed Map extends its force throughout this entire solar system; therefore, that is why the ancients, who developed a Third Eye and the gift of the pineal, were able to travel to Mars, Venus, Neptune, Jupiter, and the many Moons and rings that exist therein. These things were all obtainable and all achievable. They are obtainable and achievable for you, Dear one, Dear heart, if you but apply yourself.

There is also a wealth of information and education that can be obtained through such an understanding of the Many-Ringed Map but always understand its limitation in duality and the force of that teaching that it does bring forward. It brings a gathering for a certain particular lesson, or force, if you will. Those who are working to overcome personal selfishness will be drawn to one particular area geographically of the Many-Ringed Map, for they're in sympathetic vibration and harmony with that area. That is why you will see in one area, those who will come under a collective type of karma, for instance, in your great Earth Changes. You will see many, many examples of this and yet, you know there are no mistakes that happen in this great schoolroom. As your great Master Teacher has said, "Things do not happen to, they happen with a person." Of course, this all happens through sympathetic resonance. Now, before I proceed, we should take a break. Do you have questions?

Question: *Yes, does the sympathetic resonance gravitate toward the individual consciousness or the individual consciousness gravitate toward the sympathetic resonance?*

It is systemic in this nature but there is no mistake ever, ever, ever. Through these mighty Laws of Duality, people are drawn to those that they are like. That likeness brings its vibrational gravity to certain locations upon the Earth itself. This sympathetic resonance draws everything unto itself with a scientific precision, in the same way the oceans are under the influence of the Moon. Do you understand?

Answer: *Yes. In a sense I have a sympathetic resonance with you.*

It is true, Dear child. It is the same as in marriage . . . it is the same as in a birth of a child . . . it is the same within the death of a soul. All is brought in sympathetic resonance.

Response: *Yes it is. I have no other questions at this point.*

These vibrations must be understood in their entirety. It will bring a greater harmony and understanding throughout this Time of Testing, throughout this time of understanding Divine Wisdom. Now, Dear one, Dear heart, I shall take my leave from your density. It is important that you review these lessons and I shall return again for more questioning upon the Map of Rings. Now, I will turn the floor back over to Master Teacher Saint Germain.

Response: *Thank you, Grandfather.*

Greetings, beloveds. I now remind you that the work of that mighty Violet Ray, when you call it into action, brings forth a most transformative effect upon the consciousness. As beloved Sanat Kumara has just reminded all of us, it is indeed the work of consciousness that is most important, Dear ones, Dear hearts. It is in this consciousness that you yourself are able to grasp and understand these new realities, these new understandings. The Violet Flame is like water that is given to a new seedling. It allows consciousness to grow it roots deeper and deeper, grasping, shall we say, new understanding, the ability to assimilate and absorb. Not only does it transmute, but it also expands. As I have said before:

Violet Flame expand,
Violet Flame command,
Violet Flame I AM.

This brings that mighty law into a greater cosmic action . . . a cosmic action which allows your own consciousness to grow and expand. It brings, again, a greater command of the great I AM. And now you have questions for me. Please proceed.

Question: *Yes, some dietary guidelines for the channel would be very helpful to keep her health and energy levels up. Do you have any suggestions?*

[Editor's Note: Saint Germain suggests nutrition particular to the channel that is not applicable for all people.]

Question: *Thank you. This will be very helpful in the maintenance and sustaining of the body. Another set of questions that I have concerns the mixing of differing vibrations. Do you have any guidelines for this?*

As beloved Sanat Kumara has explained, everything is in its own sympathetic resonance. When a vibration is not to be mixed, you know it immediately. The same as when gasoline is put upon a fire, there is a complete explosion. There is disharmony; there is discord; there is a feeling of discomfort, right?

Response: *Yes there is.*

That is always the first key; however, know this, that at all times there is no mistake that can be made that cannot be undone. Know that even if you should fall or falter in your endeavor, that the vibrations and the energies are there to give you the assistance that you require. Call upon the mighty I AM to bring balance in situations where you feel there has been the vibration of mixed energy. Create the handshake of Brotherhood that I have spoken of to you, Dear ones. Know always that in that mighty Violet Ray is the Violet Ray of Diplomacy and Ordered Service. To minimize conflict is to call upon those mighty Laws Divine and to bring forward, as beloved Sanat Kumara has said, the birth of the Christ Divine. Questions?

Question: *Even though there are many colors in the Ray System, I have noticed when you come through, Saint Germain, you are only of one Ray; when El Morya* comes through, he is only of one Ray; when Sananda comes through, the same, and also with Sanat Kumara. Is this something chosen when moving into the unity of Unana and the Christ?

As it works, Dear one, in the field of duality, we are recognized only as we are distinguished. We put upon the Ray Force for the work that is at hand . . . for the work that is accepted . . . for the consciousness in its own expansion. Beyond this, there are times where we work upon other Ray Forces when it is called upon us; however, at that time, then we utilize that Ray Force in its entirety. The Ray within itself is a stream that is used to travel, shall we say, along with the consciousness. It assists and gives movement to that as an understanding. It is true indeed that we individualize our consciousness along certain Ray Forces to get certain works accomplished and there, we are known as that.

Question: *Are you saying that to make the transition from duality into Unana, it is much simpler to take the focus into one Ray to make that transition of Ascension?*

It is easier to move out of duality through taking that one focus. It is easier then to birth only as ONE, as the Christ, the child of a pure Immaculate Conception. To move from duality to, shall we say, a multi-faceted reality, requires a single focus.

Response: *I see. This is very interesting. I have noticed that the work that we have done has been of the Blue Ray and the Pink Ray going into the world and yet, of the sponsorship of Violet and Green.*

It has been dispensed not only on the Violet Ray, but primarily upon the Green Ray, to bring healing and understanding.

Response: *Yes. This is most enlightening. I have no further questions at this moment.*

Then I shall take my leave from your density and know that, I AM.

Response: *Thank you, Saint Germain, blessings.*

Hitaka

Response: *Hitaka*

Study Guide for Secret Teachings on the Map of Rings

Terms and Topics:
Archetypal Knowledge
The Map of Rings
The Elements
Sympathetic Resonance
Harmony of the Spheres
ONE Focus for Ascension

Insights on Sanat Kumara's Teachings of the Map of Rings
1. The current level of consciousness of humanity is quickly changing. As the old level of consciousness leaves and a new level enters, the new light of wisdom opens spiritual and scientific vistas for humanity.
2. Sanat Kumara is the teacher of Saint Germain as well as many other contemporary Ascended Master teachers. Because of this he is often referred to as a "Grandfather Teacher" of the ancestral knowledge of the Great White Brotherhood.
3. The Map of Rings depicts how the elements of the Earth interact with one another and illustrates how the underlying energies of Mother Earth interact with human consciousness to obtain the Ascension.
4. Through understanding, one can master the elements within (inner world, physical body) and without (astrology, Feng Shui), and an integration process of the soul occurs. This Mastery lays significant groundwork for spiritual transcendence of dual forces—the Ascension Process.
5. The Map of Rings plays an integral role in support of the Golden City Vortices. Sanat Kumara refers to the Golden City Vortices as the Crystalline Cities. Spiritual ceremonies and rituals performed within the Map of Rings help the initiate to realize the knowledge of the Great Mystery. The Map of Rings carries the heartbeat of Mother Earth to our ears.

FIGURE 1-E
The Exhortation to the Apostles
Jesus the Christ, as the archetype of the Master Teacher and Spiritual Teacher in *The Exhortation to the Apostles*. In this painting by French painter James Tissot, (circa 1886-1894), Jesus instructs his twelve apostles as they carefully listen.

6. Accessing the forces of the Map of Rings can give one the ability necessary for astrally traveling to other planets of our solar system as well as develop the potential of the pineal gland.
7. The Map of Rings functions on the principles of Sympathetic Harmonies and duality. Its implication is always karmic. For example, certain geographic areas hold particular karmic lessons or energies; therefore, these locales will attract certain populations whose karma is aligned to a specific karma. This understanding is one of the underlying principles in collective or group karma.

Archetypal Knowledge

The spiritual knowledge and teachings of the ascended Masters are often based upon archetypes. This form of universal spiritual knowledge quickly enters the human psychology, and deeply affects spiritual growth and evolution. Swiss psychiatrist Carl Jung identified five basic archetypes that comprise the human mental framework:[1]

1. The Self (Individualization)
2. The Shadow (the Dark Side)

FIGURE 2-E
Aphrodite from Pompeii
Both Aphrodite and The Birth of Venus, (following page), depict the Divine Feminine. Many Ascended Beings and Spiritual Teachers draw from this archetype, including Lady Master Venus, Mary Magdalene (Magadha or Magda), and Portia. (Fresco from Pompei, Casa di Venus, 1st century AD. Dug out in 1960. It is supposed that this fresco could be the Roman copy of famous portrait of Campaspe, mistress of Alexander the Great, before 79 CE. From the archive of Stephen Haynes, photographer.[2])

3. Anima (Feminine image held by the masculine.)
4. Animus (Masculine image held by the feminine.)
5. Persona (the Masked Self)

The works of William Shakespeare are renowned for the use of archetypes, and the Tarot is perhaps one of the best-known esoteric versions of universal myth. Archetypes weave in, through, and around the art of storytelling, and the Ascended Masters apply their exacting simplicity for humanity's spiritual growth and transformation. Here are some of the underlying archetypes of the teachers of Ascended Master lore:

- El Morya: The strong, silent type; Divine Father.
- Saint Germain: The Magician; Divine Brother.
- Soltec: The Scientist.
- Hilarion: The Physician and Healer.
- Sanat Kumara and Lord Macaw: The Sage.
- Lady Portia: The Wise Woman; Divine Sister.
- Kuthumi: The Agrarian and nature-lover; the Ecologist.
- Mother Mary: The Western feminine archetype; Divine Mother.

FIGURE 3-E
The Birth of Venus
Depicts the goddess Venus, having emerged from the sea as a fully grown woman, arriving at the sea-shore. The seashell she stands on was a symbol in classical antiquity for a woman's vulva. Thought to be based in part on the Venus de' Medici, an ancient Greek marble sculpture of Aphrodite. Circa 1483 to 1485.[3]

FIGURE 4-E
Mercury
Mercury is the archetype of Hermes and Ascended Masters Hilarion and Soltec who are both associated with this healing and scientific knowledge.

FIGURE 5-E
The Dream of Saint Joseph
Circa 1773 to 1774. Joseph, the legal father of Jesus receives instruction from an Angel in a series of dreams regarding Jesus's conception and imminent danger.[5]

- Kuan Yin: The Eastern feminine archetype; Divine Mother.
- Sananda and Lord Macaw: The realized Christ/Quetzalcoatl; Divine Masculine; Divine Son.
- Mary Magdalene: Divine Feminine; Divine Daughter.
- Lady Nada: Feminine archetype of justice, strength, and equality; Divine Sister.
- Lady Master Venus: Feminine archetype of beauty and harmony; Divine Feminine.

FIGURE 6-E
The Ancient of Days
Sanat Kumara is also known as the *Ancient of Days*, an archetype of Divine Father. (A fresco from Ubisi, Georgia, 14th Century.7)

The Map of Rings

The *Map of Rings* depicts the Earth covered with a worldwide grid of interlocking circles. The circles portray the elements of the Earth: air, water, fire, and earth, and how their interaction with one another result in the physical manifestation of the Earth. According to the teachings of Sanat Kumara, the Map of Rings is not to be confused with the Golden City Map, although the electromagnetism of the Map of Rings plays a role in the formation of the Golden Cities which manifest primarily in the realm of Angels, Archangels, and Ascended Masters (the Fifth Dimension), but are also detected in the Fourth and Third Dimensions.

The circle symbolizes the unity of life, the ONE, and the Map of Rings is built upon this spiritual knowledge. The secret of its grid has long been venerated in indigenous teachings, and although its forces are dual, it initiates consciousness to understand the Christ or Quetzalcoatl energies, which

FIGURE 7-E
Merlin and the Knight
Saint Germain is both the alchemist and magician, whose symbology is also represented as the Chariot in the Tarot. He is also an archetype of Divine Father, as Joseph, the father of Jesus. ("Merlin and the Knight," an engraving from an English gift book, *The Rose*, published in 1847.[6])

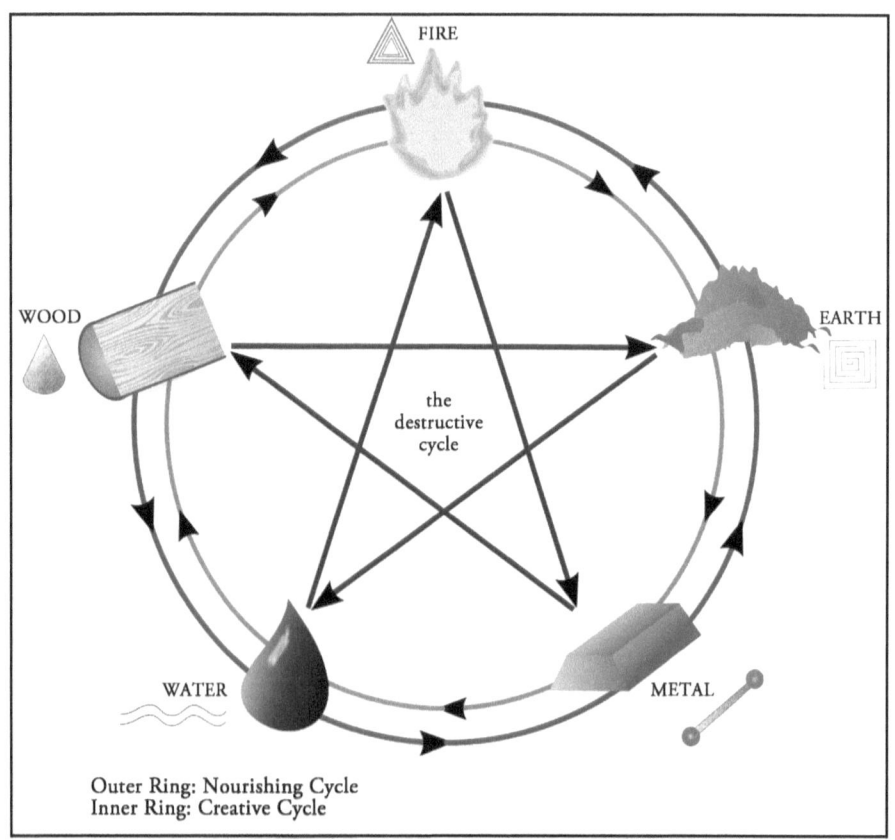

FIGURE 8-E
The Cycle of the Elements

are foundational to the Ascension Process. Its energies allegedly initiate the human soul through various stages, allegorically categorized as iron and bronze, onward to the higher states of silver and the ultimate state as gold.

Geometrically built upon a matrix of circles, the energies of this transformative grid originate at the center of the Earth and radiate to the Galactic Center—the Great Central Sun. The interlocking circles pulsate both a polarity of negative (feminine) and positive (masculine) energies. It is claimed that where two circles of feminine and masculine meet, a third ring of creative, new energy manifests. This pristine energy is claimed to physically hold and manifest the energy of unity—the Christ Consciousness. These sensitive areas of Earth influence human consciousness and are alleged to produce a sense of peace and meditative stillness that "transcends time and duality." The ability to achieve deep meditative states and astral projection is common in these geophysical areas.

FIGURE 9-E
Kuan Yin
Kuan Yin is considered the Eastern Divine Mother.
Great Master, Guan Yin Chao I (fl. late 14th c.), Yuan Dynasty Hanging scroll. Depicts: Shan Cai (center walking on waves), The Filial Parrot (above), Guan Yin and Long Nu.[8]

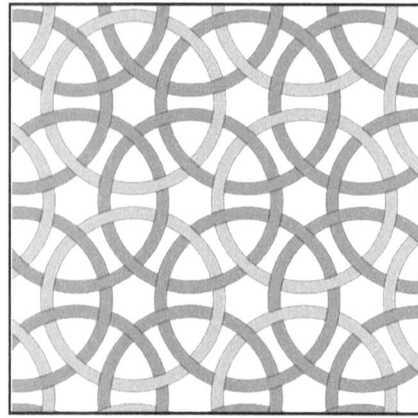

FIGURE 10-E
Map of Rings
The Map of Rings is an overlapping series of circles that feed vital ley lines and create the sacred *Flower of Life*. This energy grid feeds the matrix of Golden City Vortices.

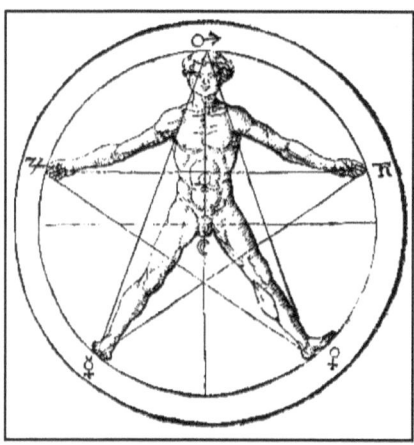

FIGURE 11-E
Humans and Elements

Sanat Kumara's teachings on the Map of Rings claim that the centers (apexes) of Golden City Vortices radiate an electromagnetic current of energy to the center of Earth. This emission of flowing energy functions through the metaphysical principle of sympathetic resonance and its presence births the ethereal series of rings upon the Earth's surface.

The energetic rings instigate a cycle of the elements on Mother Earth which is dualistic—both masculine and feminine, and constructive or destructive. According to the classical Chinese system of Feng Shui, the interaction of the five elements (metal, wood, water, fire, and earth) follows this creative-nourishing cycle: metal creates and nourishes water; water nourishes wood; wood feeds and nourishes fire; fire creates earth; earth creates and nourishes metal. The creative counterpart of this cycle is destructive: metal destroys and weakens wood; wood weakens earth; earth contains and weakens water; water destroys or weakens fire; fire melts and weakens metal.

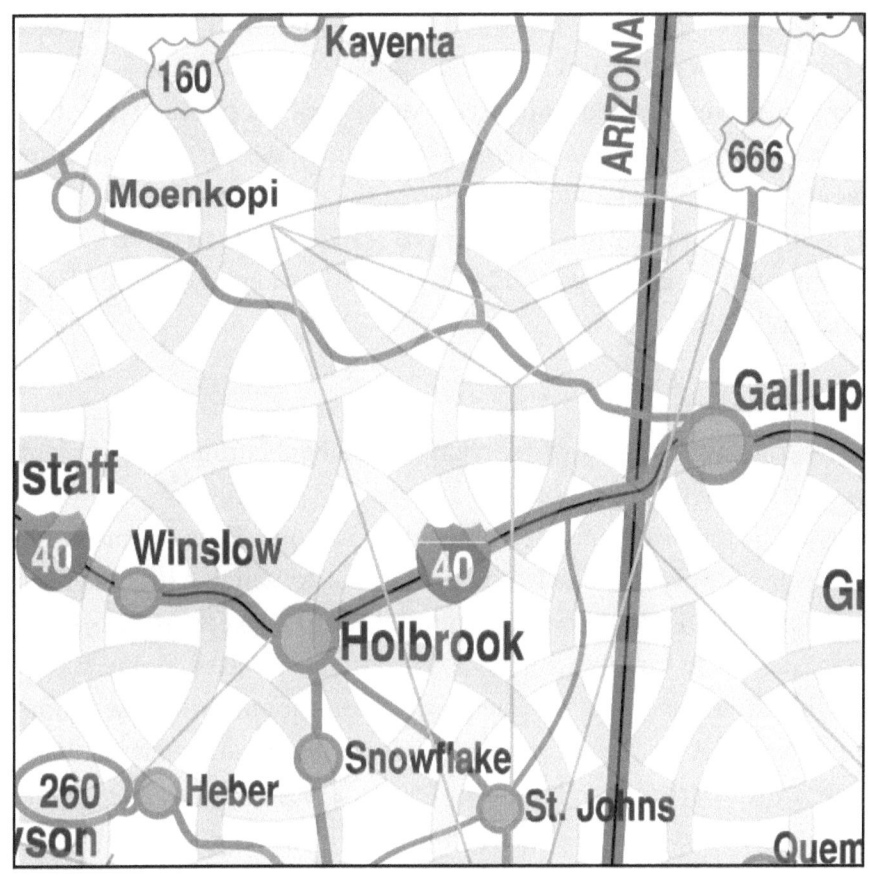

FIGURE 12-E
Golden City of Gobean Northern Door with Map of Rings

Each singular ring in the Map of Rings holds the Elemental Kingdom as both the Western four elements and as the esoteric Gnomes (earth), Sylphs (air), Undines (water), and the Salamanders (fire), plus Earth as Babajeran. Mother Earth Babajeran has a four-fold process in the four seasons that generate the creation. This Map also represents the Eastern four elements as the Wu Xing, commonly known as the Five Agents (wood, fire, metal, water, and earth).

The Divine Man based on fifteenth-century artist and occultist Henri Cornelis. The planetary forces, however, are changed to correlate with the Taoist Five Elements and their cycles. Manly Hall writes regarding the human body: "As man's physical body has five distinct and important extremities—two legs, two arms, and a head, of which the last governs the first four—the number five has been accepted as the symbol of man." [2] The Western ancients considered the elements in a different order than Taoist teaching. The two legs or feet are ruled by water and earth (Venus and Saturn). The arms and hands represent fire and air (Mars and Mercury). The head is ruled by aether (spirit), represented by Jupiter. [3] Man is held within the Map of the Rings in the cycle of death and rebirth through the destructive cycle of the elements. Through the Golden City Matrix, the elemental life force of the body is initiated into spiritual growth and realization. Man evolves to the HU-man through both fourth and fifth dimensional energies, initiating the Ascension Process.

Sympathetic Resonance

A physical phenomenon where a passive material (stringed instrument, glass, and tuning forks) responds to an external vibration from another source, as the two share similar likeness. The response is due to the sympathetic resonance between the two materials that contain a harmonic likeness. [4] This is both scientific and esoteric terminology, often used by the Master Teachers to explain why two forces may be attracted to one another. And while these two forces may be drawn to one another, this law is not limited to personal rapport or shared affinity. This anomaly may explain one person's attraction to a certain geologic location or landscape, how a guru chooses a certain student, and even personal preference. Sympathetic resonance is the underpinning of the Law of Vibration and is also known as the subtle, yet forceful Law of Resonance.

Harmony of the Spheres

An ethereal orchestra often comprises numerous stringed instruments. Many report hearing this spiritual music while dreaming or just upon awakening. The Harmony of the Spheres is also an esoteric term that refers to an exacting form of balance and synchronization, often realized through the hidden geometric and mathematical perfection of all created forms. The movement of the heavenly bodies is said to be timed to such mathematical precision and perfection that the planets create a celestial music. The Ancient Pipes of Pan are alleged to represent the natural, innate Harmony of the Spheres. It is said that Pythagoras heard the divine music of the spheres and that all men heard the rhapsody that Job describes as "when the stars of the morning sang together." [5] Manly Hall writes:

"The Pythagoreans believed that everything which existed had a voice and that all creatures were eternally singing the praise of the Creator. Man fails to hear these divine melodies because his soul is enmeshed in the illusion of material existence. When he liberates himself from the bondage of the lower world with its sense limitations, the *Music of the Spheres* will again be audible as it was in the Golden Age. Harmony recognizes harmony, and when the human soul regains its true estate it will not only hear the celestial choir but also join with it in an everlasting anthem of praise to that Eternal Good controlling the infinite number of parts and conditions of Being."[6]

Sanat Kumara's Prophecies of Change

1. The Earth Mother, Babajeran, will play a significant role in helping humanity to rise in vibration. This Divine Intervention is carried through the knowledge of the Map of Rings and its wisdom will help initiate further knowledge of the Ascension Process and the Golden Cities.
2. The Golden Cities' purpose is to assist each individual to obtain innate knowledge of divinity and destiny. The Golden Cities are also prophesied to assist the healing process of body, mind, and spirit, and initiate understanding of the Oneship.
3. Sanat Kumara prophesies that during this time three great wars will be experienced. He alludes that two great wars have already been fought, (World Wars I and II), and that the third and final battle is the battle within, "where the soul seeks unity, and victory over duality."
4. During the Time of Testing, the Akashic Records are opened for all who have developed "the eyes to see; ears to hear."

Akashic Records

Timeless, immortal records of all created things, especially souls and their many lifetimes. There are many varying accounts of Akashic Records, however, in the I AM America Teachings these records are held individually and ethereally (Fifth Dimension) in Golden City Vortices. The Seventh Light

Body is an egg-shaped ovoid with extremely strong threads of light that form a golden grid. This energy body contains both the Golden Thread Axis and Tube of Light that connect to the I AM Presence. It is alleged that this light body holds personal Akashic Records that are key to past-life memory. Akashic Records contain the accounts of all created things and events from time immemorial, both significant and insignificant. These records are constructed from the fifth cosmic element: ether. [For more information about this light body see *Fields of Light: An Introduction to the Ascended Masters of the I AM America Teachings*. For more information regarding Golden Cities and Akashic Records of Ancient Cultures see *Points of Perception*.]

Teachings of the Unity Consciousness of the Christ

1. Most wars that are fought on the Earth Plane are fought with the sword of self-righteousness. Sanat Kumara asks that we abandon the dualistic "good versus evil" and pursue the Christ Consciousness.
2. Through Unity Consciousness, war is abandoned and healing begins.
3. Through Unity Consciousness the soul's quest for truth and understanding is satiated with the light of wisdom.
4. Humanity meets the Ascension Process through the attainment of Unity Consciousness.

Saint Germain on the Violet Flame

1. Use the Violet Flame when you encounter spiritual information you cannot absorb or comprehend.
2. Use the Violet Flame when your spiritual growth is "stuck."
3. The Violet flame is like water irrigating a freshly planted seedling. The Violet Flame helps our spiritual roots to develop and grasp new material, and to assimilate and absorb new levels of spiritual consciousness. He suggests the use of this decree specifically for our spiritual growth:

> "Violet Flame expand,
> Violet Flame command,
> Violet Flame, I AM!"

1. "Jungian Archetypes." Wikipedia. Accessed August 19, 2016. https://en.wikipedia.org/wiki/Jungian_archetypes.
2. Hall, Manly. "The Human Body in Symbolism." In The Secret Teachings of All Ages, 75. Diamond Jubilee Edition. Los Angeles: Philosophical Research Society, 1988.
3. Ibid.
4. "Sympathetic Resonance." Wikipedia. Accessed August 19, 2016. https://en.wikipedia.org/wiki/Sympathetic_resonance.
5. Hall, Manly. "Atlantis and the Gods of Antiquity." In The Secret Teachings of All Ages, 35. Diamond Jubilee Edition. Los Angeles: Philosophical Research Society, 1988.
6. Ibid. "The Pythagorean Theory of Music and Color," 83.

Illustrations:
1. Tissot, James J. *The Exhortation to the Apostles*. Digital image. Wikimedia Commons, 4 May 2011. Web. 7 Aug. 2012. Between 1886 and 1894; Brooklyn Museum.
2. *Aphrodite Anadyomene from Pompeii*. Digital image. Wikimedia Commons. December 12, 2008. Accessed August 29, 2016. https://commons.wikimedia.org/wiki/File:Aphrodite_Anadyomene_from_Pompeii_cropped.jpg.
3. Botticelli, Sandro. *The Birth of Venus*. Digital image. Wikimedia Commons. November 2, 2012. Accessed August 29, 2016. https://commons.wikimedia.org/wiki/File:Sandro_Botticelli_-_La_nascita_di_Venere_-_Google_Art_Project_-_edited.jpg.
4. DeMorgan, Evelyn. *Mercury*. Digital image. Wikimedia Commons. January 1, 2014. Accessed August 29, 2016. https://commons.wikimedia.org/wiki/File:Evelyn_de_Morgan_-_Mercury,_1870-1873.jpg. Circa 1870 to 1873.
5. Mengs, Anton Raphael. *The Dream of Saint Joseph*. Digital image. Wikimedia Commons. February 22, 2015. Accessed August 29, 2016. https://commons.wikimedia.org/wiki/File:Anton_Raphael_Mengs_016.jpg. Circa 1773/1774.
6. *Merlin and the Knight*. Digital image. Wikimedia Commons. January 25, 2015. Accessed August 29, 2016. https://commons.wikimedia.org/wiki/File:Merlin_and_the_Knight.png.
7. Damiane. *The Ancient of Days*. Digital image. Wikimedia Commons. October 9, 2009. Accessed August 29, 2016. https://commons.wikimedia.org/wiki/File:Damian._The_Ancient_of_Days.jpg.

8. *Great Master, Guan Yin Chao.* Digital image. Wikimedia Commons. October 19, 2009. Accessed August 29, 2016. https://commons.wikimedia.org/wiki/File:Guanyin_acolytes.jpg.
9. Tomruen. *Flower of Life Square.* Digital image. February 16, 2016. Accessed August 19, 2016.
10. Dit Agrippa, Henri Cornélis. *Human Body in a Pentagram.* Digital image. Wikimedia Commons. May 1, 2008. Accessed August 19, 2016. https://commons.wikimedia.org/wiki/File:Gravure_d%27Agrippa_de_Nettesheim.jpg.
11. Toye, Lori. *I AM America United States Golden Cities Map.* Payson, AZ: I AM America Seventh Ray Publishing, 1998.

6

A New Reality
Saint Germain

Greetings, Beloved chelas in that mighty Violet Ray, I AM Saint Germain and I stream forth on that Violet Ray of Mercy, Compassion, and Forgiveness. As usual, Dear hearts, Dear ones, I request permission to come forward.

Response: *Please, Saint Germain, come forward.*

There is much work for us to complete, several lessons and discourses that need that completion brought forward to them; however, Dear ones, there is much that is happening now in your current times upon the Earth Plane and Planet. Many things that are happening . . . things that were prophesied that would occur . . . things that are happening with that Divine Timing and Divine Intent. It is important to understand that when a prophecy is brought into its fruition, to not move into fear around other prophecies that may too come into their materialization upon the Earth Plane and Planet. Instead, it is important to return to the spiritual teaching . . . important to return to that great drink that has been offered to you . . . that most refreshing drink. This is the drink of spirituality, the gift to humanity which opens the heart, opens the eyes and ears, and brings the hand into action. From there, that Great Will is brought into its alignment and humanity itself then is brought into a greater understanding.

This is the movement into the New Times, into the New Age. The New Age is indeed a time where there will be a difference in vibration overall upon the whole Earth . . . a time where humanity will be open at a whole new level of understanding. Many of the chakras upon the human body as they exist now will be opened to a finer reality and a finer understanding. Of course, as it is with any New Time that is birthed, there is also that door that must close behind it. We must bid goodbye to the old times, the old patterns, and the old paths . . . those, shall we say, ways that have held us bound into that Law and mighty Wheel of Karmic Action.

We gave to you a discourse upon the alignment of May 5, 2000 and the implication of what this would have for those upon the Earth Plane and Planet. As you know and understand, it is the work of the Rays streaming forth, as they do from the Great Central Sun to the planets and onward to Earth, where they lead humanity forward in its own evolution, timing, and intent. It is important to understand with this great opening, there is indeed an opportunity to cleanse the mistakes of the past . . . to move forward now, away from those paths of karmic retribution and into the paths of destiny and your own purpose as Divine Inheritors.

Beloved Sananda has given many discourses where he has talked about not hiding your light . . . to bring it forward at this time . . . to use all the laws in their application and complete demonstration. When you use the Violet Flame during this time period, visualize that it is lifting the cause, effect, record, and memory of all past lives and past relationships that now come to the forefront for cleansing and ultimate healing. Allow this soothing healing energy that is opened through the vibration of the Seven Rays of Light and Sound in this most wondrous alignment period. There is indeed an opportunity to obtain many demonstrations of the effect of the Violet Flame during this period. It will give an opportunity to bring the pure, transmuting Fires of Alchemy, that great sacred fire surrounding you in all things, and allow you to gain a new understanding in the time that humanity is now entering.

We have given some indication and inclination about the New Times that man is entering. Of course, there are those who would nay-say and would say, because of the time period of Kali Yuga and the time of lesser light spectrum upon the Earth Plane and Planet, that it is almost impossible, or mankind is unable, to correctly evolve at this time. That is the gift of the Violet Flame, for it transmutes the cause and effect of the Earth, not having as much light as is necessary or possible to guide and lead its evolution forward. It allows for complete alignment of the spectrum of the Rays within the Kundalini and the Chakra System, that Divine Astral Body you have known as the astral-logic. It allows for an understanding to come forward in a greater evolution and a greater revolution of the Sun.

This grand acceleration, and especially now, at this time in conjunction with the Golden Ray of Harmony and Completion, is a most wondrous time, Dear ones, Dear hearts. It allows one to release the past in a most forgiving manner and allows one to move forward and face the glorious gift. Dear Sananda has also said that the seconds and the minutes of the clock tick . . . the time is at hand . . . the time is now for man to receive the gift. The gift awaits, Dear ones. It is now given to you, wrapped in its perfect wrapping paper, tied with the most elegant of bows. Now, let us unwrap it and look inside and see this great gift that has been given to humanity . . . the true Divine Inheritor . . . the true God-man . . . the HU-man that resides within.

Do not get sidetracked by those who would say that because you have been bred as a body, crossed-genetically by alien genetics, that it is impossible for you to reach your Ascension. Know this, Dear ones, Dear hearts, that the work of the Violet Flame has been brought forward during this time of supposed great darkness so that you can and will make that evolutionary leap in consciousness and understand the true Oneship of Unana, where all is united as ONE beating heart.

Dear ones, Dear hearts, in the New Times, mankind, through this Collective Consciousness of Unana, will be indeed as ONE, telepathically linked to one another and the Information Age will take on a whole new understanding, a whole new vibration. Imagine the whole idea of thought transference and your ability to communicate day to day with your loved ones, based only upon single perfected thought. This is what awaits mankind at the higher levels of understanding and reality. As you have begun to understand the difference between descending and ascending cultures, you will realize that there were times upon the Earth Plane and Planet, times not in your recorded history, yet recorded in those records of Akasha, that this has existed before. All of these things are indeed possible, Dear ones, as we transcend into a new reality.

We have alluded before that there is a great opportunity not only for worldwide peace but for the removal of all poverty and pure abundance to reign upon this planet. There are those who would say that these are such lofty ideas, that these are such ideas never attained in the realm of duality. But you see, Dear ones, it is the realm of the Christ that I speak, the union of both sides coming to that neutral point . . . coming to that point of Unana . . . coming to that point of unity and Oneship.

One must understand the great harmonies that lie within when one begins to leave that negative and positive charge of duality. It is important for the soul to have the experiences . . . to have the experience of negative . . . to have the experience of positive, so then it may choose what it prefers in their own great alignment. In this great choosing, in this greater alignment, which is the opportunity afforded to humanity through the uniting of the Violet and the Golden Ray, one may now choose from within. One may choose from the heart, Dear ones, Dear chelas.

Choose and align yourself to that mighty Will Divine, for there indeed is that refreshing drink . . . the drink of freedom . . . the drink of spiritual liberation . . . the drink of Ascension. All of this, Dear ones, is that great gift that has been given to you, tied up and wrapped in its beautiful bow. Unwrap it now, Dear ones, Dear hearts, for it is your destiny . . . it is indeed who you really are . . . it is the gift of I AM THAT I AM.

If you are having difficulty and trouble in uniting these two Ray Forces and bringing them forward, I suggest that you call upon the Ring of Blue Flame Angels. They serve along with beloved Archangel Michael. They will bind any type of entity that is keeping you, shall we say, distracted and away from the truth of all. These beloved angels and beings of light have been brought here to serve mankind, to assist in spiritual evolution. They are akin to the teachers' helpers, those who are there to help at all times and to give that assistance when the student is having difficulty with the lesson.

Keep your focus upon that greater harmony. Keep your focus upon the Violet Flame. Know yes, that there are the actions and the little mistakes of the past but know this too, as it has been said to you before, there is no saint without a past and no sinner without a future.

Know, Dear ones, Dear hearts, that your future in the light awaits you. Know that the path of Ascension is indeed there. A time will come when you will no longer need to take on a physical body to have your own experiences and then you will be called into a higher realm of light and sound, called to your true destiny to become a caretaker of Creation. Come forward now, Dear ones, Dear hearts, not stewards of the past . . . not stewards of misery . . . not stewards of pain and suffering. Come forward now as Co-creators of light and sound, of that greater Harmony Divine . . . a Co-creator, hand-in-hand in that of the spirit of Brotherhood and Sisterhood, the true Christ Consciousness. Come forward in the name of I AM THAT I AM. Questions?

Response: *Not at this time.*

(He is now walking over to a blackboard and writing I AM THAT I AM.)

It is important for you to understand this concept in its entirety:

> "I AM" represents the grand universal mind. "THAT" represents the bridge, or in this case, the service of the Rays of light and sound. "I AM," in the final equation, represents the seating of that light and sound from the great universal Source within you individually. As you see, in this one statement of "I AM THAT I AM," you are all related and ONE with the Source and yet, you are all within your individual expression.

How does one keep the harmony, shall we say, keep that focus of Brotherhood and Sisterhood of the greater universal mind in their travels and sojourns in the Earth Plane? Of course, this limitation called duality is expressed in race, sexuality, and all personal choices and preferences. It is expressed in religions, political parties, and the many, shall we say, patterns of duality that come forward to give their greater Lesson Divine. Realize at all times that you are indeed all related as ONE. You are indeed as ONE, Dear hearts, Dear children of my heart. Know that this unity at all times is yours. Return back into it and whenever you feel separation, whenever you feel any dissension of any sort, you can return back into this unity. It is there that the answers are given, where being gently led back into the path and the union with the spiritual hierarchies becomes complete.

There are many things that are happening now upon the Earth Plane and Planet, many prophecies which we will see come to fruition. This will give, shall we say, a new impetus to the work that has been assigned to you. However, it is important, and again we remind you, to keep your focus and your heart upon the spiritual message. It is important that humanity change first from within. This transmuted effect that this work is to have upon humanity is essential and important; for you see, Dear ones, Dear hearts, if this evolution does not come to its completion, you will then be trapped again into another cycle of death, rebirth, death, and rebirth. Gain the ever-present and all-knowing knowledge of the self that is contained within the I AM THAT I AM.

There is the finer instruction . . . there is the greater learning . . . there is indeed the wellspring of all that replenishes the source and supply. The New Times that await will indeed be times that will long be remembered. As you see, Dear ones, it is a great turning point. It is no different than that great and mighty shift of the poles. It is a shift of consciousness within you . . . a shift of understanding that you are all related to the ONE and that unity is indeed the Cause Divine. Make peace with all of your Brothers and Sisters. Now this does not mean that you enjoin them in the work that you do but make peace within your hearts . . . make peace so that you may move forward in your own harmony . . . make this peace, Dear ones, Dear hearts, as it is indeed a very important step. From this greater harmony streams that mighty abundance.

From the heart of God, the universal stream of consciousness is ever present and ever flowing. Great opportunities then await the initiate who sees the greater string of harmony played in the grander symphony. Dear ones, Dear hearts, the great times that await, even at this level of consciousness that you are now participating in, do come, even if it seems difficult to understand. Hold within yourself faith, hope, and trust in the true transmutative process. Hold always that the great Alchemy of God awaits. May it now come forward. Questions?

Question: *Yes. May harmony come forward. Harmony can be achieved with yourself and those immediately surrounding you, even though those away from you don't necessarily agree with that harmony, is this true?*

This is always true, Dear one. As we have discussed before, in the greater teachings brought forth by Sanat Kumara, there is that sympathetic resonance that attracts one to another to bring a greater teaching further. But there are always those who stand on the periphery, so to speak, of that resonance. It is the same as throwing a pebble into a pond. At the center of impact is the greatest effect but the vibration of the ripples extends clear to the outer edges of that puddle or pond. In the same way, with those that vibrate in resonance to you, are they not the closest to you? Do you not feel them closest in your heart? Then there are those that vibrate towards the outside and stand there giving you, shall we say, in this case, a definition.

Question: *Yes, this is quite true. Then there are those at a further distance who are throwing stones. I accept all of these; however, I have noted that the use of the Violet Flame keeps what we are doing, and those who have the sympathetic resonance, in a state of purity and I am very grateful for it. My question relates to the desire to extend harmony and upliftment to the entire planet. We have always been taught that we must have the permission of those that we are praying for or decreeing for, but what about the entire planet? Do we do have their permission? I do not wish to interfere.*

All is based upon the idea, again, of agreement. Through agreement comes that sympathetic resonance, the ability to enter into, shall we say, a reciprocity, an agreement, a sympathetic vibration, so that all may then respond in accordance to a Divine Plan. Of course, there are those who proceed further with their own will, seeking their own desires to be applied or indeed sometimes forced upon the desires of others but the greatest is to bring all into harmony. Where two or more are gathered, there the focus can begin for a greater Co-creation.

Response: *Yes, I see what you are saying. So it is truly that in agreement— agreement with anyone who agrees to have you pray for them or decree for their highest and best good—prayer functions in accordance with the true law.*

The Earth itself has the agreement to bring forth the Mineral Kingdom, to bring forth the Vegetable Kingdom. A flower grows in a garden through the Laws of Sympathetic Resonance, in the same way the weed would grow side-by-side. All is brought forward through a higher understanding of Agreement Formation. Through this comes a greater understanding and responsibility. Even humanity, that exists on the outside of beloved Babajeran, will come forward in a greater understanding of agreement and harmonies of sympathetic resonance.

The opening of the Golden City Vortices, in cooperation with beloved Babajeran and the Spiritual Hierarchy, again, is done through the same Principle of Agreement, of sympathetic resonance, harmonies, and vibrations that allow this Co-creation to come forward in its greater evolution. Now, Dear ones, Dear hearts, it is important to understand that all of the openings of the Golden City Vortices are indeed with their own Divine Timing and Intent. This comes forward again at the basis of the idea of Agreement Formation.

Question: *In considering agreement then, there are those who will agree to come to Golden Cities and those that will agree not to. There will be those who agree for the Golden Age to come forward and those who will not agree, is this not so?*

There are those who recognize the need for a New Time but yet they are hardly committed to such a cause. Instead their focus and their attention are still upon the duality of life, still within the little disagreements and disharmonies. Again, as it is often stated, energy goes where the attention flows. The work of the Violet Flame allows for a grander field of neutrality and openness to expand itself. There, in this great expansion of unity, lies the unity of the Christ Consciousness. It allows for a greater understanding to come forward and the New Times to move in their Divine Timing and Intent.

As you know, Dear ones, it is not easy to make a migration to a Golden City Vortex, for there the spiritual teachings of that Vortex are owned not only in the external but they must be owned internally. Have there not been those who have come to the Vortex of Gobean and there, immediately feel continuous disharmony in all of their personal relationships? But once that disharmony is transmuted and understood in its higher order, a greater agreement then flows. A greater alignment to the Divine Will is allowed and harmony then flows forward with the release of karmic ties that get in the way, shall we say, of allowing peace supreme to rule.

Response: *Yes, I have noted this. I have also noted that those who were unable to step forward into harmony leave Gobean.*

And yet, for those who have passed that first initiation, have they not been brought to a higher understanding of love supreme, a higher understanding of the true gift of harmony and the price that is paid? As I have said before, there is the great sacrifice, shall we say, of the Avatars and the Adepts. This is the sacrifice of which I speak.

Question: *Yes, I understand what you are saying. So now that we are to this point of harmony in Gobean, is it possible for the harmony of Gobean to envelop our planet?*

Of course, Dear ones, Dear hearts, for as I have stated before, all of the Golden City Vortices are interconnected. They are the new grid of the Golden Age. They are the new grid of alignment for beloved Babajeran to bring forth this New Time, this greater harmony with every possible energy that can complement and serve in agreement for that time to move forward.

Those who would travel to Malton in their spiritual migration, with the intention of the second level of initiation, would they not then encounter insatiable desires that might take them over the edge? You see, then this must be brought into its greater balance, brought into its greater knowledge of how desires in their fruition lead one to the true path of spiritual liberation. This is where one is ready to release the world and all its folly.

Response: *You are speaking of that desire for the Source or God over the desire for the world.*

You see, Dear ones, Dear hearts, one cannot be forced to want God. One must want God in the same way as the great wrath of that chela held under water: all the chela wanted, in the same breath, was to know God in God's entirety.

Response: *Again, it is choice and agreement.*

The third initiation, that of Wahanee, leads the soul to truly seek spiritual liberation. But there again, it is haunted by the past, is it not? Always, when one makes that commitment to go to the next level, are there not those who hang and cling incessantly, fearing for their life, fearing for, shall we say, embracing the totality and natural urge to know God? That within itself is the third initiation.

Question: *I see. Are you saying that in a migratory pattern, one would start in Gobean and then work through each of the Golden Cities?*

If one would choose that, it is one of the highest paths that one may take; however, it is never promised to be easy, Dear ones, Dear hearts. Each is bound by their own karma that must be balanced and particularly, if one has entered into a union, a marriage of choice and has chosen to have a family, a family must always come first.

Question: *Another consideration is, can one achieve the Ascension even staying in one specific Golden City?*

It is true, Dear ones. That is why all of the stars glisten and glow in their inner-connectivity; for you see, it is a great global grid or matrix that covers the entire planet. It extends to other planets throughout your system and from there, they are all connected to the Great Central Sun.

Response: *So, you are speaking of the great pathways, where one may move from one city to another and also one dimension or planet to another.*

It is true, Dear ones, for in each of these pathways, are they not always to know and rejoice in the one consciousness of the source of God? Are they all not ways to understand, at all dimensions available, the inner-connectivity of the expressions of the Source that extends beyond dual force?

Question: *Is it easier to have contact with you in the Star of a Vortex than on the edge or peripheral area or doorway?*

It would depend upon the quality, or shall we say, type of work that we are bringing forward. At this time, it has been decided that the work being dispensed where we are physically now within the Golden City of Gobean, is in sympathetic resonance or, shall we say, in sympathetic harmony with that area. Each area, as you know, or gateway, or doorway of a Golden City

Vortex has its own unique energy. This energy brings forward in sympathetic resonance, harmonies with that group or soul bringing them forward into their greater understanding and evolution when the time is right. And, Dear ones, the time is at hand.

Question: *If, for example, we were to spend several days in another Doorway of this Golden City and receive transmissions, would the information be of a different quality?*

Of course, as I have always said to you, take it into the grander experiment, Dear ones, Dear hearts. But it is true that there is a different resonance, a different quality in the Golden City Vortices, contingent upon the location. This I have outlined to you in great detail.

Question: *Yes, I know, I just wanted to reiterate it again for this discourse. At this moment, I have no further questions. Did you wish to continue on with the initiations for the other Golden Cities?*

I wish to bring that information forward. Shalahah, of course, is the initiation bringing one into complete healing. First experienced as dis-ease to the individual, disease is either at a mental level, at an emotional level, and sometimes manifesting at physical levels. But when the energies are properly assimilated, a greater harmony is brought forward and one is able then to actualize the Christ Consciousness. That is why the sound of "OM-She-A- Ha," meaning "I AM as ONE," is heard as the continuous sound in the Vortex of Shalahah.

In Klehma itself, one is brought forward to face the purification within the being, to release all fear that is held at the genetic level into the ever embrace of the collective ONE, the Unity Consciousness. There, the final release is found into the Ascension and service of all, for one has the inner connection, shall we say, to the grander halls, to the grander understanding of all the dimensions. Questions?

Question: *So, your point of perception will be altered in each Doorway and Star area of each Golden City and this point of perception will give the individual a more expanded understanding than before?*

The quality of the spiritual life is then refined even at a higher vibratory level. There will also be many contacts with Master Teachers, as well as Angels of great Mercy and Compassion, who come forward to bring their greater service. Each of these Golden City Vortices become, unto themselves, a great mystery school of that Master Teacher . . . each of them serving their own initiation . . . each of them serving their own vibration.

Response: *Yes, I understand because each of us individually has a specific Ray of focus that is within the auras, layers, or even in the genetics.*

This is all a refinement process that this brought through the tempering flames of the sacred fire, the Violet Flame. It is the same tempering process which turns lead into brilliant gold. It is the process of taking a man, whose spirit is broken, through the tests and trials of duality and leading him into the Golden transformation of Unity Consciousness, peace supreme—I AM as ONE. This is truly the at-one-ment or atonement, as it has been known; for indeed, Dear ones, we are all as ONE, united in our service on the threshold of true Creation.

Response: *Yes, it would be nice if we could all perceive that instead of each group having a focus of a proprietary sense of rightness over their perception of God. It would be better to harmonize.*

There are many ways to touch the Source, many ways to know the ONE unity of all. The Golden City Vortices, again, are great schools of thought, great ways of understanding at an experiential level through the Doorways, this concept of unity. May the Christ Consciousness appear upon the Earth and rule supreme.

Response: *So be it. I agree. I have no further questions.*

Then, Dear ones, Dear hearts, I shall take my leave from you and in our next discourse, we shall continue our work upon the East and Western Doors of the Golden City Vortices.

Response: *As you wish, that would be most wonderful.*

Study Guide for A New Reality

Topics:
The New Age
Overcoming Our Alien Genetics
Thought Transference
Spiritual Alignment—the Tao
Blue Flame Angels
I AM THAT I AM
Agreement
Teachings on Spiritual Migration
The Five Initiations

Saint Germain's Teachings on Prophecies and Fear
Seek to return to the underlying spiritual message in all prophecies. This opens the heart and our psychic faculties. Through this process we will know the next action to take. Realizing the spiritual heart of prophecy catalyzes the collective will of humanity, and wisely moves humanity into the New Times.

Prophecies of Change
1. The New Age will be remembered as a time when a different vibration engulfed Earth and humanity.
2. Humanity undergoes a new level of spiritual openness. This is caused by a refinement of the human Chakra System.
3. As humanity's spiritual growth opens, we individually move away from the idea of "karmic retribution" and into the ideal as "Divine Inheritors."
4. During the New Times, humanity will communicate through telepathy. This communication anomaly will link us all as ONE in the Collective Consciousness of Unana. This will initiate a new state of the advancing Information Age.
5. New vistas of human experience and communication will open for our cultures and societies as individuals perfect the experience of

Thought Transference. This form of telepathy was claimed to have existed in evolved societies that existed in our ancient worlds.
6. As the polarity of politics subsides and humanity begins to cultivate and achieve the Christ Consciousness, we enter the neutral point. This neutral point is described as unity and Oneship and ushers in a new period for humanity; poverty is removed as true abundance reigns on Earth.
7. A shift of consciousness will occur within every individual, and we will begin to recognize our shared Creator—source and innate divinity. This leads to Unity and peaceful hearts.
8. This higher state of consciousness plays a role in creating abundance for all on Earth. Presently, this prophecy may be hard to understand or actualize, but faith, hope, and trust assist this transmutative process on Earth.
9. The great Alchemy of God awaits!

Saint Germain's Teachings on the Violet Flame:
1. Many past-life memories are triggered at this time, including specific memories regarding difficulty in relationships. This is the perfect time to apply the Violet Flame's transmuting energy to cleanse and heal the cause, effect, record, and memory of past events.
2. At this time of dimensional shift and alignment, Saint Germain claims there is an *opportunity* to gain demonstration of the Sacred Fire's alchemy and to gain new insight regarding the new time of spiritual evolution.
3. Since Earth is currently in a time of overall darkness due to Kali Yuga, the Violet Flame allows us to overcome this deficit of the light by aligning our Kundalini and Chakra System with increased astral light. This allows for our evolutionary process to continue without delay.
4. The Violet Flame, along with the timely appearance of the Golden Ray of Harmony and Completion, actually assists our solar sun to also evolve spiritually. Saint Germain refers to this solar evolution as a *revolution*. The Sun's spiritual evolution influences humanity to enter into a "collective forgiveness," which further reveals our innate divinity, the Divine HU-man.

5. The efficiency of the Violet Flame is not obstructed by alien DNA that was designed to deny the natural, human Ascension Process. The Violet Flame overcomes this physical and psychological darkness to initiate an evolutionary leap in consciousness.
6. The Violet Flame helps us to understand and experience the Oneship, the uniting of human hearts in the consciousness of Unana.

Thought Transference

Coined in the nineteenth century as a form of communication that precluded any form of sensory interaction, thought transference was later better defined as telepathy.[1] Telepathy is the process of a person randomly or intentionally feeling or knowing the thoughts and emotions of another person. This ability is not limited to time or space, and those who have developed their telepathic abilities send and receive information via the mental plane—a projection of energy in the form of vibration.[2]

Thought transference, or producing thought-waves, is said to be common among developed Yogis and their students, and in fact many Ascended Masters will use this technique to contact their disciples from the higher planes of consciousness to our physical world. The mind-telepathy connection broadcasts waves similar to a radio, and the thought wave is received by those who are sensitive to the vibration. It is claimed that our personal and spiritual habits can acclimate our mind to move more ably to receive these subtle vibrations by attuning our consciousness through prayer and meditation, a vegetarian diet, positive thoughts, relaxation of the mind, and time spent in nature. The Master Teachers encourage walks or hikes in nature, and a simple lifestyle to cultivate our receptivity to the spiritual planes. Sri Swami Sivananda writes regarding the power of thought, "Thoughts are living things. A thought is as much solid as a piece of stone. We may cease to be, but our thought can never die." He elaborates on the travel of thought through time and space: "Those who harbor thoughts of hatred, jealousy, revenge, and malice are very, very dangerous persons. They cause unrest and ill-will amongst men. Their thoughts and feelings are like wireless messages broadcast in ether, and are received by those whose minds respond to such vibrations. Thought moves with tremendous velocity. Those who entertain sublime and pious thoughts help others, who are in their vicinity and at a distance."[3]

It is also important to note that in our dream state our communication is often through thought transference or telepathy, and thoughts and ideas will often appear as images or symbols. After death, it is alleged that communication in the astral and spirit worlds is telepathic, and communication mirrors the telepathic communication one might encounter in the physical world. It is claimed, however, as the soul advances to the inner planes of the spirit world, telepathic communication compresses, and vast amounts of information can be relayed between two beings. [4] This same phenomenon has been reported by channels who telepathically download large amounts of information from Spiritual Masters or the spiritual planes which will later be "decompressed" or conveyed in trance sessions or automatic writing.

Practitioners of thought transference or telepathy claim that this mode of communication can be learned and, like all things, one must first have a natural inclination towards its practice. Start by learning to listen to the inner voice. [Editor's Note: For more information regarding the cultivation of the inner-dialogue, see: *Divine Destiny*.]

Saint Germain's Teachings on Spiritual Alignment

1. Alignment from the Ascended Masters' viewpoint is a mental and emotional state of balance, or inner harmony. To achieve this we must first identify and see our experiences that are either negative or positive. This allows us to begin to see "the great harmonies that lie within.
2. Experience is the key to gain a working knowledge of Unity. Through both negative and positive experiences the soul learns about duality, so they may come to understand the role of personal choice.
3. Like the Yin and Yang, Saint Germain sees the Violet Flame and the Golden Ray as two profound spiritual catalysts that unite to assist humanity's spiritual evolution at this time.
4. These two forces assist personal choices made through the heart (feeling) and the Divine Will (thought). Integrated thoughts and feelings lead to harmonious, worldly action.

5. The cultivation of alignment, through harmonious action, leads one to Spiritual Freedom. Saint Germain often refers to freedom as the "refreshing drink," the elixir of life which incites the Ascension Process.

FIGURE 1-F
Seeking the Tao

The Tao

The Chinese philosophy that emphasizes living in harmony is perhaps the underlying notion in Saint Germain's spiritual insights on alignment. The Tao, also known as "The Way," in simpler terms is based on the Cycles of the Five Elements and the Hermetic Principle of Yin and Yang, or shadow and light. In Taoist philosophy the Tao is nameless and is not God. It is instead a universal principle that is expressed or observed in the world. Some phrases describe the Tao as: the source of creation; the ultimate; the indefinable; the natural universe as a whole; the way of nature as a whole. [5]

Since Taoist practices embrace alchemy, physically and spiritually, no doubt its tenets have a profound similarity to many Ascended Master teachings. Taoist spiritual practices also embrace meditation, breathwork, energy flow—both in physical body and in our habitats (Feng Shui), martial arts, chanting prayers and religious texts, and the pursuit of spiritual immortality.

FIGURE 2-F
Saint Michael and Souls
(1858 engraving.[2])

Ring of Blue Flame Angels

Archangel Michael's Ring of Blue Flame Angels is perhaps one of the most efficient forces to call upon for assistance with the Co-creation process. To invoke the angels' power for any sort of manifestation Co-creation process, write your decree or intention by hand; write two copies. Before you read your words, begin by invoking the angels' presence:

"In the name of I AM that I AM, I call forth the assistance of Archangel Michael and his Ring of Blue Flame Angels." (Insert your petition, and close your request.)

"In that Mighty Christ I AM, may the Ring of Blue Flame Angels and the Mighty Blue Ray protect and surround my request. So Be It! (or amen)

This formula is not exacting, and given only as an example. You may add to it if you choose, or use any other manifestation-decree language you are familiar with. The most important factor is that you notice results!

Burn both copies of the decree by either candle light or electrical light for seventy-two hours (three full days). If the petition is accepted, the light will stay lit for the duration. [Editor's Note: For safety, I recommend using an electrical light placed at least twenty-four inches away from the paper. For watchful purists, use candles (preferably in glass). One candle will suffice, but I have heard students will use up to seven candles for this intention.]

If during the entire seventy-two–hour period there were no power outages, accidental turn-offs of the electric bulb, or (if using a candle) no extinguished flames, the Angels have accepted your request. Immediately burn one copy as this allegedly carries your petition to the ethereal planes. Place the remaining copy on your altar or in a sacred location, i.e., behind a Master's photograph, in a family Bible, or a treasured spiritual book. You should note results within seven to ninety days. Some practitioners report instant results through the spiritual intervention of the Blue Flame Angels, but in my experience it takes about three months.

During your waiting period, have patience and faith! You can continue to read your petition out loud on a weekly basis (preferably on Saturday, the day of the Blue Ray) until answered; however, in most cases this is not absolutely necessary. Your intention, along with the focused attention of the Ring of Blue Flame Angels is especially helpful for problems or challenges surrounding important decisions, relationship issues—especially those surrounding intimate partners, business partners and associates, attracting a spiritual guide or mentor, attracting a soulmate, and any sort of family problem.

Some esoteric teachers claim that four Blue Flame Angels can be involved to constantly protect you and focus your spiritual growth towards Archangel Michael's Blue Flame. Spiritual healer and counselor Catherine Robson calls the four angels your "Warrior Angels," and she suggests "Your (Blue Flame) Angels will go wherever you send them to serve . . . send your angels to those in harm's way. If you desire something in your world to be manifested, ask your heart. If the answer from your heart is 'yes, it is constructive for my growth,' then send an angel to clear the path. Angels will go ahead of you and move things around so that you are protected." [6]

To call in your Blue Flame Angels, light a blue candle while facing east. Visualize either a protective circle or square of white light surrounding you. Then decree:

> "I call forth a Protective Blue Flame Angel to my front,
> to my back, and to both of my sides!"

Visualize and the see the Four Personal Blue Flame Angels, standing either at all four cardinal directions of the protective circle or all four corners of the protective square. You are located in the middle of the stream of white light.

Through Geraldine Innocente, channel of the Ascended Masters in the 1950s, Archangel Michael instructs, regarding the Blue Flame Angels: "the great Angelic Kingdom comes to your Planet Earth primarily as protectors—as amplifiers of the virtues of God . . . they stand yet within the auras of men and women who are enmeshed in their own human creations and through the Power of Radiation, help them to continue to place one foot before another, moving onward and upward until the Cosmic Day dawns, when more help can be given . . ." [7]

Saint Germain says, "They will bind any type of entity that is keeping you distracted and away from the truth. These beloved angels and beings of light serve mankind, to assist in spiritual evolution. They are akin to teachers' helpers (and) are there to help at all times to give assistance."

I AM That I AM

This classic Hebrew phrase from the Torah translates into English as "I Will Be What I Will Be." [8] In Ascended Master Teachings the I AM is known as the individualized presence of God. In "A New Reality," Saint Germain breaks down this spiritual phrase:

- "I AM": represents the Universal Mind.
- "That": is the rainbow bridge, through the service of the Rays of Light and Sound.
- "I AM": the final I AM represents the seating of the Rays of Light and Sound into the individual.

From this context, God is seen as both the universal Creator and the Creation.

The "OM" (pronounced A-U-M) is a Sanskrit word used in both Hinduism and Buddhism as a name for God. The three letters of AUM signify the three aspects of God as beginning, duration, and dissolution: Brahma, Vishnu, and Shiva.

The AUM syllable is known as the omkara, which is a name for God that translates to mean "I AM Existence." [9] *Soham* is yet another mystical Sanskrit word for God, which translates into English as, "I Myself," or "It is I," or "He is I." The teachings of the I AM Activity, brought through Guy and Edna Ballard, use this aforementioned translation as the meaning of "I AM." In Vedic philosophy it is claimed that when a child cries "Who Am I?" the universe replies, "Soham—you are the same as I AM." [10]

Saint Germain's explanation of the I AM That I AM states that all members of humanity are related to ONE source, even thought we are each an individual expression of the God-source. He explains, "Know that this Unity, at all times is yours (your heritage). Return back into it whenever you feel separation or dissension of any sort . . . it is here where answers are given and you are gently led back into the path, and the union with the Spiritual Hierarchies becomes complete."

Agreement Formation

Agreement Formation is an early tenet of the I AM America Teachings, as the Law of Agreement is also known as the First Jurisdiction, Harmony. Agreement is the sacred meeting of two minds which on one formative side reflects our intent and commitment. The results of our agreements with others reflect our choices and our responsible actions that ultimately define the quality of our life force. Since our actions illustrate our motivations, agreements reflect our ability to Co-create with others and the level of harmony we enjoy from the interaction. Saint Germain explains that the metaphysical underpinning of Agreement Formation is sympathetic resonance. That is, the combined effect of two in harmony will create the greatest vibration, from which many more will respond. This is physical law—pure and simple. As a "unison or octave will provoke the largest response as there is maximum likeness in vibratory motion." In simple terms this means: the greater the harmony, the greater the vibration. This spiritual maxim is described and explained in the Jurisdiction Harmony. Abundance follows Harmony, and Saint Germain says, "Where two or more are gathered, there the focus can begin for greater Co-creation." So undoubtedly, prolific partnerships begin with the formation of clear intent and commitment-filled agreements.

Saint Germain's Teachings on Spiritual Migration

1. Before traveling to a Golden City Vortex to integrate spiritual principles, make sure that you are proficient in the spiritual qualities of that particular Vortex. That is, through your agreements and actions you have exemplified to the best of your ability the characteristics you are now willing to integrate.
2. First, be prepared to face the negative aspects of the spiritual attribute you are focused on integrating. This is part of duality, and your willingness to release karma will smooth your alignment and transmutation process.
3. Recognize and be thankful for each sacrifice you have made to receive your initiation. This is the same Great Sacrifice made by the avatars and adepts.
4. Through each subsequent initiation through the Golden Cities and as you release karmic out-of-balance desires, cravings, and energies, you are realizing the New Times through your alignment process. Saint Germain reminds us "that the path of spiritual liberation is for one ready to release the world and all of its folly."
5. While it is best to follow the Migrations of the Golden Cities as they have been outlined in the I AM America Teachings, this may not be possible. Do the best you can, and do not forget previously made agreements. This is especially true for those who are married and committed householders. According to Saint Germain, the commitments of marriage and family come first.

6. The Ascension Process can be initiated by traveling to and applying the energies in just one Golden City. This is the primary purpose of the Golden City Stars, which are spiritually connected to every other Golden City Star throughout the world. The worldwide connection of Golden City Vortices "glistens and glows in their interconnectivity." This global connection extends to the Great Central Sun, or Galactic Center.
7. The Master Teachers dispense teachings and share this work with others through certain areas, i.e., Golden City Doorways, Golden City Stars. This teaching is specific for that geographic Vortex area and matches it in vibration and unique energies.
8. Saint Germain shares these personal insights regarding how Golden City Vortices assist individuals to integrate and self-realize certain qualities. They are:
    a. Gobean—the first initiation: Harmony and the creation of agreements. Alignment to the Divine Will.
    b. Malton—the second initiation: Identification of personal desires, and the ability to realize them.
    c. Wahanee—the third initiation: the desire for spiritual growth and spiritual liberation.
    d. Shalahah—the fourth initiation: Release of dis-ease—mentally, emotionally, and physically (in some cases). The harmony process realized in Shalahah allows our consciousness to be as "ONE." This is the beginning of the Christ Consciousness.
    e. Klehma—the fifth initiation: Release of genetically held fear. This purification process allows one to embrace Unity Consciousness—Unana. This allows one to enter into service for all and access the "Great Halls," the school which resides in the Fourth and Fifth Dimensions.
9. Throughout all of the Golden City Vortices, contact with the Master Teachers and Angels of Mercy and Compassion of each particular Golden City Vortex is possible. Masters and Angels prepare us individually to enter into the mystery school of that Golden City. Each

Golden City Mystery School serves the Golden City's Master and their unique teachings and initiations.
10. The initiation through the Golden City Mysteries is really the at-one-ment process whereby the man—broken through the tests and trials of duality—is tempered by spiritual fire. The sacred fire—the Violet Flame—produces the HU-man, through transformation and the brilliant gold of Unity Consciousness. This is peace supreme—or I AM as ONE.
11. The Golden City Vortices and the initiations and great mystery schools they contain are just one of many ways to realize unity and the appearance of the Christ Consciousness on Earth.

Great Sacrifice

This philosophical notion is based on the idea that the entire universe originates as an act of sacrifice, known as The Law of Sacrifice. Sacrificial acts are mirrored throughout life from the great adepts and avatars who take human form to assist humanity, to the spiritual sacrifice of our individuality as we evolve into the ONE, to a mother birthing a child, and even to lower levels of life that sustain a food cycle in an ecosystem. The Great Sacrifice is known in esoteric circles as the Law of Life. H. P. Blavatsky once spoke about the law that rules life: "Life is built by the sacrifice of the individual to the whole. Each cell in the living body must sacrifice itself to the perfection of the whole." [11] Some theosophists view the Great Sacrifice as the essential fuel that moves humanity forward. Theosophical leader and teacher Annie Besant wrote: "Man, then, cannot even live in the world of forms, as he performs acts of sacrifice. The revolving wheel of life cannot go on, unless each member, unless each living creature, helps to turn it by the performance of acts of sacrifice. Life is preserved by sacrifice, and in sacrifice all evolution is rooted." [12]

Householder

According to many religious traditions and mystery schools, until one has fulfilled one's obligations to spouse and children, it is difficult to solely devote life and energies to spiritual asceticism and spiritual liberation. The householder is held by the tradition of duty, that once fulfilled, may move the student onward to seek renunciation.

1. "Telepathy." Wikipedia. Accessed August 22, 2016. https://en.wikipedia.org/wiki/Telepathy.
2. Ibid.
3. Sivananda, Sri Swami. "Thought Power." Accessed August 22, 2016. http://www.dlshq.org/download/thought_power.htm.
4. "Telepathy or the Ability of Thought Transfer." Our Ultimate Reality. Accessed August 22, 2016. http://ourultimatereality.com/telepathy-or-the-ability-of-thought-transfer.html.
5. Myss, Caroline. "Taoism at a Glance." Caroline Myss. Accessed August 22, 2016. https://www.myss.com/free-resources/world-religions/taoism/taoism-at-a-glance/.
6. Robson, Catherine. Calling Your Blue Flame Angels to You. http://www.angeliclight.co.uk.
7. Innocente, Geraldine. "Archangel Michael." Accessed August 22, 2016. http://www.ascension-research.org/michael.html.
8. "I Am That I Am." Wikipedia. Accessed August 22, 2016. https://en.wikipedia.org/wiki/I_Am_that_I_Am.
9. "Om." Wikipedia. Accessed August 22, 2016. https://en.wikipedia.org/wiki/Om.
10. "Soham (Sanskrit)." Wikipedia. Accessed August 22, 2016. https://en.wikipedia.org/wiki/Soham_(Sanskrit).
11. "The Great Sacrifice." Accessed August 22, 2016. http://sociedadteosofica.es/?tribe_events=european-school-of-theosophy-the-great-sacrifice.
    Besant, Annie. "The Laws of Higher Life." Accessed August 22, 2016. http://www.anandgholap.net/Laws_Of_Higher_Life-AB.htm.

Illustrations:
1. Seeking the Tao. Digital image. Wikimedia Commons. July 7, 2011. Accessed August 22, 2016. Circa, 10th Century. https://commons.wikimedia.org/wiki/File:Ju_Ran_Seeking_the_Tao.jpg.
2. Martinet, Joseph. Saint Michael and Souls (Sa. Miguel E Almas). Digital image. Wikimedia Commons. May 31, 2016. Accessed August 22, 2016. https://commons.wikimedia.org/wiki/File:Sa._Miguel_e_Almas.jpg. Engraving, 1858.

7

The Golden Cities
Saint Germain

Greetings, Beloved chelas on that mighty Violet Ray, I AM Saint Germain and I stream forth on that Violet Ray of Mercy, Compassion, and ultimate Forgiveness. As usual, Dear hearts, I request permission to come forward.

Response: *Do, Saint Germain. You are most welcome and please come forward.*

As I step forward to this lectern to give discourse, I remind you, Dear ones, Dear hearts, that the work of the Violet Flame is the most important that you can do of all the spiritual practices and principles that you apply. When you use this mighty Violet Ray, it imbues a vibration about you at an energetic level that is throughout your whole Human Aura. This gives a transcendence, a transformation, and ultimate alchemy to any situation that you may be facing. It is through this science and principle that Divine Intervention flows forward and you are lifted from the burden of karma, from things that hold you back. These things, actions, or shall I say, events that are predetermined to happen, are then lifted and raised to another level of consciousness or understanding.

I give this teaching to you so that you may understand how to use the principle of time in a better way. Know, Dear ones, Dear hearts, stalwart chelas of mine, that you are then able to move above and beyond things that seem impossible . . . things that seem to hold you back . . . things that seem to tire you in the work that is presented to you. Always use this wondrous Violet Flame. It is truly that Alchemical elixir that I have always spoken about.

Dear ones, visualize the Violet Flame in, through, and around your office . . . in, through, and around your business . . . in, through, and around your home . . . in, through, and around all of your activities . . . in, through, and around employees and volunteers . . . in, through, and around your children. Even in the trips that you take when you travel, visualize this Violet Flame in, through, and around all experiences that you have . . . in, through, and around business acquaintances. It is through this mighty work that then you can move forward unencumbered with that great ease and grace that is the work of the transcendence of the Violet Flame. May the Violet Flame now move among us in this discourse. So be it.

The Golden City Vortices have been brought forward as a great Divine Intervention. Alongside the Violet Flame, beloved Mother Babajeran serves with great grace and ease with this hierarchy of teachings. This energy serves to move humanity at a time when spiritual crisis and, not only that, cataclysmic Earth Changes, are facing all. It is important to understand that the Golden City Vortices represent a higher knowledge, a higher vibration, and a higher energy. Dear ones, Dear hearts, we have given you many teachings regarding the Golden City Vortices and as I had promised in past discourses, now I shall bring forward information regarding the East and the Western Doors.

I have given you information of the North and the Southern Doors in previous discourses. This was important, for this is the way that the teaching is given, from North to South and from East to West. This contains within it, its own cosmology that you will later begin to understand. It moves, shall we say, with the movement of the energy alongside even the movement of chakras on the body and the entryway of energy from the North to the South Pole and the rising of the Sun from East to West. This is most important, even in understanding how to utilize the Vortices to gain a greater understanding of energy movement into the New Times.

You see, Dear ones, Dear hearts, with the shifting of the poles and even the shifting of the magnetic poles, there will be many new rifts and shifts even within the Third Dimensional physical energy. I define this as Third Dimension so that you understand it, so that you are able to define it. We are talking about a Third Dimensional energy and a shift that exists within that. These are the energies of duality moving towards the consciousness of the Christ, the plane that you know as Unana.

The Eastern Doors are used for the gathering of friends and families. It is where the Sun rises in the morning and the Rays of the Great Central

Sun then meet all who are ready to serve that day. Therefore, within the Eastern and Western Doors, these are places where the invocation for the Violet Flame at sunrise and sunset can occur to give a stronger effect. The use of the Violet Flame in the Eastern Door allows one to create anew, to bring new creations forward for greater harmony and in this effect, create a greater resonance in relationships, marriage partners, and families.

The Eastern Door of Gobean is a prime example of one, where harmony can then be achieved where there has been disharmony. As you well know, it is the work of beloved El Morya, bringing through the energy and radiance of that mighty Blue Ray and Blue Flame into the Vortex of Gobean that allows a greater peace and transcendent harmony to ensue. Dear ones, Dear hearts, the time that you spend in contemplation on this great principle within an Eastern Door will bring peace and harmony in any family situation. It will bring you to a greater understanding and a greater experience of all consuming peace.

> May peace reign supreme within the hearts of man.
> May we move now onward to Unana,
> humanity's true residence.

You see, Dear ones, the Eastern Doors are brought forward at this time to bring this greater and higher vibration. Therefore, these are wonderful places to have meetings, to bring a true harmony, and, shall we say, a meeting of minds. These are also places where young children can receive their beginning instruction into the higher laws . . . those higher laws that govern the human spirit and bring one forward to a greater unity in knowing the true and only God, the mighty I AM.

Western Doors also bring a great service, for they allow a greater understanding to come forward, one that is first engendered in the Eastern Doors and allowed, through spiritual migration, to move, to grow, and to expand. Therefore, Western Doors are for the expansion; whereas, Eastern Doors are always for the beginning of things.

> May light expand on Earth.
> May the heart of God serve all.

This is the decree of the Western Door; for there, within the Western Door, light indeed expands and the consciousness of the mighty I AM Presence becomes all pervading. Dear ones, Dear hearts, this is why within a Western Door, particularly that of the Golden City of Gobean, connections with the other realms then begin to occur. People will begin to sense the other dimensions and the great halls and schools of learning, sometimes referred to as the Great Cathedrals of Learning. This is also where many of the great Akashic Records or, shall we say, the libraries of Egypt, also exist within that Western Door of Gobean. For this reason, that is why beloved El Morya has given you instruction upon building and completing a school in the physical, to mirror that mighty record that once existed in Egypt.

This Mighty Hall of Records was once all that remained of the remnant of the continent of Atlantis and now, many of these records have been moved by the Brotherhood to exist here, in the ethereal template, for those who have the eyes to see and the ears to hear. These records of this lost civilization can now be attained by one who is readied through the Seventh Seal and can travel in the finer bodies and perceive with a finer will. Dear ones, Dear hearts, the Western Door of Gobean will bring a greater understanding to the workings of peace and, at one point in time, will become a centralized post for those among humanity who will bring a great synergy of peace to the entire world.

As you know, when one door closes, another one opens. Of course then, this great record of another time, of a people that existed long before the times that you know now, their memory would be served here. So this Western Door serves as a record of the ancestors of which we now speak, a culture and a time which served its own Ray Force, served its own timing and intention. There is much to be gleaned by understanding these records . . . much to be gleaned about the true history of humanity and the interaction with the Spiritual Hierarchy throughout this time.

Let us now move on to the Golden City of Malton, which is served by beloved Mahatma Kuthumi, that mighty Master of the Ruby and the Gold Rays. The Eastern Door, you see, brings a great fruition to families. This again, is where families can be brought together to bring their dreams and their desires into manifestation, into that great wonderment.

As you have also understood, this Golden City Vortex of Malton also holds the energy for the great purification of the Elemental Kingdoms. This includes the Vegetable, Mineral, and Animal Kingdoms and also, many of the unseen forces, such as the gnomes, the sylphs, the undines, the fairies, and many more of those invisible areas of life which do indeed exist. This great purification brings all to a greater vibration and understanding.

In this Eastern Door, there will be many celebrations which unite humanity as ONE to all of Earth. This Eastern Door of Malton brings a greater understanding, a unity, shall we say, with all the Kingdoms. Many people who will travel to this area will have many experiences with these invisible Kingdoms and will be able to unite and see that they are indeed all as ONE, for Unity Consciousness is the great teaching contained within all Golden City Vortices.

The Western Door, again, will bring forward great schools of understanding and there will be great research that will be brought along the lines of understanding the higher uses of the Mineral Kingdom, the higher uses of the Plant Kingdom, and the higher uses of the Animal Kingdom. This will bring, shall we say, great schools forward for the healing of animals through the use of plants and minerals and in this higher vibration, many new great discoveries will be made in this Western Door of Malton. Many of the secrets of Alchemical knowledge of nature will then be unlocked but again, Dear ones, only in its own direct timing and intention.

What a wondrous gift to humanity the Golden City Vortices will be. As you gain and grow in your understanding, share this information with many. There will be those who will come into complete and direct resonance with the truth that you speak and they too will receive the gift.

That mighty Violet Ray aligns to the heart of the Golden City of Wahanee and it is there that I shall serve, along with my beloved companion, arcing the Ray Forces with beloved Portia from the Golden City of Eabra, which exists in the Yukon area, near what you would call present day Alaska. This is to bring forward a greater understanding of healing in relationships between man and women. For you see, Dear ones, Dear hearts, it is through the misuse of the sexual chakras that many become trapped, shall we say, within the confines of the physical body.

It is important to understand that the use of the sexual energies are to be brought to the higher use at the heart level and onward to the opening of the Third Eye. The use of these energies, when brought to a greater understanding, can be used in conjunction with the finer transcending energies of the Violet Flame. There, one is able to access the hurts and the wounds of the past. They are able then to Alchemize and release the effects of past life experience and move into the ever present now, into the consciousness of Unana.

The Eastern Door is indeed a beautiful place to start with this work, for this is where a man and a wife may move forward, and I shall also say a woman and a husband, to bring that perfect balance. Balance is the key, Dear ones, Dear hearts, and within the Eastern Door, those who are having problems in their marriage unions, who wish to move to a higher understanding of unity, may call upon that mighty Violet Flame and bring about a great healing within. All can call this forward, as it calls the I AM. The Eastern Door will bring much healing forward for those having troubles in their relationships.

The Western Door will bring forth, again, an expansion of this understanding and there will come forward a greater understanding of united Brotherhood and Sisterhood. Therefore, in the Western Doors of Wahanee, there will be many great meetings from many nations. Also, in the ethereal realms, the Great Halls of Justices reside and those again, who have the eyes to see and the ears to hear can move into these great halls and access the Records of Eternity, the records that are related to the great laws that have served all civilizations that have existed upon this Earth, also known as Terra.

> May the Violet Flame blaze forth
> from the heart of the Great Central Sun.
> May the Golden City of Wahanee serve all
> for united Brotherhood and Sisterhood.

This brings a greater purpose in understanding the work of the Violet Flame, for it brings a great unity of all peoples, a great unity to a greater cause.

In the Golden City Vortex of Shalahah, the Eastern Door opens that great energy, not only for at-one-ment, but to bring a Oneness with all energy bodies for great healing. It is here in the Eastern Door, that those who have physical ailments or problems existing within the body, which are encumbering a family, a relationship, or a friendship, may travel. Traveling not as one, but as many in groups, you see, will then move those into Unity Consciousness and into finding the healing power therein. Om Sheahah is the sound mantra that comes forward from the Golden City of Shalahah.

The Green Ray in its glory brings healing at many levels, not only just at the physical but is able to get to the root of all causes, that which is the mind itself. Also, for those who have had problems in the past of financial blockages, those unable to have the true aboundness of God and the true experience of Golden Age abundance, may find healing in the Eastern Door of Shalahah. Dear ones, Dear hearts, the Eastern Door of Shalahah is always to be used in this type of group movement, to bring this forward in a greater understanding of at-one-ment.

The Western Door, again, brings the greater school forward and as a purveyor of that mighty and wondrous healing Green Ray, this is where many new scientific and technological developments will take place. Shalahah will become a leader in the New Times in bringing new technologies forward . . . in bringing a greater awareness and understanding that moves consciousness beyond the limitation of this dimension. That is why Ascension Valley and the Transportation Vortex have also been identified in this Western Door area. These energy anomalies, as they appear now to you, are actually templates of energies which will be known and harnessed in the New Times to bring forward, shall we say, a greater understanding that leads us into that great Age of Transportation.

Again, those who have the eyes to see and the ears to hear may access the great schools of learning and an understanding of these higher technologies and learn how they can be used for a greater good, not again for the coveting of treasures and the monies of Earth. These higher technologies will bring an end to suffering and allow the consciousness, the true at-one-ment, to expand.

Shalahah becomes a preparatory ground at a spiritual level for the process of Ascension. The Eastern Door unites many groups that are drawn to the Law of Attraction to begin this preparatory work and those who desire to walk the path of Ascension will begin many of their studies and work within this Eastern Door. As you well know, Dear ones, Dear hearts, healing is always required before one can face the great tempering fires of purification. So within this Eastern Door, there will be the location of many new schools of thought which introduce these teachings of Ascension.

Now, Dear ones, Dear hearts, let us move to that wondrous Golden City of Klehma, served by beloved Serapis Bey of the White Ray. Because this Golden City vibrates to the ancient Native American cultures and communities, these teachings will pervade throughout all of the Doorways in the levels of Akasha.

Within this Eastern Door of Klehma will come some of the first gatherings of many of the tribes, not only of the United States but also of North and South America. Here, cultures may gather and bring their greater offering, their great bundles of truth to be understood in a greater and grander teaching. Therefore, within this Eastern Door, the energies are prepared to greet and meet them. The energies are prepared to bring about that great sound of one drum as one heartbeat. This again, is not limited to genetics or just the color of the skin; however, Dear ones, Dear hearts, in this great collective gathering comes forward a great healing of many wounds of the past.

Ultimately, Dear ones, Dear hearts, the Golden Cities have been brought forward to give great healing at a dimensional level, to lift humanity to a new understanding beyond duality. The Western Door of Klehma is given to bring the schools forward, the teachings forward, of the great purification. This purification exists within, Dear ones. It is the uniting of the dark side - which is within every person, every human - with that of the higher side - that higher side of All Mighty Reasoning. This unification of the self, through control of the dualistic forces, places one upon the path of Ascension and, in later teaching of the Stars, I shall talk about the process of Ascension, which will occur here in the Golden City Vortex of Klehma. And now I shall pause for questions.

Question: *When you talk of Ascension, do you mean the actual movement of the body into the other realms?*

Dear ones, Dear hearts, it is not just the body that we are concerned with; it is the movement of the consciousness. For you see, the energy always goes where the attention flows. A great teacher once said in your realm that mind is the builder. This is most important to understand, that the physical energy will follow once the mind has been sharpened and honed.

It is important to understand within the process of Ascension, that it is the drawing of all energies into another realm or dimension of understanding.

You see, Dear ones, Dear hearts, when we moved into the realm of Ascension, all energies of past lives have to be brought to their final balance or, shall we say, that neutral point in juxtaposition. It is important to understand that all must be brought to a balance and then one may move forward. I hope this gives you explanation.

Question: *Yes. Does Ascension occur where the consciousness moves through a specific chakra into that realm?*

Ascension occurs, of course, through gathering the energies through the lower chakras and expanding them through the heart. For you see, Dear ones, it always is the Law of Love that brings us to that point of neutrality. Then, the energy is developed through the finer use of the higher chakras, through the Throat, through the Third Eye, and finally the Crown.

Question: *I see. So in a past discourse, where you spoke of a thousand eyes, and how each of the life experiences was a thread for the creation of the seamless garment in the Ascension Process, it requires the thousand eyes of all of those life experiences to be brought to a time of balance?*

To be brought into the great Heart of Love, where all is seen for what it truly is. Have you not been taught when all is said and done, all that remains is love. Is this not true, Dear ones?

Question: *Yes. Is that a reference to the world we have our consciousness focused in at this moment, this Third Dimensional world, so to speak?*

Indeed it is, for the Law of Love is the great atoner. The Law of Love brings all disparity into balance. All becomes equal within this mighty Law of Love. Have you not noticed that when you love so deeply, you care not what you give? Do you keep a balance sheet of what was given through love? Of course not, for all is brought into infinite balance.

Question: *Yes, does this include life experiences from different worlds and the heart is the thing that brings all to balance?*

The heart brings all to balance but the Ascension here, at this level of consciousness, is from the experiences here, from this world only.

Response: *I see, so this is the world of the heart. This is the world of the Law of Love, where love becomes an action.*

It is true, Dear ones. It is love in that expression of action and creation.

Response: *So basically, what you are saying is that the experiences collectively create the seamless garment, each one of them being a thread, each one of them having their own set of eyes.*

The thousand eyes refer to the multitude of experience found in the maya of time. The thousand eyes come as great witnesses to this experience. Even though they are experiences within illusion, they are experiences that educate and temper the soul and prepare it for the Great Work. They come forward lending many, many experiences of the dual forces to show that there can be many perceptions to one experience.

Question: *I see. So then the Ascension, which is created by the balance of all of those experiences through the use of the heart, takes us to the next world and is that the world where you reside?*

This is the world that no longer requires the physical body to serve the great and mighty Heart of the Logos, that great and mighty Plan of Love Eternal. Then one is prepared to move further onward in greater understanding and evolution. The body brings with it its own limitations, its own understanding, encased within the Laws of Duality. When the consciousness is freed, liberated shall we say, from dualistic thinking, then the physical law simply responds.

Response: *I see, so when the sense of separation is no longer the focus of the individual and the sense that we are all ONE, also ONE with you and the rest of the hierarchy, when that becomes an admitted focus of each soul, then the lifetimes can be brought to balance through that love.*

Yes, Dear chela!!!

(He is now very happy; he has a very wide grin on his face)

Response: *Very few times do you smile as such. We truly are all ONE.*

> May the Violet Flame blaze in, through, and around
> all those who seek the path of Ascension.
> May it move all into that crystal consciousness
> of greater understanding.

Response: *So be it.*

And now, Dear ones, Dear hearts, are there further questions?

Response: *It is my sense that this is more than enough to ponder for one visit. And those who will hear this tape and read this transcription, may their hearts and minds be uplifted to that ONE.*

Study this discourse carefully, for indeed upon reflection, there will be many more questions, as such is the nature of evolution, is it not?

Response: *It most certainly is.*

OM Manaya, Pitaya, Hitaka!

Study Guide for The Golden Cities

Topics:
Microcosm and Macrocosm of the Teachings of the Four Doorways
The Four Doorways and the Human Energy System
Eastern and Western Doorways of the United States Golden Cities
Hall of Records
Hall of Justice
Ascension

Prophecies of Change
1. With the Earth facing cataclysmic Earth Changes, humanity's need for spiritual grace is increased. The Golden City Vortices help to ease this crisis. The Golden Cities increase Earth's spiritual vibration and energy.
2. As the poles shift—magnetically and physically—many new physical-spiritual shifts and rifts occur within humanity. Increased polarity in our economic, social, and political systems move many forward to seed the Christ Consciousness, also known as the plane of Unana.

The Four Doorways and the HU-man Energy System

The infrastructure of the four doorways of the Golden City Vortices is specially designed to evolve the human energy system to the HU-man. Northern and southern doors represent the North and South Poles of the activated Kundalini system, and play a role in opening and evolving the Seven Chakras. Eastern and Western Doors, respectively, evolve the feminine and masculine currents of the body. This evolves the open heart chakra and the chela's ability to consciously enter into world service. Hearts and Hands represent the "Heart to Love . . . Hands to do."

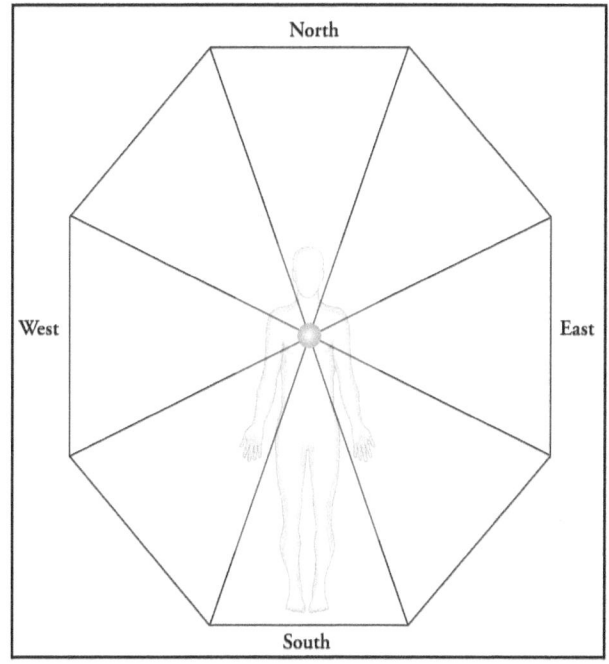

FIGURE 1-G
The Four Doorways of a Golden City and Human Energy
The North and South Doors of Golden Cities open chakras along the Golden Thread Axis. East and West doors of Golden Cities open our hearts and our ability to serve.

Golden City of Gobean Eastern Door

Since Eastern Doors symbolize our relationships with friends and family, Saint Germain claims that the use of the Violet Flame in this Golden City Doorway—especially the invocation of the Violet Flame at sunrise and sunset—is much stronger. This helps to create harmony in relationships, with marriage partners, and among families. Saint Germain suggests that the use of meditation in Eastern Doors will create peace in relationships. This prepares the mind to receive the consciousness of Unana.

Golden City of Gobean Western Door

Energies developed towards the principle of service are expanded in the Western Door. To cultivate or to understand your unique spiritual service, say this decree in the Western Door of any Golden City Vortex,

> "May light expand on Earth,
> May the Heart of God serve all!"

It is claimed that this specific decree expands the consciousness of the I AM Presence. This creates connections to the spiritual schools hidden in the Fourth and Fifth Dimensions. Saint Germain claims that the esoteric libraries of Egypt exist in the Fourth and Fifth dimensions of the Western Door of Gobean—the Golden City located in the United States's southwest. Apparently the Great White Brotherhood moved the esoteric library and its many spiritual teachings, along with the renowned *Hall of Records,* to the ethereal planes of the Golden Cities.

The *Hall of Records,* which once existed in Atlantis, contains records and information of Earth's lost civilizations. Time spent cultivating spiritual energies in Western Doors develops the Crown Chakra and the light bodies and makes astral travel to these venerated schools possible. Saint Germain prophesies that the Western Door of Gobean will play a synergistic role in creating peace on Earth in the New Times.

Golden City of Malton Eastern and Western Doors

Prayers and meditation for Family Unity and the manifestation of family dreams and desires are answered with contemplative time spent in the Eastern Door of Malton. While Malton's forces can help on an individual basis, perhaps it is its universal purpose that is most important. In this Golden City Vortex, the unseen kingdoms of the gnomes, fairies, and elementals are eager to interact and share their culture and customs. This process is claimed to be inordinately enlightening, and schools and research facilities for animal and plant science may develop in Malton's Western Door. An underlying purpose of Malton unveils the alchemical secrets of nature.

Golden City of Wahanee Eastern and Western Doors

Right use of sexual energy for spiritual development and healing is the primary focus for this pair of Golden City doors. Some Taoist teachings claim that the sexual organs and kidneys store energy that can be transformed into energy—vital chi. Referred to as "inner alchemy," this form of sexual energy is conserved and leveraged for healing and regeneration through various practices.[1] In addition, Saint Germain suggests the use of the Violet Flame to harmonize relationships. Here are some suggestions from the I AM America Teachings:

Violet Flame Decree to Dissipate Anger and Hostility
    I invoke the assistance of the Violet Flame.
    I AM a being of the Violet Flame,
    Cleansed in the harmony of all that is.

    — from *A Teacher Appears*

Awakening to Love
    I AM loved.
    I AM awakened to my true being.
    I AM loved.
    I AM part of my whole being.
    I AM loved.
    I AM loved within that love.

    —from *Sisters of the Flame*

Violet Flame Decree for Perfection
    I AM a being of Violet Fire;
    I AM the perfection God desires.

    —from *Fields of Light*

Violet Flame Decree to Remove Obstacles
    Mighty Violet Flame, come forth
    And blaze your transmutation into this situation,
    And into this circumstance.
    Remove all obstacles and let the power of the Mighty Divine
    Set all free,
    Beloved I AM.

    —from *New World Wisdom, Book Two*

I AM the Healing Heart
> I AM the heart,
> I AM the healing heart.
> I AM the love,
> The love that heals.
> I AM the heart that binds all as ONE.
> I AM the heart that heals all in that Mighty ONE I AM.

—from *New World Wisdom, Book Three*

The Western Doors of Wahanee contain the Fourth and Fifth dimensional (ethereal) Halls of Justice. This library contains the Akashic records of every form of government and associated law that has served mankind. Accessing this type of information creates clarity and direction for the Violet Flame and its metaphysical purpose of creating a United Brotherhood and Sisterhood on Earth. Wahanee's Western Door unifies all peoples to this work.

Golden City of Shalahah Eastern and Western Doors

The Eastern Door of Shalahah helps and assists individuals to attain the at-one-ment. This is especially important for healing crises, or couples seeking healing of a relationship. This doorway benefits groups, as its power can quickly move group consciousness into the ONE. It is suggested to use the mantra, "OM Sheahah," when working towards the at-one-ment in this Golden City Doorway. Saint Germain claims that meditation and focus on the Green Ray in this doorway can remove financial blockages, while reasserting the "true aboundness of God" through the principle of choice. He also states that the Eastern Door of Shalahah is the best location for mystery schools to prepare for the Ascension, and this process naturally completes in the Western Door location—Ascension Valley.

Saint Germain prophesies that as we enter the New Times, universities located in the Western Golden City Doorway will innovate "Many new scientific and technological developments" that create the "awareness and understanding that moves consciousness beyond the limitation of this dimension." The Transportation Vortex and Ascension Valley are energetic templates which will be harnessed in the New Times, and they will help to usher humanity's consciousness into the great Age of Transportation.

Golden City of Klehma Eastern and Western Doors

The Eastern Door greets all who are ready for Unity Consciousness and the family of ONE. This is assisted and built on the Native American principles of truth, tolerance, and healing through the tenets of the Great Purification, found in the Western Door. Unification of the self, through facing our shadow, is the necessary process before entering the White Flame of Ascension located in the Star of Klehma.

Hall of Records

Specific records associated with humanity's histories that are located in the Fifth Dimension of Golden Cities and in the Astral Plane. This heavenly location is similarly known as the Akashic Records and is a palatial building containing an account or record of each individual lifetime for every soul on Earth. The Hall of Records allegedly works in tandem with the Hall of Justice, a spiritual location where each soul meets their "Council of Elders," a group of spiritually advanced teachers and guides who help to oversee and guide each individual lifetime. It is claimed we meet with this collective energy in between each lifetime. [2]

The Ascension Process

The Ascension Process, according to Saint Germain, gathers the energies of the individual chakras and expands their energy through the heart. The Law of Love calibrates the energy fields (aura) to Zero Point—a physical and philosophical viewpoint of neutrality. From there, the subtle and fine tuning of the light bodies is effectuated through the higher chakras, sequentially including the Throat Chakra, the Third Eye Chakra, and finally the Crown Chakra. Zero Point is key in this process and it is here that the energies of all past lives are brought to psychological and physical (karmic) balance. Then the initiate is able to withdraw their light bodies from the physical plane into the Astral Light of the Fourth Dimension. Saint Germain reminds students of this process that "Mind is the builder" and that the physical energy of the light bodies will follow a honed and sharpened mind. Finally, Saint Germain reminds us that in simple terms the Ascension

Process is the activity of the great Heart of Love: "When all is said and done, all that remains is love."

Love creates balance, releases injustice, and is the great equalizer. Love frees our mind from dualistic thinking and as our consciousness is free, the physical law responds. Saint Germain shares this prayer to remove separation and initiate the Ascension Process:

> "May the Violet Flame blaze in, through,
> and around all those who seek the Path of Ascension.
> May the Violet Flame move all into the
> Crystal Consciousness of greater understanding. So Be It!"

Maya Time

The illusion of time, while consciousness is focused in the physical, Third Dimension.

Thousand Eyes

In Ascended Master terminology, this phrase refers to the endless rounds of death and rebirth the soul encounters before entering the Ascension Process of spiritual liberation.

Law of Duality

All of creation in the physical plane has two expressions: feminine or masculine, with each expressing a degree of polarity. Perhaps the best way to understand the Law of Duality is within the principle of light, which cannot exist without the scientific presence of darkness. Since our life experience is created through the tension of the world of opposites, the human challenge is to spiritually achieve balance. From this position, our consciousness is freed from the seesaw of duality and is able to enter into a viewpoint of peace and harmony—a vital component of Christ Consciousness.

1. Chia, Mantak. Awaken Healing Energy through the Tao: The Taoist Secret of Circulating Internal Power. New York, NY: Aurora, 1983. Print.
2. Browne, Sylvia. Psychic Sylvia Browne's Near-Death Experience Revelations. N.p., 2016. Web. 26 Oct. 2016.

8

Integrating Golden City Energies
Saint Germain

Greetings, Beloved chelas in that mighty Christ, I AM Saint Germain and I stream forth on that mighty Violet Ray of Mercy, Compassion, and Forgiveness. As usual, Dear hearts, I request permission to come forward.

Response: *Please, Saint Germain, you have permission.*

It is with great delight that I come forward this evening; for you see, Dear ones, I have promised that if you require my help, even on a daily basis, there I AM. Call upon me, for there is much work that can now move forward. There is much information that can now be shared. In our last discourse, I gave information on the Doorways of the Golden City Vortices, so that you could begin to understand how to use the energies, even at the most subtle levels. This information is being given at this time, for there are many who ask the question, "What is the use of moving to a Golden City area? Why would I even be concerned to move myself to such a place?"

Dear ones, Dear hearts, not only is there the energy of the Ray Force itself but there is the energy that exists in each of the Doorways and the energy of the Stars. But let me explain even so much more. You know, Dear ones, Dear hearts, that the Earth itself is composed of many energy points, many small Vortices. These energy centers exist throughout the whole planet. Rivers exist as lines of energy, even creeks and small ponds emit a type of energy. A fault line is emitting again another type of energy. Every fissure, crack, and cranny of the Earth is showing and emitting a type of energy that can be utilized for a certain and special purpose.

In the ethereal levels, there are also many other energies: As above, so below. These energies, as they exist in the physical, are mirrored in the ethereal, or for better words, from the ethereal, these energies are mirrored to the physical. And from there, humanity may participate and partake with these energies and understand how they have been brought forward for this great Time of Global Awakening and Global Ascension.

Dear ones, Dear hearts, it is important to understand that even within the Earth itself, at the central core of her being, is a great white fire emitting itself to the outer crust of the planet. There, that energy emits itself and sends itself throughout the entire universe. This is indeed how the Ray Forces arc themselves from that Great Galactic Center or Great Central Sun and are sent to your Sun and into the white core of the Earth. There, these energies are sent through different vortices, rivers, lakes, meridians, if you will, or acupressure points of the Earth herself. The Golden City Vortices are indeed a very interesting energy force, as they exist to bring forward the purity of the Rays and how the Rays can then move forward for spiritual liberation and Global Ascension.

This work upon the Earth Plane and Planet is a very important. Tarry not in your work, but let this move forward, so that many will gain a greater understanding and a greater opening and awareness. This time of great spiritual evolution or, shall we say, Spiritual Awakening, is one of great timing and order and this timing and order comes forward in the activation of each of the Golden City Vortices.

The subtle energies, as you have understood, come forward in the Doorways. These Doorways, as I have discussed, bring a different understanding to the Ray Force and how that Ray Force is then utilized at an even greater work of awakening. Within the Golden City Vortex structure itself exists, as you have always known, a cross within a circle. Each of the Doorways shows itself as the four directions. I have spoken about the adjutant points, or the gateways, of each of these Doorways (I have given these in past discourses and if you refer back to this information, you will understand this). The area between the two outer points is indeed where the energy itself is the strongest for each of the Doorways of the Golden Cities. This energy brings itself, shall we say, coalescing to the Star and there you will find a greater energy of that Ray Force.

So, for instance, let me give you this example: In the Eastern Door, between the two outer points, there the energy finds itself at the strongest in the East and as you move in the triangular section towards the Star, you will feel the energies coalescing with the other gateways. So, for those who wish to move to an area to participate in the energies of the gateways of the Golden Cities, it is important that they use the energy first towards the outer portion of the Vortex.

We have spoken about this before and for those who move in their intention to gain spiritual liberation . . . Spiritual Awakening . . . spiritual growth and evolution . . . it is very important to understand that you live first towards the outside of any Golden City Vortex; that is, within a ten to twenty-mile range prior to entering the Vortex. This is the flux of the Vortex itself and there you are able to feel the energy in its fluctuation. As you absorb this energy, shall we say, through the air that is breathed, through the water that is drunk, through the food that is eaten, there is a gradual assimilation of the energies of that Vortex. Slowly but surely these energies begin to assimilate within the being.

Now, if one would only like to retreat to a Golden City Center for ceremony, prayer, or reflection, this is a different idea within itself. However, Dear ones, Dear hearts, for those who intend to live there, coming forward to give their hearts and their hands to this work, it is most important that the energies are completely assimilated. This will allow for lesser discord within the body itself . . . lesser discord in the emotions . . . lesser discord within the mind. Have you not noticed that those who move immediately to the Gobean Vortex, seeking that center of harmony, seeking that great peace, find in their first entry in to the city, without the proper preparation, much discord within themselves . . . discord in personal relationships . . . problems with those that they are in partnership with?

Answer: *Yes, this is true. I have noted this.*

The reason for this, Dear ones, Dear hearts, is because there is not yet the proper assimilation of the Ray Force and not only at the physical level. It does indeed take some time for the Ray Force to be properly assimilated. Through gem elixirs, we are hoping to bring a greater efficiency to the absorption of the Ray process but we do recommend that no less than one year is spent within ten to twenty miles of the outer side of the Vortex before entry. After that, then one may pick one of the Doorways. Again, remember that the energies are the strongest within the gateways themselves and then the energies coalesce as they move towards that great Star. After three to four years of understanding and knowing the energies within the different Doorways, then one is prepared at the great inner level to enter into a Star.

Those who wish to live in the Star will notice that they are then to hold the great intent of the light of that Ray Force. That Ray Force then becomes integrated and part of their being. They will be taught on the inner levels at the great schools of that Golden Crystal City. You see, Dear ones, Dear hearts, when we speak of the Akashic Records that lie above each of the Golden Cities, we are speaking of the great Crystal Cities that lie above. These are the great schools where the Master Teachers bring forth their discourses.

Some souls in their dream states travel to receive inner instruction in these Crystal Cities. There are even those who have crossed over to the other side through the process of physical death and reside in the Crystal Cities, preparing themselves for the next embodiment. You see, Dear ones, this all serves for a great evolution and a greater understanding of the human soul itself. Now, before I proceed with any more information, do you have any questions?

Not at this time.

The Crystal Cities are very important, Dear ones. You see, they exist in the ethereal alongside the Vortex itself. As we have always stated in these teachings, it is in complete cooperation with beloved Mother Earth, Babajeran, and the Ascended Masters that we are able to bring this information forward. This is how the Golden City Vortices are brought in their greater understanding; this is how they are brought in their great structures. We explained in the earliest information how they are constructed as a series of pyramids. As we taught, it is through the triangle that the geometric language is then replicated unto itself. This causes, shall we say, an inversion of the energy and allows the great energy of the Crystal Cities to permeate the minerals, vegetables, airs, rivers, and all that surrounds Mother Earth in that vicinity.

It is our hope over time, after the activation of the fifty-one Golden Cities, that the great process of expansion shall occur. At that moment in time, each of the Golden Cities will radiate at a greater distance. Soon they will all touch one another with each of the Ray Forces coalescing. This great force will be a momentum unto the universe and allow the Earth then to change in its own revolution about the Sun, its own revolution about its own pole. Of course, this is hundreds of years into the future in terms of Earth time but it is important for you to understand the importance of the Golden City Vortices and why their activation and purpose is there to assist, help, and heal humanity. Questions?

Response: *Yes. With the Golden Cities expanding to that distance, to where they're actually touching one another, that would require the inhabitants to be very, very different than they are today.*

This process is accelerated through the energies of the Golden Cities. You see, they reflect as a mirror reflects the energies of the great Crystal Schools; therefore, every waking moment, conscious or unconscious, that is spent in the Golden City Vortex, the energy of the great Crystal Cities is vibrating at a resonance that is much higher than if you are not located within one. Have you not noticed that when you leave a Golden City, a difference in the vibration?

Answer: *Oh, yes.*

This is because you have left the radiance of the great etheric Crystal Cities; however, when you enter back in, you hear a hum . . . you hear a pitch . . . you sense a vibration. This is the resonance of Mother Earth in cooperation with the work of the hierarchy, arcing these energies of these great cities to humanity to bring their help and healing love.

Response: *Yes, I understand this now. Do you have further discourse?*

Proceed for questions.

Question: *Are we complete?*

Proceed, Dear one.

Question: *We have a dear friend, whom you are aware of, who lives in Switzerland and Arizona. We feel that he is not well and would like to know what he can do to affect a cure?*

This beloved Dear Brother has a blockage, a blockage not only in the physical body itself, but a blockage within the Chakra System, as you have well noted. This blockage is related not only to his feelings or insecurities about being safe but also related to the lower chakras, worrying about money and worrying about caring for his family. He is in constant worry and struggle. How shall I provide? How shall I do this? How shall I do that? This has brought great conflict to this individual and this is the reason for such a blockage. It is time to release at another level, time to let go, shall we say, of all that holds one back. In this case, fear . . . fear of not being able to provide . . . fear of not having enough . . . fear that one may be thrust into poverty. It is important to use the Violet Flame for such a problem; for you see, this type of problem is one that is carried through many, many lifetimes.

This is a type of fear that many individuals face. Many humans on the Earth Plane and Planet, seeking their Ascension in the great Light of All, carry such fear. This is carried at the genetic level, coming not only from parents that give us birth but carried over from lifetime after lifetime after lifetime. This beloved Dear one must let go of this fear. It must be let go through the use of the Violet Flame. Please remind this Dear one to increase his use of the Violet Flame. To call it forward:

Mighty Violet Flame, release all fear within my system.
Mighty Violet Flame, may I move now into the Heart of Love.
Mighty Violet Flame embrace my entire system.
Mighty Violet Flame, in love I AM.

When this Dear one uses this decree, tell him to call forth this sacred fire from the white fire core of the Earth itself. Let him resonate also to the Great Central Sun and there he shall find this sacred fire moving along the Kundalini current of his entire system. It is important to move into the Heart of Love . . . to move into unconditional acceptance and surrender to that mighty Will. It is also important for this one to realize that within himself is his own choice. As you well know, we shall never tell another what to do. We can only give a suggestion that can give help and assistance.

There is a choice that lies for this Dear one, this Dear Brother. He has a choice to release at many levels, the many, many lifetimes of fear that have been held within the being . . . fear from not being accepted from traditional beliefs . . . fear of not being accepted by those who would want other things for this person's life . . . fear of not being loved by those close to him. All of these bring a karmic burden. This must come forward in that mighty Violet Flame and there is the ultimate release. But now I shall scan the physical body and see if I can make a further suggestion.

(He is now moving his hands up and down as if the image of this individual is right in front of him).

[Editor's Note: Saint Germain offers medical suggestions particular to the individual with the problem—not generally applicable.]

Questions?

Response: *I have no further questions.*

Then, Dear ones, it is with great joy that I now depart your dimension. Know that I AM here and always available for further discourse.

Response: *Thank you.*

Study Guide for Integrating Golden City Energies

Topics:
The Ethereal Mirror
Golden City Adjutant Points and Lei-lines
Coalescing of Golden City Energies

The Ethereal Mirror

The physical Earth, with every fissure, canyon, prairie, lake, and river is similarly mirrored on the ethereal Astral Plane. Saint Germain explains this spiritual phenomenon as similar to Hermetic Law, "As above, so below." The ethereal mirror also creates energy anomalies with physical and spiritual energies emitting through earthly lei-lines, energy points, and both minor and major Vortices. While the energies slow down as they move through the dimensions, a blueprint for each level of energy is detected. This is one of the underlying principles of the Golden City Vortices, which mirror energies from the Fifth Dimension to the Fourth Dimension, and onward to the Third Dimension. The energies step down through each subsequent dimension imbued with unique qualities and different vibrations.

Saint Germain's Prophecies and Teachings on the Golden City Vortices:

1. Ray forces originate from the Great Central Sun—the Galactic Center—and travel through space to our solar Sun and then to Earth. They are absorbed through our Earth's core, said to be a core of fiery white light, and then the energies emit from Earth's energy meridians, lei-lines, small Vortices, faults, rivers, lakes, and fissures.
2. Since Golden City Vortices are created though the crossing of eight major Galactic Ray lei-lines, these are areas that manifest the purity of certain Ray Forces. The Ray Force can be easily accessed in a Golden City for spiritual liberation.
3. As each Golden City activates, humanity encounters leaps in spiritual evolution and growth. Saint Germain prophesies that Golden Cities are locations for Global Ascension. (See *Golden City Vortex Activation Dates*, "Light of Awakening," Appendix E.)

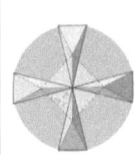 # Golden Cities Through the Dimensions

	THIRD DIMENSION	FOURTH DIMENSION	FIFTH DIMENSION
EVOLUTIONARY ARCHETYPE	The awakened, conscious human.	The HU-man Nature Beings	Ascended Masters Elohim Archangels Evolutionary Archetypes
COMMUNITY	Golden City Community. Harmonious connection to Mother Earth. Stewardship	Elemental Kingdom Mineral Kingdom Plant Kingdom Animal Kingdoms Nature Kingdoms	Shamballa (Spiritually perfected community.)
ACTIVITY	Longevity Slower aging process. Greater healing and recovery ability. Physical Regeneration (Cell replication)	Telepathic Ability Psychic Ability Development of the Super Senses. Lucid Dreaming Multi-dimensional awareness.	Unana Consciousness of the ONE. Fellowship through the ONE and Oneship.
PLANE	Physical	Astral	Causal
TIME	Duality Linear Time Continuous time is a series of transactions.	Time Compaction Time Warp Deja Vue Peak or Zone Experience	Timelessness The Abiding *Presence* Ever Present Now Continuous Flow
SOCIAL	Human Rights Civil Rights Twelve Jurisdictions	Group Mind Collective Consciousness Brotherhood and Sisterhood	Unity
CULTURE	Cultivation of the Four Pillars: Arts, Languages, Sciences, Ancient Religions and History, Philosophy	Beauty, Harmony, Cooperation	Grace Peace

FIGURE 1-H
Golden Cities through the Dimensions

4. The subtle, individualized energy of the Ray Force is best experienced in each of the four Golden City Doors—the four cardinal directions. Each door, also known as a gateway, allows the individual to experience the energy of the Ray through the four directions.
5. At the Gateway Adjutant Points, the Ray's energy is at its maximum force. This is the best place to experience the energy of the Golden City Ray.
6. Adjutant Points play an important role initiating an individual's Spiritual Awakening.
7. The geometric and energetic line that connects the two gateway adjutant points forms a lei-line in the gateway energy. This is a vital part of the Golden City infrastructure. The energies of the Golden City Gateway are strong along this entire lei-line; however, its peak energies concentrate in the middle of the lei-line, this is known as a Peak Adjutant Point.
8. A second lei-line is formed from the Peak Adjutant Point to the Golden City Star. The energies of the Golden City Gateway coalesce to the Star through this energy current. While energies of the Golden City Gateway can be felt and accessed throughout the entire geophysical Golden City Gateway, the doorway's Peak Adjutant Lei-line contains the most intense, condensed energies of each individual gateway and the Ray Force.

Science of the Maltese Cross

Recent scientific research has created the first ever hologram of a single light particle—the photon. Einstein resolved the argument about whether light was wave or particle when he created the quantum theory of light that conceived that light exists in microscopic packets or particles that he called photons. He also knew that the flow of photons is a wave—so light contains its own form of polarity, it is both particle and wave. These two properties allow light, as a photon, to create both refraction and diffusion.

So when scientists wanted to view exactly what a photon would look like, they knew that they would be looking at something that might be tricky to detect: the shape of the wave fronts of a single photon. [1] Physicist Erwin Schrodinger, an Austrian scientist, disliked the dual terminology of wave and particle, and set out to theorize in waves only, which led to the basis of wave mechanics, wave equation, and quantum wave function that has corroborated the recent research of physicists at the University of Warsaw. After

FIGURE 2-H
Photon Hologram

reconstructing a series of 2,000 repetitious flashes of two photons intersecting and their subsequent interaction, they were able to create a hologram image and the shape of the photon's wave function: a Maltese Cross. [2]

The four directions of the Golden City represent the refraction and diffusion of light into the four doorways. They are: Northern Door, black; Eastern Door, cyan; Southern Door, magenta; and the Western Door, yellow.

Since a Golden City is prophesied to be 400 kilometers or 248 miles high, its elevations contain both terrestrial and spiritual significance that relate to atmosphere and planes of consciousness. It breaks down like this:
- 0 to 28 miles in elevation: Physical Plane (stratosphere)
- 28 to 191 miles in elevation: Astral Plane (ionosphere, mesosphere, thermosphere)
- 191 to 400 miles in elevation: Causal Plane (ionosphere, exosphere)[3]

Adjutant Point
Power points that form where the lei-lines of the geometric Maltese cross formation of a Golden City traverse or intersect. Adjutant points support the infrastructure of a Golden City, both geometrically and spiritually, and assist and disburse the unique energies held by Babajeran, the Ascended Masters, and the Golden City's Ray Force. Golden City Adjutant Points can have up to a ten- to twenty-mile radial electromagnetic energy flux.

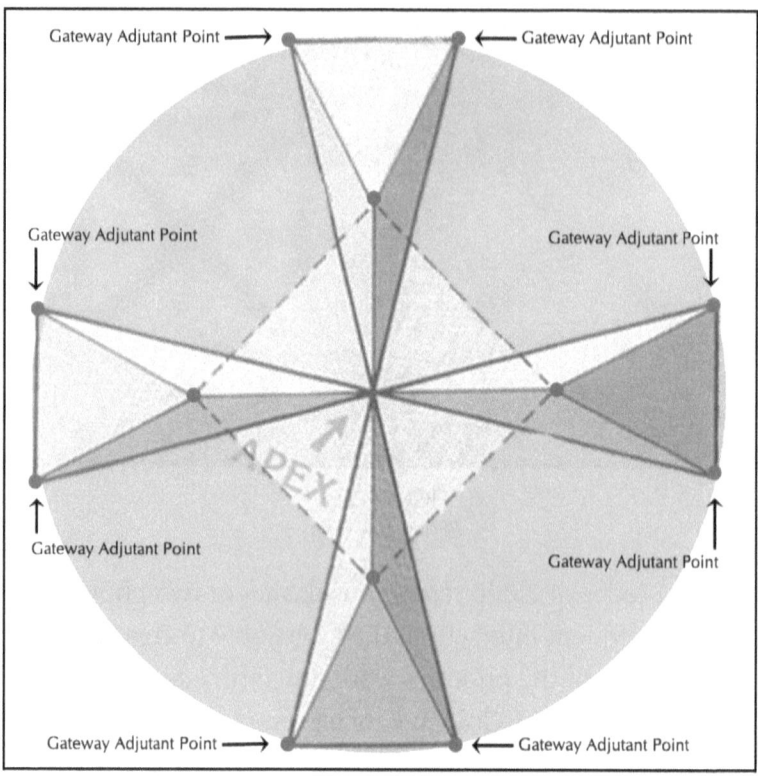

FIGURE 3-H
Golden City Gateway Adjutant Point

Gateway Adjutant Points

Two Golden City Points are locations on either side of each directional gateway of a Golden City Vortex and situated to the outer perimeter of the Vortex. They protect the span of each gateway—103.6 kilometers, just over 64 miles. Since there is one pair of points per doorway, one masculine *Father Point* (electrical) and the other is the feminine *Mother Point* (magnetic), there are a total of eight Gateway Adjutant Points in each Golden City Vortex, two for each of the four directions. Each power point carries a concentration of the Golden City's Ray Force, and its unique attributes and qualities. Adjutant Points are alleged to step-down and distill the energies of the ethereal Fifth and Fourth Dimension into our physical Third Dimension with strength and intensity. Adjutant Points are spiritual locations for multiple, yet smaller, etheric retreats that exist exclusively within a Golden City Vortex that are overseen and inhabited by certain Spiritual Teachers, Angels, and Elohim.

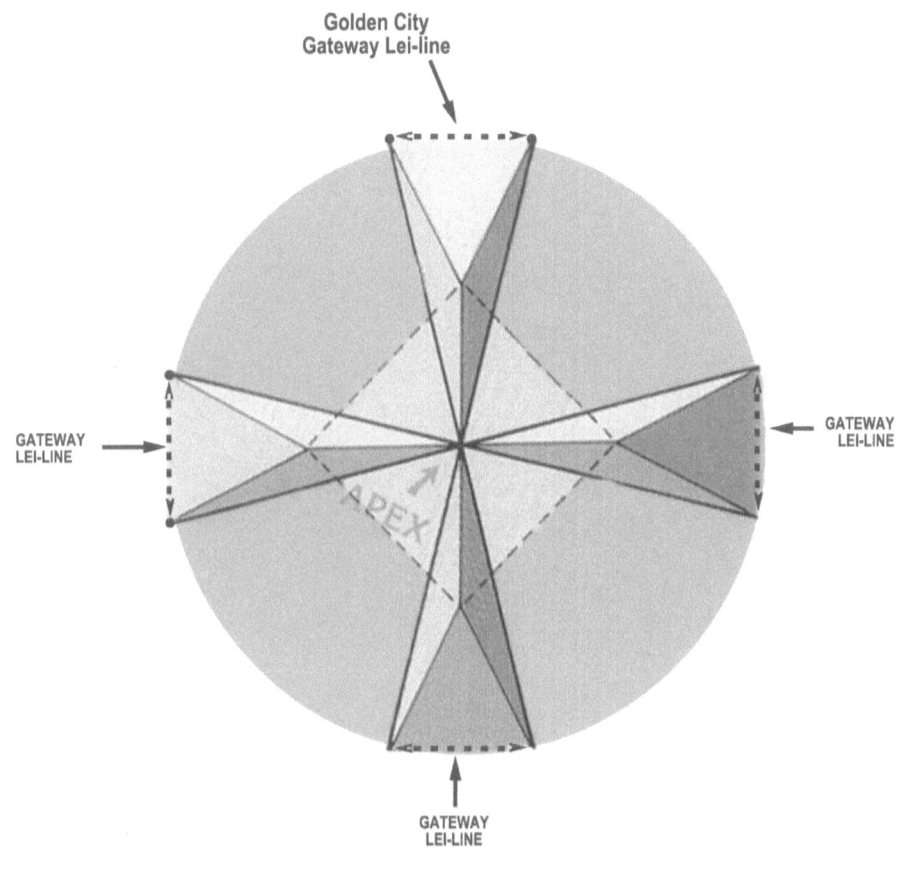

FIGURE 4-H
Golden City Gateway Lei-line

Golden City Gateway Lei-line

A lei-line is a line of spiritual energy that exists among geographical places, ancient monuments, megaliths, and strategic points. Since a Golden City Gateway Lei-line manifests between a pair of Gateway Adjutant Points—the energy of the lei-line is electromagnetic. The length of this Golden City arterial lei-line is 64 miles.

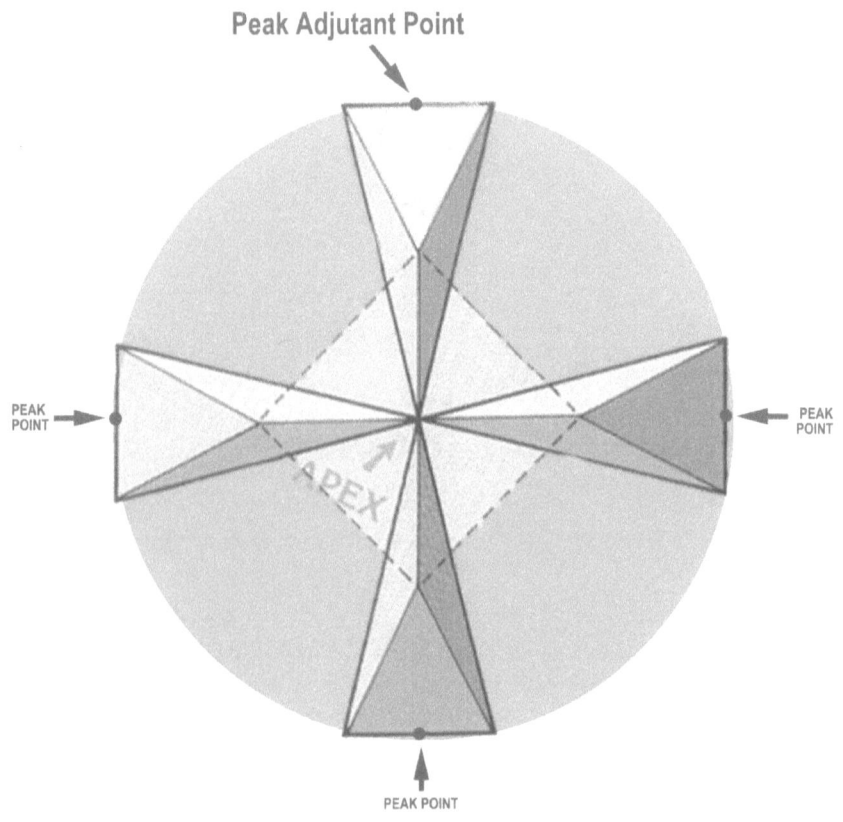

FIGURE 5-H
Peak Adjutant Point

Peak Adjutant Point

This power point is energetically defined by the merging of both masculine and feminine Gateway Adjutant Points. The Peak Adjutant Point is also referred to as a *Golden City Child Point*, as it contains and expresses a pure and concentrated energy of both points of the Golden City Doorway. It is located exactly in the center of the doorway's lei-line, approximately 32.19 miles from either side.

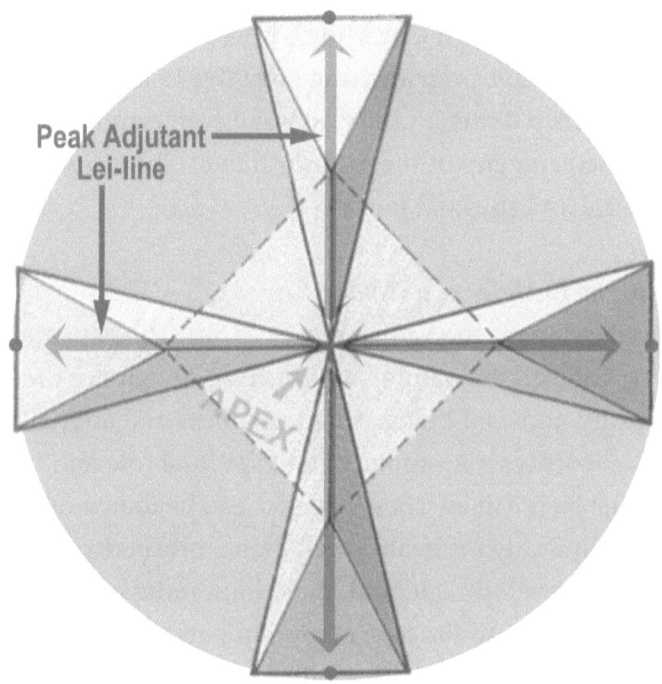

FIGURE 6-H
Peak Adjutant Lei-line

Peak Adjutant Lei-line

This arterial lei-line of a Golden City is formed through energies surging from two points. Point one is the Golden City Doorway's Peak Adjutant Point and extends to the Golden City Star, the second point. There are four Peak Adjutant Lei-lines per Golden City, often referred to as *Peak Lei-lines*. A Peak Adjutant Lei-line is 217.4 kilometers, or approximately 135 miles. This lei-line is especially dynamic, and at its approximate halfway point—about 67.5 miles—Golden City Fifth Dimensional energies can be easily detected and utilized.

Coalesce

To grow together into one body, or to unite into one mass. [4] The principle of the coalescing energies in a Golden City Vortex, Golden City Gateways, and along the various adjutant points and lei-lines is profoundly important in order to grasp how a Golden City Vortex gathers, harnesses, and distributes the energies of the Ray Force. The etymology of the word "coalesce" comes from the Latin word *coalesco*, which means "to grow up."[5] It is important to remember that Golden City energies may be sensed throughout the entire Golden City Vortex, however, to harness the essential energies of a Golden City Doorway, one must live in a Golden City. The two major lei-lines of each doorway, the Gateway Lei-line and the Peak Lei-line, contain condensed energies of the gateway that can be tapped into for a variety of physical and spiritual purposes.

Tapping into the Energies of a Golden City

For thousands of years, the Vedic practice of Vastu Shastra and Chinese Feng Shui have utilized the natural and intrinsic energies of the Earth for balance, harmony, and well-being. Adjutant points and arterial lei-lines of the Golden City Vortices play an important spiritual role and help humanity move into the New Times. These energies can be drawn upon both spiritually and physically for health, well-being, prosperity, dynamic relationship, spiritual development, and, most importantly, initiating the soul's journey into the Ascension Process. Many students of the I AM America Spiritual Teachings travel to specific Golden City Vortices to spiritually attune to certain energies and the Ray Force of the Vortex.

It is also important to know that you can physically employ the Golden City energies through the use of Golden City mineral elixirs. Here is the recipe:

- Collect these types of rocks from the geophysical doors of Golden Cities: silicon rocks (obsidian, granite, diovite, and sandstone), felds par, and quartz or quartz crystal. (Use only activated Golden City minerals; for more information see *Light of Awakening*.) Use about 16 ounces per batch.
- Three gallons of water
- One cup salt (any type)

Technique: Soak the rock in the salt water for at least 8 hours in a glass container or stainless steel pot (no plastics of any type)—this allows for the extraction of subtle energies from the mineral. Quickly heat the water and rock to a boiling point, and immediately remove from heat. Add your essential oil of choice—12 to 20 drops. (See following suggestions.)

Golden City Elixirs interface the energies of Golden Cities utilizing both the Mineral and Plant Kingdoms. Apply 4 to 8 drops of the Elixir on pulse points (wrists are best). This allows for contact with the Human Aura—energy field. It is claimed that the Golden City energies remain inert or inactive until they come into physical contact with the individual. Saint Germain suggests that the mineral (rock) should be used no more than seven times total, and then all rocks, minerals, and crystals are to be returned to the Star of the Golden City of origin. He teaches that after returning the rock to the Star, that the rock set undisturbed for a total of twenty-four hours and placed to properly receive a cleansing bath of both sunlight and moonlight. Then perform the "Sacrament of the Fire." After this ritual, return the rocks to the Golden City Star, where they should remain undisturbed for a minimum of two years. Here is an excerpt from Saint Germain's lesson, "Golden City Elixirs," [6] that describes this important process:

> "And so, only seven times for this process and then a recharging . . . after purifying the substances (rocks) in the sunlight and moonlight, then rinse in water to bring a purification and set within the Sacrament of the Fire."

Response: "The Sacrament of the Fire . . . I'm confused."

> "It is a ritual. For you see, Dear one, these energies are to create a spiritual liberation. I ask you to set these, after the (water) purification, near a fire that is dedicated to the work of the Lodge, a consecration of the service of the Mineral Kingdom, and an honoring of their work. Do you understand?"

Answer: "Yes, I assume that there is a methodology and a protocol to create this fire?"

> The *Sacrament of the Fire* may be a fire set outdoors, or a fire lit within your home, even a candle. This fire establishes a spiritual intention. You see, Dear one, this preserves the agreement that the elixirs be used only for spiritual growth and evolution. Many eons have passed over Earth when men have toiled for the nature of

greed and the hoarding of power over others. This has brought great suffering to humanity. And now the humblest shall come forward and convey the greatest prize. This is also the spiritual understanding:

> All are united as ONE.
> All is as ONE in the New Time.

> This *Sacrament of the Fire*, is akin to the desire that links you as ONE to and within the Lodge."

Since the Plant Kingdom interfaces the energies of the Mineral Kingdom in Golden City Elixirs, it is suggested to pair rocks, minerals, and crystals with these specific essential oils:

1. **Rocks, minerals, and crystals from Northern Doors**: Use essential oils that are derived from plants that bloom with deep blue or purple flowers. Saint Germain suggests that violet and lavender are best.
2. **Rocks, minerals, and crystals from Eastern Doors**: Essential oils from plants that display light blue or pink flowers—rose and lavender are good.
3. **Rocks, minerals, and crystals from Southern Doors**: Use essential oils that are derived from plants with white flowers and aromatic green leafs. Any citrus oil will work well but mints, basil, and sage oil is best. You can also combine oils for a good result.
4. **Rocks, minerals, and crystals from Western Doors**: Use essential oils that are derived from plants that bloom with orange or yellow flowers. Even though lemon blossoms are white, Saint Germain claims that lemon oil is best, but you can also use calendula and neroli oils.

If you decide to physically live in a Golden City and build on an arterial lei-line, remember that these lines of detectable spiritual energy have a flux of approximately five miles; adjutant points have a concentrated flux of up to ten miles. You can tap into the energy flow of the arterial lei-line by examining the nearby landform. In the case of capturing energies from a Northern Door lei-line, look for landforms that slope to the north, and

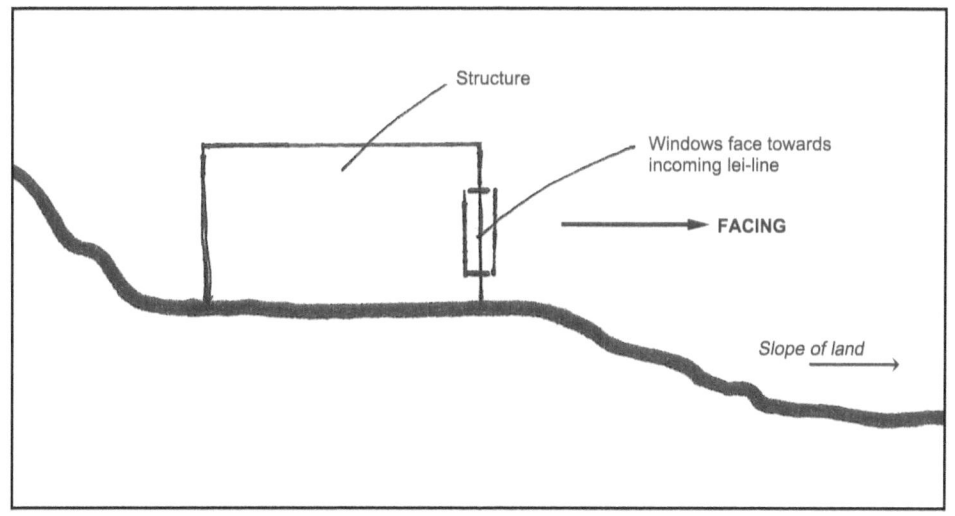

FIGURE 7-H
Slope of Land Towards Energy Flow of a Golden City Lei-line

position your home to receive supportive energy (the higher slope of the land) from the south. This is considered the *back* of the building. Position your structures' primary windows on the opposite side of your building, looking towards the downward Northern slope and Northern horizon. The structures should directly face the incoming influx of energies from the lei-line. In several schools of Feng Shui, every structure receives energy or chi from its *facing* direction.

Since Northern Doors are beneficial gateways for the manifestation process, these Golden City locations are good for business, entrepreneurs, small business, and individuals interested in the physical manifestation or self-actualization process. According to the Master Teachers, Northern Doors are good locations for small farms, orchards, and gardens. One interesting technique to pool the energies from the benefic lei-line is the creation of a *Ming Tang*—known in Feng Shui as the "Bright Hall."

This is achieved through creating a large, flat area at the bottom of a benefic slope, or if no slope is available, plant trees around the flat area to capture and hold the energies. A large front yard with plenty of grass, open towards the incoming energies of the lei-line is best. Some Feng Shui practitioners refer to this area as "virtual water" as the energy collects or pools on the flat, grassy surface. Contain the energy by embracing the "pool" with

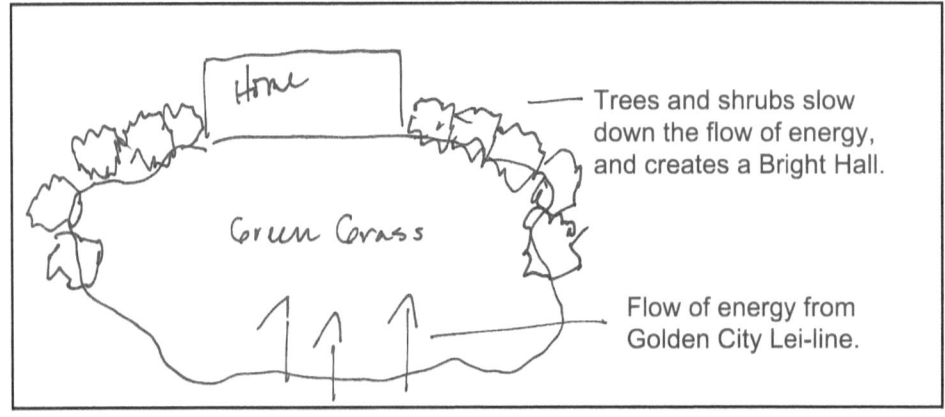

FIGURE 8-H
Creation of Bright Hall to Capture Golden City Energies

shrubbery, flowering bushes, or low-growing trees. If needed, you can also incorporate hardscape features such as pathways, fences, or walls.

Beautiful gardens, with low-growing shrubs and trees are also beneficial for capturing benefic energies. The etymology of "guardian" is the Old French word *gardien*, which translates to its Middle English version, *garden*. A properly placed garden, with flowers and edible landscape protects and shields the home with beauty, while capturing the ambient, subtle energies of the Golden City Lei-line.

There are many different ways that a bright hall can be constructed for efficient energy collection, and this example is simplistic. Please employ an authentic Feng Shui practitioner to help engineer your collection pool for Golden City energies. When picking a practitioner, question them thoroughly about their background and training. My practitioner and Taoist teacher once counseled that a properly trained Feng Shui practitioner must literally "walk a thousand miles" to gain the important knowledge associated with landform. A Feng Shui practitioner can also assist you with the Flying Stars, an assessment of how the five elements are interacting in your living or business space, along with any appropriate remedial measures. My practitioner once advised me, "Any negative circumstance or situation can be neutralized." So if a practitioner tells you that they cannot remediate your situation or suggests that you should move or sell your property, they likely do not have complete knowledge about the cycle of the elements. There are cases, however, when the Feng Shui becomes corrupt on a property—but these cases are inordinately rare.

Another technique for capturing Golden City energies is building a series of cascading pools down the gradual slope of the facing of your building. This design will sufficiently pool the energies and hold the vital chi; be sure to add trees, shrubs, and flower plants. [Editor's Note: My husband designed a similar configuration for the facing of our home, recommended by a Feng Shui designer. When our practitioner saw the cascading garden, filled with apple, plum, and almond trees, she commented, "Every living plant is capturing and distributing vital energy to your property." This design technique is especially helpful for hilly or sloped land, and effectively slows energy down before entering the property or leaving it.]

Southern doors are beneficial for healing processes: spiritually, mentally, emotionally, and physically. It is also claimed that they are good for physical and spiritual regeneration. Locate spas, retreats, and sanctuary communities to embrace the restorative energies of Southern Door Peak Adjutant lei-lines.

Eastern Doors create loving relationships with family members, and are the best locations for residences. Face your home to the East with a bright hall for energy collection of the vital lei-line. Remember that large windows open your home to the energy of the lei-line through sunlight. Keep your blinds and curtains open during the day so your home will benefit from the harmony-inducing spiritual energy.

Western Doors help us to assimilate, learn, and self-actualize through the experience of higher knowledge. This may occur through scholastic endeavors or through the integration process with the I AM Presence. Western Doors prepare our consciousness to receive the vital, spiritual integration processes of Ascension, prior to our entry into the energies of the Star—the center of the Golden City Vortex. Through their affiliation with wisdom and higher knowledge, Southern Doors are good locations for schools and universities. The energies of the Peak Adjutant Lei-line assist mental and intellectual processes which are claimed by the Ascended Masters to be ideal locations for the Capital Cities of the countries of the New Times.

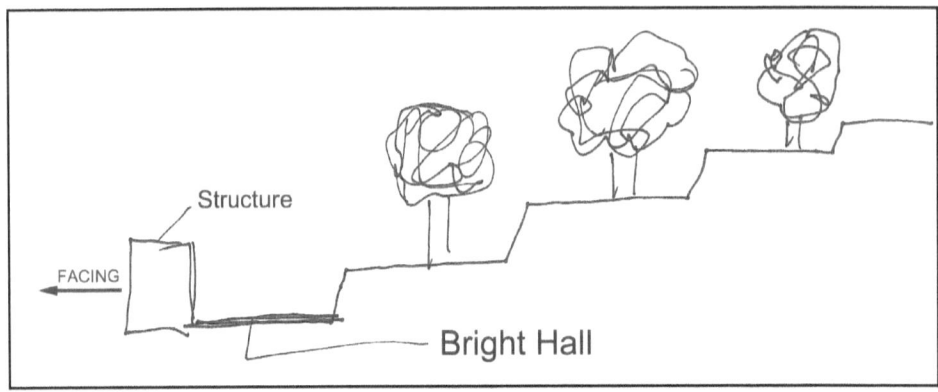

FIGURE 9-H
Cascading Bright Hall for Energy Collection

The thirty-third degree, or the meeting point of the Peak Adjutant lei-lines, is also known as a Peak Adjutant Point. At the Thirty-third Degree Point, Fourth- and Fifth-dimensional energies enter the Golden City Vortex. This is also known as the neutral or zero point of the Golden City Vortex. Energies of the Golden City Zero Point embrace the ONE, Unana, and prepare our physical body and light bodies for Ascension. The Thirty-third Degree Point—also known as the center of the Golden City Star—has a concentrated influence of about one mile in diameter. Golden City Stars have an overall influence comprising a forty-mile radius, centered on the Thirty-third Degree Point.

1. Jessa, Tegga. "What Are Photons—Universe Today, December 24, 2015. Accessed November 14, 2016. http://www.universetoday.com/74027/what-are-photons/.
2. O'Connell, Cathal. "What Shape Are Photons? Quantum Holography Sheds Light." Cosmos Magazine. July 20, 2016. Accessed November 14, 2016. https://cosmosmagazine.com/physics/what-shape-is-a-photon.
3. Zell, Holly. "Earth's Atmospheric Layers." NASA. July 30, 2015. Accessed November 14, 2016. http://www.nasa.gov/mission_pages/sunearth/science/atmosphere-layers2.html.
4. "Coalesce." Wiktionary. Accessed November 13, 2016. https://en.wiktionary.org/wiki/coalesce.
5. Ibid.
6. Toye, Lori. Gem Elixirs by Saint Germain, August 10, 1998. I AM America Archive, Payson, Arizona.

Illustrations
1. FUW. "Photo Hologram." Digital image. Cosmos Magazine. July 20, 2016. Accessed November 14, 2016. https://cosmosmagazine.com/physics/what-shape-is-a-photon. Hologram of a single photon reconstructed from raw measurements (left) and theoretically predicted (right).

9

Golden Ray Compassion
Saint Germain

Greetings, Beloveds in that mighty Violet Ray. I AM Saint Germain and I stream forth on that mighty Violet Ray of Mercy, Compassion, and Forgiveness. As usual, Dear hearts, I request permission to come forward.

Response: *Please, Saint Germain, please come forward.*

Greetings and salutations, Dear chelas, Dear students of mine. It has been some time since our last lesson and there is much information for me to impart to you this day. As stewards of this mighty ray of teaching and understanding, as this information is being dispensed through you, it is important that it is brought forward within a rhythm, or sattva. We realize of course, at times it is important for you to conclude or carry out your daily activities; however, it is also important for you to understand the rhythm and the harmony of the lessons that are being given to you. We ask you to schedule time into your life to bring this information forward in that harmony and absolute rhythm of the spheres.

Dear ones, Dear hearts, we shall be of assistance to you, so that this important information may be carried forth for the chelas and the students whose ears and eyes are now open. This is most important, as the mighty Golden Ray has opened its vibration upon the Earth Plane and Planet and there are many now who are readied in their vibration to receive this higher information, to receive this higher knowledge. As you understand, the Golden Ray is bringing forth many new discoveries in your scientific community, many new discoveries that are coming forth in the Information Age. This is of course very important to those whose eyes and ears are on the pulse of this information but it is also important for the student, the chela of the Ascended Masters, to understand the importance of the Golden Ray.

Not only does this great alignment force of the Golden Ray bring forth an understanding of the past karmas and the past lives that have now been brought to a conclusion in their understanding, but the Golden Ray readies one to understand a new vibration, a new level. This Golden Ray is being brought forward to bring a higher frequency and vibration to the spiritual awakening.

Dear chelas, now listen, for this is of great importance. Understand that the Golden Ray brings forth its higher frequency vibration within the Stars of all Golden City Vortices. But know this: that if one were to hear this information and try to utilize it for the first time, it would take a great integration of the higher frequency of the Violet Flame to be able to bring the Golden Ray forward. So those who wish to utilize the Golden Ray in its higher frequency must have applied and used the Violet Flame for at least a two-year period, that is a full twenty-four months.

Those who are prepared know that they can now move to the Stars in this higher frequency and utilize the energy of the Golden Ray to bring a greater understanding and knowledge of the new dimensions. Now when I say "the new dimensions," understand this, Dear ones, Dear chelas, that there is no such thing as a new dimension, for all dimensions have always existed. Since time was created for your knowledge and understanding, also know that this higher frequency does exist and it is important for you to access it. In accessing this greater knowledge of the dimensions, the soul is then readied to move forward into the completion of the Ascension. This has always been the purpose and the intention of the Stars of the Golden City Vortices, to prepare the body for the Ascension process.

Now that you have brought several of the stalwart chelas to this great center, the Star of Gobean, you will hear reports from them that they will begin an alignment process in their physical, astral, mental, and emotional bodies. This great alignment process is very important to bring a greater purity, to bring a purification forward. Honor and allow this purification process to flow throughout your being, Dear ones, Dear hearts, for this brings one to that alchemy of the true soul. The union with the soul is most important at this time; for you see, the monad in its journey in illusion begins to over-identify with the body, over-identify with the illusion. But understand, in the grand interplay of the rays, that there is more that lies beneath, as you have always known. It is this contact with the soul that is most important, for one begins to understand the consequences of past lives and the consequences of past actions, and then moves them all into the transformation of that burning and alchemizing Violet Ray.

> May the Violet Ray stream forth into the hearts and souls
> of those who are ready to serve the Cause Divine.
> May this Golden Ray, in its greater harmony,
> adjunct to this mighty Violet Ray,
> now bring its own harmony forward.
> May the Golden Ray now initiate the consciousness
> to move into the new dimensions.
> May this new initiation now serve this grand and greater plan.

Dear ones, Dear hearts, the Brotherhoods and the Sisterhoods of Light and Sound eagerly await your arrival . . . eagerly await your presence.

> Mighty I AM Presence, stream forth
> into the heart of the Great Central Sun.
> Mighty I AM Presence, stream forth
> into that mighty service of the Great White Brotherhood.

Dear ones, Dear hearts, this initiation into this greater consciousness will not only increase your telepathic abilities but you will notice, in your dream states at night, more lucidity coming to your consciousness. A greater understanding of the interplay of past lives and how these journeys now serve this greater cause will unite your soul with an understanding of true compassion . . . of true peace . . . of true united Brotherhood and Sisterhood. You see, Dear ones, Dear hearts, this has always been our cause, to bring peace upon this Earth; to bring a greater understanding, a greater evolution, and the knowledge that the true self is a Divine Inheritor of the Kingdom.

Beloved Brother Sananda was sent, in his journey to the Earth Plane and Planet, as Jesus the Christ, to bring this teaching and knowledge forward. And Buddha followed this great teaching, to show that these teachings could be internalized, that compassion could truly be felt among one another. You see, Dear ones, this greater compassion is a truth among those who come to the Earth Plane and Planet, even those of the alien consciousness. What they seek is this knowledge of true love, true compassion, and how the heart-felt emotions open and initiate the consciousness into a greater understanding.

Until one enters into the path of the heart, the "true blood that washes the feet," one is not truly and absolutely prepared to understand the higher consciousness. Understand that there is no remote viewer . . . understand that there is no mind control . . . understand that there is no unlawful government out there that can take, steal, or even listen in on any information of this type until they have opened that heart of compassion. It is truly the heart of compassion that opens all to this greater understanding, the greater love, and the journey that awaits within.

Dear ones, Dear hearts, open . . . open to this greater compassion . . . open to this greater understanding. This is only done through that mighty path of experience, is it not? As I have always said, "it is in the laboratory of the self where one truly carries out experience." Test the law for yourself and know yourself. Then and only then will you know the truth that I speak.

The experiences that one has here on the Earth Plane and Planet at times, yes, open terrible horrors and fears that are held lifetime after lifetime. Those terrible karmic connections, however, have woven a handshake through pain and suffering. Where is that drink of refreshment? It lies in that Cup of Compassion. When one has truly suffered, then one truly understands and can offer their hand, a helping hand in understanding and knowledge. But until one opens the soul, until one opens the heart and sees that bank of the past experience of tears, of suffering, one may think, "I shall just move forward for myself this day. I shall only serve my common desire." Beyond the common desire lies the truth of all. Beyond the common self, beyond just this one embodiment, lies the true self, the Divine Inheritor.

One may ask, "How do I open Akasha? How do I open the template, so I may peer within and see this mighty truth in action?" Dear ones, Dear hearts, it is as simple as the use of the Violet Flame. At a scientific level, the alchemizing fires transmute the cause and the effect of all past actions that may keep you from your eternal gift and blueprint of Ascension. For you see, Dear ones, consciousness was never meant to be trapped. Consciousness is meant to unfold, to grow beyond the limits of the flesh, and spring free. From that once seed, eternally it branches onward and upward into greater understanding of unity and the realms of beauty. When one views this true effect, they see the beauty that lies within and without . . . they see, understand, and know the harmony of the great eternal spheres . . . they realize that the journey is not a journey in pain and suffering but the journey is one of joy and ultimate glee. Only in this dance of consciousness can the soul truly then be free to understand its true self, the divinity within.

Compassion is truly the way of understanding and relating to another. Develop compassion within and share it among yourselves. Work hard to stay out of the lower vibrations of judging one another, of saying and sharing hurtful thoughts toward one another. For you see, the thought is a vibration. Even to think such a thought brings it forward in a manifestation, as if it were a spoken word. Understand, Dear ones, Dear hearts, that only in harmony, only in true compassion, does the soul then surrender to its ultimate victory. The new dimensions await. The Violet Flame and the Golden Ray are both here now to bring you this glorious assistance. Now I shall open the floor for questions.

Question: *What is the difference between the Divine Complement, the soul mate, and twin flames?*

There is this desire among humanity to know itself. For you see, within the dual consciousness, the soul is only allowed to take one sex at a time. It is either male or it is female; however, there are those of course who work to embrace the two types of consciousness at once and the body holds on the left and the right hand side, the female and the male consciousness. However, the dominant consciousness expresses itself in the embodiment and, therefore, the lessons are brought forward, are they not? For as we have known, there are those cultures that honor the feminine and then those cultures that honor the male.

The monad, in its great journey and the remembrance of itself, works to bring a greater unity forward, so it may move into that glory and power of the Ascension. Prior to the advent of the Golden Ray coming forward, the soul must meet its other half, its twin half. That other half was brought forward at the time of its first expression into physical embodiment. For, you see, when a soul first enters into the Earth Plane and Planet, it enters not as one but it enters as two: "and two shall come forth from the breath of the holiest of holies." This is the law that is written eternal. This was the law that was brought forth for the embodiment of humanity. These two twin rays or twin souls share that great Garden of Existence. This is the story of Adam and Eve, as you would know now in your culture. One does not come first but they are brought forward in that one great and mighty breath. They are brought forth from their Mighty Logos, from the Great Creator. All praises to this process. All praises and I bow to it eternally.

Dear ones, Dear hearts, this is how you have been brought forward into your existence. Now this twin beloved, through the cycles of reincarnation, re-embodiment, and that mighty web of illusion weaving itself over the soul, is brought now to a place perceived as an imbalance. Sometimes, these mighty twin rays or twin flames have not seen one another for millions of years. Now, how are they brought back together? They are brought back together through the Divine Complement of energies, through understanding and knowing that energy of the higher order will ultimately seek its own level. Now, maybe one of these beloveds has called upon this mighty Sacred Fire and used the energies for the highest Will Divine? Then and only then are they able to pull upon the vibrational level of the other, for does not like harmony seek like harmony?

Often there are those who meet one another preparing for that Ascension process. That is the process of moving to the higher levels of understanding . . . moving beyond the grasp of illusion . . . moving beyond the web of re-embodiment. Sometimes the result is a good one and the work that flows through these two streams of consciousness brings a balance and they are allowed to reunite as ONE. However, if the preparation of the souls is not completed through that mighty alchemizing Violet Ray, continuous disharmonies and conflicts within their webs of karmas, actions, and unfulfilled desires, may cast the souls deeper and farther apart from one another. And yet their unity cries for each other: "my other half . . . my twin . . . my beloved."

Now let us understand this at a greater unity of cause. You are all united, as all of you are Brothers and Sisters in the Earth Plane and Planet. You are all ONE within this mighty kernel of great truth and light. Perhaps you seek this energy only through that special one; you seek to know and understand yourself only through the uniting with that mighty soul that is the other half of you. The work of the Golden Ray has been brought forward to complete this process, so limitation is no longer on the Earth Plane and Planet. For those souls that have been trapped in this web of time, the Golden Ray is now brought forward to bring a higher vibration, a higher frequency and understanding. Open your heart to compassion, Dear ones, Dear chelas, and the mirror of illusion cracks and you face your eternal self. Questions?

Question: *I am still a little confused. The soul comes through into experience as one half and one half and is it only through re-aligning their energies that they are reunited?*

This is true, Dear one, Dear heart. When energy is taken and understood at its higher frequency, the consciousness understands that it was the true sense of separation that parted the two halves in the journey of time. Now, how do we gather forces together but through understanding the unity of all of consciousness. In this greater unity and harmony, the web of illusion is cracked and the soul no longer feels the separateness. It feels the completion. This begins the process of Ascension. This Divine Arcing, this Divine Harmony of the rays, comes forward now and serves a greater plan. For you see, then that Law of Sympathetic Resonance and Sympathetic Harmonies supersedes the Law of Duality, does it not? Understand, know, and apply these greater laws and the journey continues in its upward ascent of joy.

Dear ones, Dear hearts, the work of the Golden Ray is now allowing many souls that have not seen one another for thousands of journeys into the Earth Plane and Planet to reunite with a great joy and understanding of this higher completion. Of course, there will be those brief encounters and perhaps one is not ready to join and move forward. But understand, now the Law of Unity prevails. Unana, a higher consciousness that is brought forward through this Golden Ray, has a greater understanding and will now lead many souls into the path of Ascension.

This greater unity and harmony comes forward through the service of beloved Mother Earth, Babajeran as we know her. Babajeran has offered, in the same way that she offered to clothe you in your physical bodies, to release this hold and allow the higher frequencies that come through the Stars of each of the Golden City Vortices to unite the consciousness into a higher understanding of a collective unity and consciousness. As Dear Sananda has said, "the time is at hand, the awakening is here. The seconds and the minutes tick." Make your choice, Dear ones, Dear hearts.

The work of the Golden City Vortices and the work of the Stars of these great focuses of higher energy come to assist in that alignment process. Now realize this: do not take the limitation into your consciousness of meeting your other half before entering into that path of Ascension. Know that your other half awaits there, beyond the web of illusion. Know that your true self is complete within itself. Wait not to find union in the Earth Plane but find that union of Divine Harmonies. Questions?

Question: *The very fact that the Golden Cities now exist energetically and that we can even communicate with you, is that not a crack in the illusion?*

It is the Divine Order and Timing, as it always has been and always shall be. SO BE IT!

Question: *So are you saying, it is time for the global graduation and moving on from this realm of consciousness to the other realms?*

Only consciousness held at a certain frequency or vibration can limit itself. You see, Dear ones, it is as simple as pouring the consciousness into the cup. Is this cup half full or is this cup half empty? What is the perception of how I see things? Am I complete or am I incomplete? Am I ready to move forward or am I still filled with fears? Is my consciousness blocked? Can it no longer receive? Is my consciousness moving forward? Can I see the Divine Interplay and Harmony? This is the work of the alignment process that I have explained in previous discourse. To understand and accept the past and then use it as a building block, will move you into a greater understanding and knowledge. Then the past will no longer serve as a karmic detriment, as a path of previous action to be stuck in, as muck and mire.

Dear ones, Dear hearts, this alignment process brings us into understanding that the work and the Divine Intervention of that mighty Violet Ray is there at all times to lift you into higher consciousness, to lift you into higher frequency. The Golden Ray comes as a twin ray in service with the Violet Ray, to bring an even greater harmony for those who can embrace such consciousness. You see, Dear ones, consciousness must move forward. Consciousness moves beyond the illusion of the physical and moves into its greater creation. This, Dear ones, is the gift that awaits all.

Question: *So, in the ever-expanding consciousness, there must be a Golden City that is more aligned for each individual, maybe even a specific Doorway?*

This, Dear ones, of course shows within the astral body but also it shows within the Chakra System. If one vibrates to lower chakras, then perhaps it is better to work first with the Elemental and Deva Kingdoms, to understand the harmony that exists within the creation of Mother Earth. For those who wish to have sympathetic harmonies through sustenance and abundance, work upon that mighty Green Ray. Go to the Golden City Vortex of Shalahah and work to understand the higher frequency of at-one-ment. Work to understand that greater knowledge leading one to the path of Ascension. The soul will be drawn to where it needs to be.

Know that even in that mighty law, all are where they need to be at any given moment. For as you understand, Dear ones, Dear hearts, all is brought in Divine Order and in Divine Timing. It is important to know, though, when the soul feels uneasy, feels disharmony or dis-ease, these are the feelings that lead one to seek harmony, are they not? This is the little "a-ha" that puts one gently back upon the path, with feet now walking toward that mighty light that it had long forgotten.

Yes, it is true, that there is a better Ray Force . . . a better Master Teacher . . . a better Golden City Vortex for each and every one. But know this:. each will be led through the process of seeking the great internal self. One is led through that great journey within. There is no greater way to begin this process, no greater joy that I can share than that moment in time when the voice then whispers to the soul, "It is time for you to move; it is time for you to go here." Those gentle nudges from within are the ones that should be listened to. Those are the gentle nudges that open the eyes and the ears and lead one into the path eternal. Questions?

Question: *So, would that make it relatively simple for a person to visit at least one Golden City?*

The answers always lie within, Dear one, Dear heart. The Master always awaits in that great softness. When the student is ready, the Master appears. As above, so below, Dear hearts, Dear ones. Let us honor these laws eternal.

Question: *Yes, I see what you are saying. Then, since we are populated by many Star seeds, is there a group consciousness or a group karma that exists as a pattern?*

A group karma, or a group consciousness, comes from the perception of separation . . . comes from the perception that only one shall unite me to my true self . . . comes from the consciousness of separation from the eternal ONE. You are all as ONE, Dear one, Dear heart. You are all united as ONE. Yes, in the annals of history, there have been those groups that have come in to suffer the consequences of a group karma. There have been those who have come in to celebrate the great dharmic paths that await. There are those who come in higher frequencies of consciousness and we know these as the Seventh Manu, do we not? But know, beyond this, there is that greater law eternal and that is the unity of all. You are all a Oneship, Dear ones, Dear hearts.

Question: *There have been discussions about individuals or groups who seem to have the desire to control others or to control the entire group and I would like to know if this is really true and can we do anything about it? Do things like mind control exist?*

This comes from handing over one's will. When one recognizes that the law eternal is within, alignment is to that greater and grander will; there is the truth eternal. As I have stated before, sympathetic resonance is very much the key here. Those who have fears of their own will being subjected to another will are those who have not yet defined their own will, is this not true? Those whose will is developed to an understanding of alignment to the greater will, to the greater harmony, to the greater at-one-ment, truly understand that all control is God control. God control is that ONE mind. The ONE mind that exists among us all is the consciousness of that mighty eternal ONE, Unana. How could one force control over that mighty all force? Again, this is the greater understanding of that mighty Violet Ray of Mercy, Compassion, and Forgiveness. The Violet Ray brings forth a development of the will, does it not? For within the Violet Ray is that mighty Blue Flame.

Response: *Yes.*

Use of that mighty Violet Ray and alignment to the mighty Golden Ray will bring one into a greater harmony and frequency of alignment. Yes, there are those dark frequencies, those dark forces that play at will with scripted or ended laws, but there are the laws eternal . . . the laws that exist within . . . the law that brought you here . . . the law that shall return you to the heart of God and to that all-encompassing embrace and breath of love. Know the law eternal supersedes. Questions?

Question: *Yes, do you have a decree that could be shared for the sense of apprehension about the subject of mind control?*

> I AM as ONE mind.
> I AM as ONE heart.
> I AM the mind of God complete.
> I AM the love of God eternal.

Repeat this as seven times seven, then invoke that mighty Violet Ray about you.

> Mighty Violet Ray come forth in the eternal Heart of the Logos.
> Mighty Violet Ray come forth and unite my mind as ONE.
> SO BE IT!

Response: *Thank you.*

Study Guide for Golden Ray Compassion

Topics:
Rhythm
The Golden Ray
Stars of the Golden Cities
Heart of Compassion
Twin Rays
Garden of Existence
Evolution through the Ray Forces of the Golden Cities
Mind Control

Steward
One who is entrusted with the care of another or the management and protection of land, another's finances, or something in need of supervision.

Sattva
Harmonious response to vibration; pure and spiritual in effect.

Law of Rhythm
This ancient understanding is one of the Seven Hermetic Laws and is based on the timely flow of creation. According to the Kybalion, a metaphysical text published in 1908 by the Yogi Publication Society—whose philosophies and teachings are based on Hermeticism, "Everything flows, out and in; everything has its tides; all things rise and fall; the pendulum swing manifests in everything; the measure of the swing to the right is the measure of the swing to the left; rhythm compensates." When the Master Teachers advise to use the Law of Rhythm, it is a suggestion to move us out of extremes or lethargy, and to recognize the Divine Order and Timing in our lives. In simpler terms, it is spiritual advice to return to a level of personal balance. This is often achieved through various spiritual practices such as meditation, decree, or contemplation. As we move forward in our Mastery, we begin to understand that balance is achieved through mental direction of negative or positive patterns of thought. If we are engaged in negative patterns, we can redirect the

course of our thinking with gratitude and appreciation. Or, if we our overly positive attitude leaves us ungrounded, we begin to deal with and face everyday problems through common sense and practicality. This is the necessary mental underpinning to understand the Law of Compensation—based on the notion of karma—where each and every person is compensated in a like manner for their contribution. Simply states, "What you sow, you shall reap."

Ralph Waldo Emerson writes in his 1841 essay "Compensation," "Every act rewards itself, or, in other words, integrates itself in a two fold manner; first, in the thing, or in real nature; and secondly, in the circumstance, or in apparent nature. Men call the circumstance the retribution. The causal retribution is in the thing, and is seen by the soul. The retribution in the circumstance is seen by the understanding; it is inseparable from the thing, but is often spread over a long time, and so does not become distinct until after many years. The specific stripes may follow late after offence, but they follow because they accompany it. Crime and punishment grow out of one stem. Punishment is a fruit that unsuspected ripens within the flower of the pleasure which concealed it. Cause and effect, means and ends, seed and fruit, cannot be severed; for the effect already blooms in the cause, the end preexists in the means, the fruit in the seed."[1]

Rhythm of the Spheres
The pattern and the movement of the planets; astrology.

Gold or Golden Ray
The Ascended Masters Kuthumi and Saint Germain prophesy that perhaps the Gold Ray is the most important spiritual energy currently present on Earth. While its presence catalyzes the spiritual growth of the HU-man, it is also associated with Karmic Justice and will instigate change at all levels: Earth Changes, economic, political, and social change.

Use of the Gold Ray accelerates spiritual evolution and growth and should be used alongside the Violet Flame. Since the Gold Ray enters the Crown Chakra, it travels along the Golden Thread Axis where it affixes and strengthens the overall spiritual dexterity of the kundalini. This reinforces and evolves the chakra centers, and, more importantly, helps one to develop the Eighth, Ninth, and Tenth Energy Bodies that support the Ascension Process. Because of its higher frequency and vibration it is suggested to use its energies after one has faithfully applied the Violet Flame for at least two years—a full twenty-four months.

The Gold Ray increases the alchemy of the Violet Ray (the foundation of the Violet Flame) through the spiritual processes of transformation and purification, and initiates the consciousness to perceive and move forward into the new dimensions of co-creative experience. Saint Germain suggests the use of this prayer:

> "May the Violet Ray stream forth into the hearts and souls of those who are ready to serve the Cause Divine. May this Golden Ray, in its greater harmony, adjunct to this Mighty Violet Ray, now bring its own harmony forward.
> May the Golden Ray now initiate consciousness to move into the new dimensions.
> May this new initiation now serve the grand and greater plan."

Daily Use of the Violet Flame and Gold Ray

- Call forth the Violet Consuming Fire: "In that Mighty Christ I AM, I call forth Saint Germain's Violet Transmuting Flame of mercy, transmutation, and forgiveness. Alchemize my lower energy bodies into the perfection of the Christ! Almighty I AM! (3x)" Then proceed with any Violet Flame decree. (Use seven times.) Suggestions are: "Violet Flame I AM, God I AM Violet Flame," or "I AM a Being of Violet Fire, I AM the Purity God desires!"
- Invoke the Gold Ray: "Beloved Helios and Vesta, I call forth the Golden Ray of Divine Protection, Strength, Courage, God Authority, and Ascension! Stream into and around my kundalini and chakra system, strengthening my energy bodies to move me into the liberation of the Ascension! Almighty I AM! (3x)"
- Call upon the Tube of Light: "Beloved Mighty I AM Presence, surround me now with the Tube of White Light, ever-sustained, ever-maintained, throughout this day and onward into night! Almighty I AM! (3x)"
- Invoke Archangel Michael's Blue Flame: "Beloved Archangel Michael, surround me now with the Blue Flame of Protection! Protect my Violet

Flame in its action and activity, protect my Golden Ray in its perfection and strength, protect my Mighty Tube of Light, giving me multiple layers of protection! Almighty I AM! (3x)"
- Complete this spiritual practice with thanks and gratitude: "I love you, I love you, I love you! I bless you, I bless you, I bless you! And I thank you, I thank you, I thank you! Almighty I AM! (3x)
- Close with Almighty I AM that I AM (9x) and OM HUE (9x). (This properly seals the decree and affirmation.)

Saint Germain's Teachings on the Gold Ray:
1. The Gold Ray guides the reception of higher understanding and this notion is not limited to the spiritual planes. This Ray forces guide scientific knowledge and technology, especially discoveries related to computer science and the Information Age.
2. The Gold Ray helps the individual to understand past lives, and along with the Violet Flame, induces transformation of the soul into higher frequency and vibration, instigating new levels of Spiritual Awakening.
3. The Gold Ray is present and detectable in the Stars of the Golden Cities.
4. Those who have spiritually prepared can move to the Stars of Golden Cities to utilize the Gold Ray and consciously enter the Fourth and Fifth Dimensions. This includes moving through many subtle levels of energies with these dimensions. This readies the soul for Ascension.
5. After entering the Stars, the Gold Ray initiates an alignment process with physical, astral, mental, and emotional bodies.
6. This spiritual initiation increases telepathic ability, lucid dreaming, feelings of peace, compassion, and the openness of spiritual Brotherhood and Sisterhood.
7. The Gold Ray helps to bring together Twin Rays, whose identities may have been lost to one another for thousands of years. The Gold Ray helps to reunite and merge their energies.
8. Through the energies of the Twin Rays uniting, the two Twin Rays are united in a rapport where separation is no longer felt and their light becomes complete. This initiates Ascension.
9. The Law of Sympathetic Resonance states that passive energy responds to external vibration that has a harmonic likeness. It is claimed that the Gold Ray activates one in this manner toward its Twin Ray.

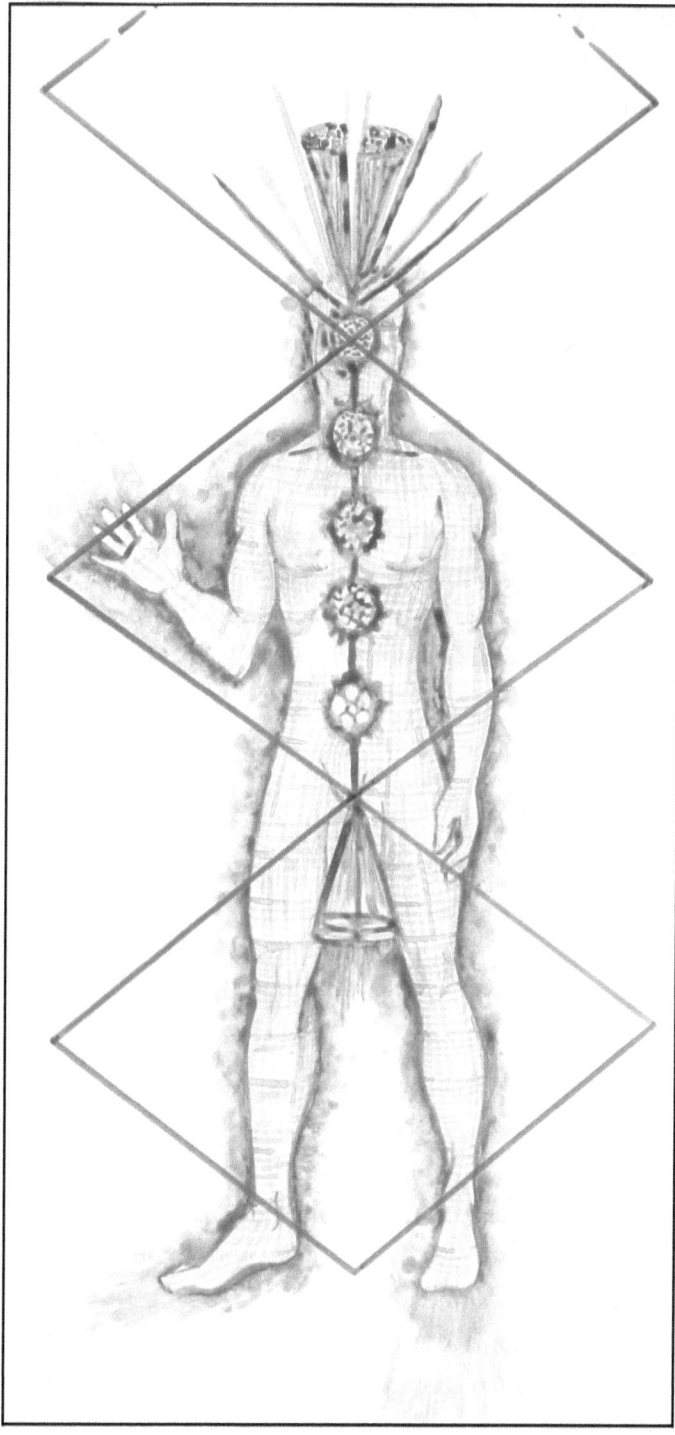

FIGURE 1-1
The First Layer of the Human Aura also known as the Electronic Blueprint

10. The Gold Ray instigates further evolution into Unity, experiences with the ONE, group mind, and Unana. This process affects both individuals and our planet. As we personally experience periods of higher frequency and harmony, Mother Earth —Babajeran—further activates the Stars of Golden Cities. This ramping up of energy through the force of the Gold Ray initiates collective unity and consciousness, especially in Golden City Vortices.

Layers of the Field of the Human Aura

First Light Body

The Electronic Blueprint holds the electrical impulse in the light body; therefore, it is similar to the Auric Blueprint. It is charged with the energy of the Seven Major Chakras, the energy grids, meridians, and nadis. It resembles a grid and is blue in color. This layer of the human aura contains a distinctive pulse that is synchronized with the individual's heartbeat, and lies within several inches of the physical body.

Second Light Body

The Emotional Field holds our instincts, feelings, and emotions. This light body is normally a vibrant pink in color. It is associated with the magnetism of the physical body. This light body is most affected by sound, especially mantras and decrees. Because varied emotions can change the characteristics of this light body, the light body can fluctuate in color. Extreme anger or violence can turn the light body dark red, while spiritual feelings of devotion can alter it to a visible light pink with hues of green. This light body is observed four to six inches from the physical body.

Third Light Body

The Mental Body carries our distinct thoughts, ideas, and perceptions. This energy field, to some degree, is associated with intelligence and our capability to process and implement information. This light body is associated with the color yellow, although some individuals display mental bodies that are vibrant gold. It is located six inches to one foot from the physical body.

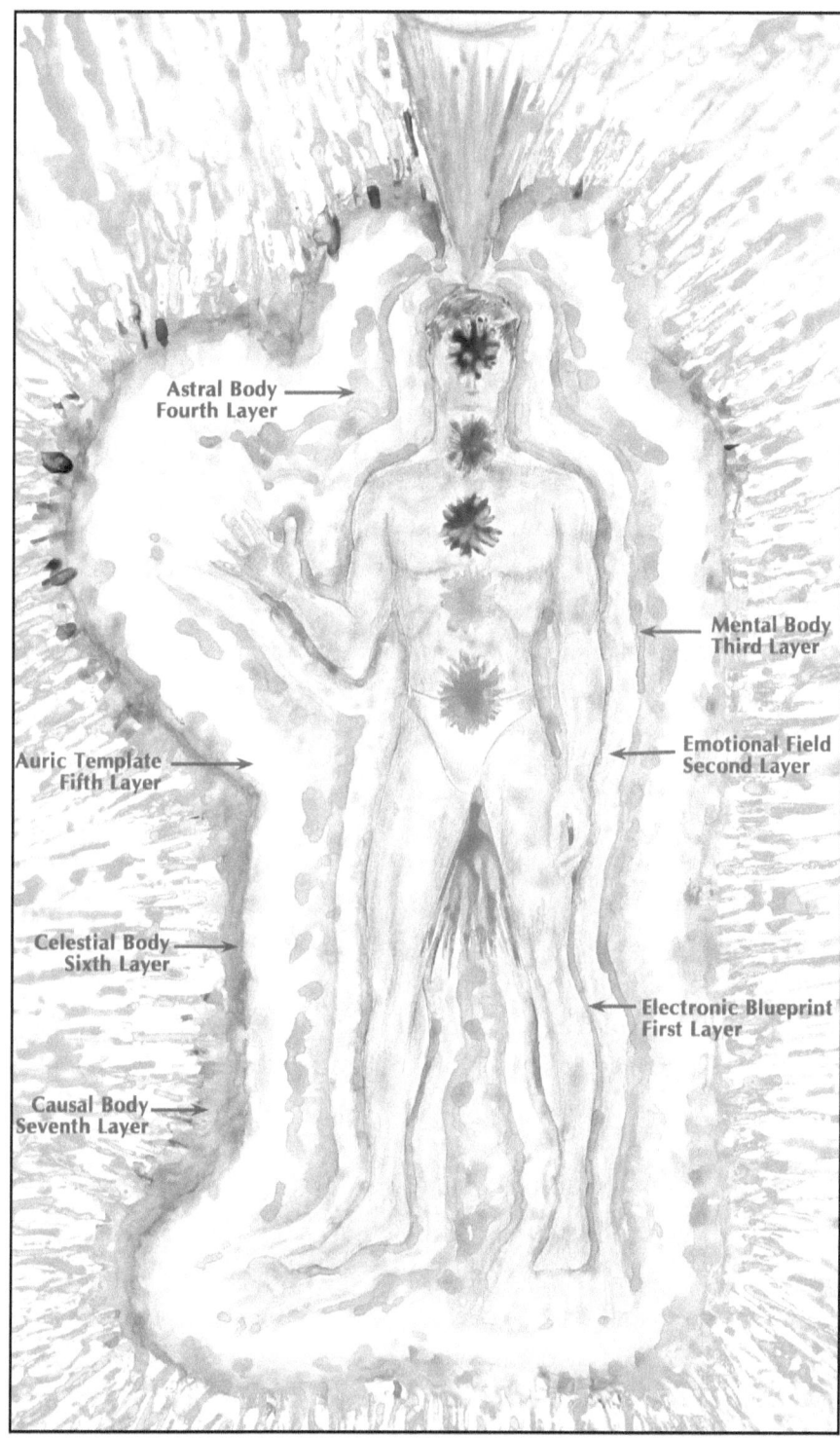

FIGURE 2-I
Layers of the Human Aura and the Seven Chakras

First Three Light Bodies

The first three light bodies represent Action (electronic blueprint), Feeling (emotion), and Thought (mental). These three primary colors also represent the Unfed Flame of Power, Love, and Wisdom, respectively. The first three light bodies of the human aura endure throughout the Earthly incarnation, and dissipate with the death of the physical body.

Fourth Light Body

The fourth light body of the human is the Astral Body. This is the energy body that we use when we dream and travel at night. This energy body is also cultivated through various spiritual techniques for astral travel, commonly known as astral projection. It is varied in color, but often displays a rainbow of pastel colors: blues, pinks, greens, and purples. It is located a foot, to a foot and a half, from the physical body. Advanced souls often display a larger Astral Body of luminous white light, with iridescent pastels. This light body, along with the next three higher light bodies, survives the death of the physical body, and then resides in the Astral Plane for further spiritual development to prepare for the next incarnation.

Fifth Light Body

This body of energy is known as the Auric Template and is similar to the Electronic Template. However, this field of vital energy gives form according to individual states of consciousness. It radiates approximately one and a half to two feet from the physical body. It is the energy layer from where a seasoned energy practitioner can detect and treat disease. The color of this energy body can vary depending on the individual strength of Ray Forces.

Sixth Light Body

This energy body carries the individual's aspirations and beliefs. Many refer to this energy body as the Celestial Body, but it is also known as the Spiritual Emotional Body. This body is often connected to feelings of bliss, unconditional love, and interconnectedness. It can be reached through meditation. This layer extends two to nearly three feet from the physical body. It is colored with opalescent pastels. Some energy practitioners report a gold-silver light shining throughout this energy body. Master Teachers, Spirit Guides, and Spiritual Teachers often enter this energy field to communicate with an individual or to revive and heal the physical body. The Sixth and Seventh Light Bodies hold varying levels of the Akashic Records.

Seventh Light Body

The Causal Body is the last of the human energy bodies. It is an egg-shape ovoid that holds all of the lower energy bodies in place with extremely strong threads of light that form a golden grid. This energy body is also known as the Spiritual Mental Body, and contains the Golden Thread Axis, also known as the Tube of Light that connects one to the I AM Presence. Energy practitioners allege that this energy body holds the Akashic records that are keys to past-life memory. This energy body extends approximately three feet around the body but can be larger, depending on the spiritual evolution of the individual.

As human spiritual evolution advances, we begin to develop new energy bodies of light, sound, and experience. The Spiritual Teachers mention that the HU-man, the developed God Man, can acquire eight new distinct energy bodies beyond the initial, primary Seven Light Bodies. The Fifteenth Energy Body propels the soul out of duality, free from both physical and astral restraint.

An Ascended Master contains and influences twenty-two light bodies. Apparently, Light Bodies Eight through Ten have the ability to contend with varying light spectrums beyond Third Dimension and can manage space-time, including time contraction, time dilation, and time compaction. But more importantly, the development of the HU-man Energy system implements the ever-important Ascension Process. The following information shares descriptions of the HU-man Energy Bodies Eight, Nine, and Ten.

Eighth Light Body

Known as the Buddha Body or the Field of Awakening, this energy body is initially three to four feet from the human body. It begins by developing two visible grid-like spheres of light that form in the front and in the back of the human aura. The front sphere is located three to four feet in front of and between the Heart and Solar Plexus Chakras. The back sphere is located in front of and between the Will-to-Love and Solar Will Chakras. These spheres activate an ovoid of light that surrounds the entire human body; an energy field associated with harmonizing and perfecting the Ascension Process. This is the first step toward Mastery. Once developed and sustained, this energy body grants physical longevity and is associated with immortality. It is known as the first level of Co-creation, and is developed through control of the diet and disciplined breath techniques. Once this light body reaches full development, the spheres dissipate and dissolve into a refined energy field, resembling a metallic armor. The mature Eighth Light Body then contracts and condenses, to reside within several inches of the physical body where it emits a silver-blue sheen.

Ninth Light Body

This body of light is known as The Divine Blueprint, as it represents the innate perfection of the divine HU-man. It is an energy field that is developed through uniting dual forces, and requires an in-depth purification of thought. In fact, this energy field causes the soul to face and master those negative, dark, forces that the Spiritual Teachers refer to as a type of mental purgatory. This energy body processes extreme fears and transmutes them. The transmutation completely restructures beliefs, and purifies energies held in the lower mental bodies accumulated throughout all lifetimes. This produces an alchemizing, divine, HU-man Mental Body that develops approximately thirty-six feet from the human body.

This energy field first appears as nine independent triangular-gridded spheres. Apparently, the nine glowing spheres grow in circumference and, inevitably, morph into one glowing energy body. As the Ninth Light Body develops, it is extremely responsive to telepathy and group thought, and progresses to act and influence collective thought and consciousness. In its early to mid-stages of development, this energy body emits a high-frequency violet light that evolves into the alchemic Violet Flame. The Spiritual Teachers claim that the decree, "I AM the Presence of Collective Thought," is its energetic mantra. The refined energies of the mature Divine Blueprint inevitably contract and concentrate in a similar manner to the Eighth Light Body. As it draws its auric field closer to the physical body; within two to four inches, it radiates gold and then a bluish-silver light that reflects the strength of its protective shield.

Tenth Light Body

This is the final level of three protective HU-man light bodies, which is formed through the purification of desires, and is known as the Diamond Mind. Because this energy body gathers thought as light, it is a substantive and sizeable light body. The Spiritual Teachers often refer to the three protective HU-man energy bodies as the Triple Gems, and together they are strong enough to pierce human illusion. Combined with the four higher primal energy bodies—the Fourth Light Body to the Seventh Light Body—the total sum of these energy bodies produces the alchemic number seven. In this septagonal order, the Diamond Mind helps to produce the Lighted Stance and the inevitable attainment of the Seamless Garment.

The Lighted Stance is a state of conscious perfection—a precursor to Ascension. The soul's ability to manifest the Seamless Garment bestows the Master with the ability to travel and experience the Astral and Physical planes without spiritual corruption or physical disintegration. This mature energy body compacts itself to reside approximately six inches from the physical body, and is alleged to have the strength and brilliance of "ten-thousand diamonds." This energy body also exhibits complete Mastery over thought, feeling, and action—the first three primal human Energy Bodies—and can dissolve or manifest their physical presence at will; or, it can take form for whatever cause, circumstance, or "task at hand," without any limitation. [Editor's Note: For more information on the human aura, light bodies, and their relationship to the Ascension Process, see, "Fields of Light."]

Monad

In theosophical thinking, the Monad represents the unity of a metaphysical triad: Atman (as a form of I AM that I AM; Love); Buddhi (the ability to comprehend, reason, and to choose; Power); and Manas (the higher mind; Wisdom).[2] Atma or Atman is the soul itself; Buddhi is the spiritually awakened intellect; and Manas is the Mind. From an Ascended Master viewpoint, the Monad is the spark or flame of life of spiritual consciousness and it is also the Awakened Flame that is growing, evolving, and ultimately on the path to Ascension. Because of its presence of self-awareness and purpose, the Monad represents our dynamic will and the individualized presence of the Divine Father. Ultimately, the Monad is the spark of consciousness that is

FIGURE 3-1
The Monad within the Eight-Sided Cell of Perfection

self-determining, spiritually awake, and drives the growth of human consciousness.

According to spiritual philosophers, the Monad is both ONE and many. It fuels the Eight-Sided Cell of Perfection, whose movement gives birth to the perfection of the Unfed Flame. It also explains our solar system whose heart is our Sun. David Pratt writes, "Monad literally means 'unit.' In its broadest sense, it can therefore refer to any natural system or entity, any unitary individual—from the vastest solar system to the tiniest atom. In general, every entity, on any plane, has within it a nucleus, a control center or nerve center, of more highly developed energy substance to that plane, and this nucleus, too, can be call a monad. The term is commonly used in a still more restricted sense to refer only to the highest spiritual portion of any entity's multileveled constitution."[3] The Monad is the indivisible, whole, divine life center of an evolving soul that is immortal and contains the momentum within itself to drive consciousness to learn, grow, and perfect itself in its evolutionary journey.

Heart of Compassion

A deeper and more evolved form of empathy, kindness, tolerance, and charity that is self-aware and operates with spiritual intelligence. It is the evolution of the common self, once held in illusion, that awakens to the true self—the Divine Inheritor.

Twin Ray

It is alleged in Ascended Master Creation stories that upon the creation of the soul, its innate light is split into two halves, and each of these aspects that create the soul assist one another in their spiritual growth and evolution throughout many lifetimes. As the soul begins the Ascension Process, it is common to encounter the beloved Twin Flame. This can greatly assist and escalate the union into light. However, because of the dual nature and expression of life, it is common that one twin of the dynamic pair may not be ready to initiate personal spiritual growth or enter the Ascension Process. There are several teachings that address this spiritual problem:

1. The enlightened person of the twin pair can continue to hold spiritual light and energy for their twin aspect and can also achieve ascension without the reuniting of the twin forces with the assistance of an Ascended Master.
2. The soul can also begin the arduous journey to develop self into the ONE by entering Christ Consciousness. This allows the attraction of yet another partner in Ascension and service known as the Divine Complement. This is achieved through the balance of a least fifty-one percent of the personal karma.

Divine Complement and Twin Ray are terms that are used interchangeably—but there is a subtle difference. The Twin Ray is present at the creation of the soul. The Divine Complement often appears as one enters the Ascension Process and fulfills the place vacated by the unreadied Twin Ray.

Twin Rays may still united after both have achieved Ascension with altogether different, but harmonizing Divine Complements. This may explain why some Ascended Beings have a Divine Complement, but may still be united in service alongside their Twin Ray. An example of this is Portia and Saint Germain, both Divine Complements of the Violet Ray. Portia achieved her ascension thousands of years before Saint Germain and held conscious light for his ascension. During Saint Germain's ascension process, he purposely united his energies with Mary, to fulfill his mission as Joseph, the father of Jesus, the Christ. Lady Nada is the Divine Complement of Sananda; however, beloved Mary Magdalene is often taught as the Twin Ray of Jesus. The point is that as we grow and evolve, the right person at the right time is always available to assist our spiritual growth and ascension. Every soul on schoolroom Earth is growing and learning at their own pace, and to force evolution prematurely can create illusion, pain, and suffering. The veritable truth is that as one aspect of a Twin Ray grows and evolves, the other Twin Ray undoubtedly receives benefit.

Ascended Master creation myths place the origination of the human soul from the heart of the Sun God-Goddess who constructs at the end of a Ray the Three-Fold (Unfed) Flame. This generates a Divine Presence, or a God-Flame, a Co-creator with the Source, the Cosmic I AM Presence. According to esoteric historians, some God-Flames choose to remain in the eternal embrace of the loving aura of the parental Sun; those who choose to progress further project their spiritual essence into two Rays—Twin Rays. The Twin Rays develop a new light substance: an electrical light field which separates the Rays into two distinct individuals. The I AM—the individualized presence of God—dwells within the newly formed soul, and the electrical field of light is known as the I AM Presence.[4] According to Saint Germain, the Golden Ray accelerates the light held by the Twin Rays, and begins their metaphysical unification process into the Cosmic I AM Presence.

Garden of Existence

Ascended Master terminology for the Christian idea of the Garden of Eden. The etymology of existence is linked to the word "exist." This means to come into being (BEing) and to stand forth in the light. The two Twin Rays share this common light, and when united, live in Gold's perfection, united through ONE breath. This is the perfected state of harmony and bliss of the Fifth Dimension where the Twin Ray transforms into ONE.

Law of Unity

Another name for Unana—indivisible, complete, and whole; as ONE.

Limitation

The process whereby consciousness is held at a particular fixed level of frequency or vibration. Limitation can be somewhat self-defining and calibrated through perception. That is, only an ability to see a situation or set of circumstances in one particular manner (i.e., the glass is always empty, not half full). Often limitation is the result of fear and the inability to see the Divine Plane and Divine Harmony through blocked or unaligned reception. Expansion of consciousness moves us beyond self-limiting, karmic illusion.

Seventh Manu

The word Manu comes from the Hindu word "to think," an apt root for this highly evolved society of young souls prophesied to incarnate on the Earth during the New Times. But the idea of Manu is expansive; its significance reaches far beyond the context of the I AM America Prophecies.

Manu refers to a root race or a group of souls inhabiting a vast time period (era or epoch) on Earth. The concept of Manu is found among Native American tribes, too. The Hopis describe this term as "worlds," e.g., fourth world, fifth world. Manu is also a mythical, cosmic being who oversees the souls during their incarnation processes throughout the duration of that specific time period. Some consider Manu a type of spiritual office, not unlike a "World Teacher." For example, one evolved cosmic being will serve as Manu for one world cycle, and when it ends, it moves on in the evolutionary process. A different entity serves as Manu for the next group. Each group of souls has a different energy and purpose. Seventh Manu children will possess advanced capabilities—astute intellect, vast spiritual knowledge, and

HU-man Chakras and the Golden Cities

First Chakra (Root Chakra)
Ruby-Gold Ray

Malton (Illinois, Indiana, USA)
Gobi (China)
Shehez (Iran, Afghanistan)
Gandawan (Algeria)
Kreshe (Botswana, Namibia)
Unte (Tanzania, Kenya)

Second Chakra (Sexual-Creative Chakra)
White Ray

Klehma (Colorado, USA)
Sircalwe (Russia)
Arkana (Russia)
Sheahah (Australia)
Afrom (Czechoslavakia, Hungary)
Zaskar (China)

Third Chakra (Solar Plexus)
Ruby-Gold Ray

Amerigo (Portugal, Spain)
Malton (Illinois, Indiana, USA)
Gobi (China)
Shehez (Iran, Afghanistan)
Gandawan (Algeria)
Kreshe (Botswana, Namibia)
Unte (Tanzania, Kenya)
Andeo (Peru, Brazil)
Adjatal (Pakistan, Afghanistan, India)

Fourth Chakra (Heart Chakra)
Pink Ray

Klehma (Colorado, USA)
Sircalwe (Russia)
Arkana (Russia)
Sheahah (Australia)
Afrom (Czechoslavakia, Hungary)
Zaskar (China)
Uverno (Canada)
Andeo (Peru, Brazil)
Braham (Brazil)

Fourth Chakra (Heart Chakra) Pink Ray	Tehekoa (Argentina) Crotese (Costa Rica) Purensk (Russia, China) Prana (India) Clayje (Australia) Angelica (Tasmania)
Fifth Chakra (Throat Chakra) Green Ray	Shalahah (Idaho, Montana, USA) Pashacino (Canada) Yuthor (Greenland) Marnero (Mexico) Kantan (China, Russia) Grein (New Zealand) Gankara (Turkey)
Sixth Chakra (Third Eye) Yellow Ray	Asonea (Cuba) Purensk (Russia, China) Nomaking (China) Presching (China) Braun (Germany) Larito (Ethiopia) Mesotamp (Turkey, Iran, Iraq) Denasha (Scotland)
Seventh Chakra (Crown Chakra) All Seven Rays	All 51 Golden Cities

HU-man Chakras and the Golden Cities
Activation and Initiatory Path

	GOLDEN CITY	YEAR	INITIATORY PATH
First and Third Chakra	Malton	1994	I AM America Map
	Shehez	2028	Map of Exchanges
	Gandawan	2036	Map of Exchanges
	Kreshe	2038	Map of Exchanges
	Unte	2042	Map of Exchanges
	Gobi	2062	Greening Map
Second and Fourth Chakra	Klehma	2000	I AM America Map
	Afrom	2022	Map of Exchanges
	Zaskar	2060	Greening Map
	Sircalwe	2074	Greening Map
	Arkana	2076	Greening Map
	Sheahah	2088	Greening Map
Third Chakra	Adjatal	2030	Greening Map
Third and Fourth Chakra	Andeo	2050	I AM America Map
Fourth and Sixth Chakra	Purensk	2032	Greening Map
Fourth Chakra	Prana	2034	Greening Map
	Braham	2052	I AM America Map
	Tehekoa	2054	I AM America Map
	Crotese	2056	I AM America Map
	Clayje	2084	Greening Map
	Angelica	2086	Greening Map

Fifth Chakra	Shalahah	1998	I AM America Map
	Pashacino	2002	I AM America Map
	Yuthor	2010	I AM America Map
	Gankara	2024	Map of Exchanges
	Marnero	2046	I AM America Map
	Kantan	2070	Greening Map
	Grein	2099	Greening Map
	GOLDEN CITY	**YEAR**	**INITIATORY PATH**
Sixth Chakra	Denasha	2014	Map of Exchanges
	Braun	2020	Map of Exchanges
	Mesotamp	2026	Map of Exchanges
	Laraito	2044	Map of Exchanges
	Asonea	2048	I AM America Map
	Nomaking	2066	Greening Map
	Presching	2068	Greening Map
Seventh Chakra	All 51 Golden Cities		

[For more information on the evolution of the chakras through the Ascension Process, see *Light of Awakening*.]

keen psychic abilities. Forerunners of the Seventh Manu will pave the way for this metaphysically venerated population. Carrying less karmic burden than those of the past, these forbearers of ever-increasing enlightenment promote a sense of higher consciousness. As dharma flourishes, the Seventh Manu, sponsored by the Beloved Mother Mary, proliferates.

The majority of this Seventh-Manu generation will settle in an area of Brazil known as the Swaddling Cloth. [You can view the geo-physical perimeters of the Swaddling Cloth on the I AM America Freedom Star World Map and the I AM America Atlas.] Others will be born in the Golden City Vortices. The Seventh Manu will play a large role in raising the consciousness and the Vibration of the Earth. Saint Germain first prophesied the appearance of the Seventh Manu in a Trance-Mission on May 1, 1993.[5] [This transcript can be read in New World Wisdom, Book Two.]

Mind Control

This form of control over another has many forms that are known as brainwashing, coercive persuasion, thought control, and involuntary re-education of someone's beliefs and values.[6] Saint Germain teaches that this psychological breakdown involves the developing will, balance, and the metaphysics of sympathetic harmonies. He suggests the use of the Violet and Blue Rays to develop and reinforce the will, plus the use of this decree:

> "I AM as ONE mind.
> I AM as ONE heart.
> I AM the mind of God complete.
> I AM the love of God eternal.

Repeat this seven times seven, then invoke that mighty Violet Ray about you:

> Mighty Violet Ray come forth in the eternal Heart of the Logos.
> Mighty Violet Ray come forth and unite my mind as ONE.
> SO BE IT!"

1. Emerson, Ralph Waldo. "Compensation." September 3, 2009. Accessed February 27, 2017. http://www.emerson-central.com/compensation.htm.
2. "What Exactly Is the Monad?" Blavatsky Theosophy Group UK. December 24, 2016. Accessed February 27, 2017. https://blavatskytheosophy.com/what-exactly-is-the-monad/.
3. Pratt, David. "The Monad: One and Many." February 2003. Accessed February 27, 2017. http://www.davidpratt.info/monad.htm.
4. Toye, Lori Adaile. "Spiritual Hierarchy." In Divine Destiny: Prophecies and Teachings of the Ascended Masters, 37-46. Vol. 3. Golden City Series. Payson, AZ: I AM America Publishing, 2016.
5. Toye, Lori Adaile. "The Seventh Manu." In Points of Perception: Prophecies and Teachings of Saint Germain, 31. Vol. 1. Golden City Series. P: I AM America Publishing, 2016.
6. Kowal, D. M. "Mind Control." Wikipedia. February 22, 2017. Accessed February 27, 2017. https://en.wikipedia.org/wiki/Mind_control.

Spiritual Lineage of the Violet Flame

The teachings of the Violet Flame, as taught in the work of I AM America, come through the Goddess of Compassion and Mercy Kuan Yin. She holds the feminine aspects of the flame, which are Compassion, Mercy, Forgiveness, and Peace. Her work with the Violet Flame is well documented in the history of Ascended Master teachings, and it is said that the altar of the etheric Temple of Mercy holds the flame in a Lotus Cup. She became Saint Germain's teacher of the Sacred Fire in the inner realms, and he carried the masculine aspect of the flame into human activity through Purification, Alchemy, and Transmutation. One of the best means to attract the beneficent activities of the Violet Flame is through the use of decrees and invocation. However, you can meditate on the flame, visualize the flame, and receive its transmuting energies like "the light of a thousand Suns," radiant and vibrant as the first day that the Elohim Arcturus and Diana drew it forth from our solar Sun at the creation of the Earth. Whatever form, each time you use the Violet Flame, these two Master Teachers hold you in the loving arms of its action and power.

The following is an invocation for the Violet Flame to be used at sunrise or sunset. It is utilized while experiencing the visible change of night to day, and day to night. In fact, if you observe the horizon at these times, you will witness light transitioning from pinks to blues, and then a subtle violet strip adorning the sky. We have used this invocation for years in varying scenes and circumstances, overlooking lakes, rivers, mountaintops, deserts, and prairies; in huddled traffic and busy streets; with groups of students or sitting with a friend; but more commonly alone in our home or office, with a glint of soft light streaming from a window. The result is always the same: a calm, centering force of stillness. We call it *the Space*.

Invocation of the Violet Flame for Sunrise and Sunset
I invoke the Violet Flame to come forth in the name of I AM that I AM,
To the Creative Force of all the realms of all the Universes, the Alpha, the Omega, the Beginning, and the End,
To the Great Cosmic Beings and Torch Bearers of all the realms of all the Universes,
And the Brotherhoods and Sisterhoods of Breath, Sound, and Light, who honor this Violet Flame that comes forth from the Ray of Divine Love—the Pink Ray, and the Ray of Divine Will—the Blue Ray of all Eternal Truths.

I invoke the Violet Flame to come forth in the name of I AM that I AM!
Mighty Violet Flame, stream forth from the Heart of the Central Logos, the Mighty Great Central Sun! Stream in, through, and around me.

(Then insert other prayers and/or decrees for the Violet Flame.)

Glossary

Adjutant Point: Power points that form where the lei-lines of the geometric Maltese cross formation of a Golden City traverse or intersect. Adjutant points support the infrastructure of a Golden City, both geometrically and spiritually, and assist and disburse the unique energies held by Babajeran, the Ascended Masters, and the Golden City's Ray Force.

Agreement Formation: Agreement Formation is an early tenet of the I AM America Teachings, the Law of Agreement is also known as the First Jurisdiction, Harmony. Agreement is the sacred meeting of two minds which on one formative side reflects our intent and commitment. The results of our agreements with others reflect our choices and our responsible actions that ultimately define the quality of our life force.

Akashic Record: Timeless, immortal records of all created things, especially souls and their many lifetimes.

Alchemy: A hidden yet transformative and sacred science which bridges the world of chemistry and metallurgy with the spiritual worlds of Mastery and Ascension Process.

Alignment: Balance.

Archetype: The first form from which something is made or modeled.

Ascending Culture: A culture that emerges from the upswing of galactic light from the Great Central Sun. Ascending cultures are constantly moving towards the light of truth that is yet to be defined or fully realized.

Avatar: When an Ascended Master takes on a physical body to bring blessings to the world, he or she is known as an avatar. This perfected physical manifestation usually casts no shadow or leaves no footprints. Masters rarely appear to the general public and can become invisible if necessary.

Babajeran: A name for the Earth Mother that means, "grandmother rejoicing." Feminine form of Babaji.

Bliss of the Eternal Ocean: The state of consciousness that immerses the individual into constant bliss.

Blue Flame Angels: A group of angels associated with Archangel Michael who assists humanity with the manifestation and Co-creation process.

Chakra(s): Sanskrit for wheel. Seven spinning wheels of human-bioenergy centers stacked from the base of the spine to the top of the head.

Chela: Disciple.

Chi: Energy.

Christ, the: The highest energy or frequency attainable on Earth. The Christ is a step-down transformer of the I AM energies which enlighten, heal, and transform all human conditions of degradation and death.

Christ Consciousness: A level of consciousness that unites both feminine and masculine energies and produces the innocence and purity of the I AM. Its energies heal, enlighten, and transform every negative human condition and pave the way for the realization of the divine HU-man.

Co-creation: Creating with the God-Source.

Collective Consciousness: The higher interactive structure of consciousness as *two or more*.

Consciousness: Awakening to one's own existence, sensations and cognitions.

Cosmic Wave Motion: Belts of energy that weave a pattern throughout the universe; they originate from the Great Central Sun, also known as the Galactic Center.

Cup: A symbol of neutrality and grace.

Cycle of the Elements: The interactive cycle of the elements on Mother Earth is dualistic—both masculine and feminine, and constructive or destructive. The cycle contains a creative, nourishing cycle: metal creates and nourishes water; water nourishes wood; wood feeds and nourishes fire; fire creates earth; earth creates and nourishes metal. The counterpart of this cycle is destructive: metal destroys and weakens wood; wood weakens earth; earth contains and weakens water; water destroys or weakens fire; fire melts and weakens metal.

Descending Culture: A culture that emerges during the downswing of galactic light from the Great Central Sun. Cultures birthed in descending cycles strive to protect their traditions and spiritual heritage whose origin is from a period of greater light and enlightenment.

Desire: Of the source.

Deva: Shining one or being of light.

Dimensional Rifting: An anomaly caused by the individual absorbing evolutionary Ray Forces from the Great Central Sun. It is associated with the healing of trauma and painful experiences associated with past lives and unfulfilled desires.

This allows one to complete and liberate from karmas, initiating the liberation process of the soul, known as Ascension.

Divine Inheritor: The enlightened understanding that affirms our divine status through an innate connection to spiritual knowledge and spiritual heritage.

Divine Mind: The principle or idea that a universal mind or soul creates a rational order in the cosmos.

Divine Will: God's plan for humanity.

Divinity: Derived from the Sanskrit word *Deva*, this notion is the transcendent power of light or God.

Duality: An understanding that the world is divided into two perceptible categories.

Earth Changes: A prophesied Time of Change on Earth, including geophysical, political, and social changes alongside the opportunity for spiritual and personal transformation.

Earth Plane: The dual aspect of life on Earth.

Eastern Door: The East side of a Golden City gateway, also known as the *Blue Door*.

El Morya: Ascended Master of the Blue Ray, associated with the development of the will.

Elemental: A nature-being.

Elohim: Creative beings of love and light that helped manifest the Divine Idea of our solar system. Seven Elohim (the Seven Rays) exist here. They organize and draw forward Archangels, the Four Elements, Devas, Seraphim, Cherubim, Angels, Nature Guardians, and the Elementals. The Silent Watcher—the Great Mystery—gives them direction.

Emotional Body: A subtle body of light that exists alongside the physical body. It comprises desires, emotions, and feelings.

Ever Present Now: Time as a continuous, unencumbered flow without past or future.

Feminine: Esoteric philosophy considers the Mother Creative principle as the highest expression of being. Femininity is akin to the Goddess; it comprises one half of God whose gender is neutral. Feminine energy represents love, beauty, seduction, sensitivity, and refinement— the characteristics of the Goddess Venus. On the dark side, it reflects vanity, superficiality, fickleness, and exhaustion. Femininity is the intuition, a nurturing force which, above all, produces the first creative spark in our

Sun of Truth; the female essence serves as the inspiration and aspiration for life's goodness and purity—a devotion to truth.

Fifth Dimension: A spiritual dimension of cause, associated with thoughts, visions, and aspirations. This is the dimension of the Ascended Masters and the Archetypes of Evolution, the city of Shamballa, and the templates of all Golden Cities.

Fourth Dimension: A dimension of vibration associated with telepathy, psychic ability, and the dream world. This is the dimension of the Elemental Kingdom and the development of the super senses.

Gateway: A doorway of a Golden City.

Gateway Adjutant Points: Two Golden City power points that are located on either side of each directional gateway of a Golden City Vortex and are situated to the outer perimeter of the Vortex.

Gobean: The first United States Golden City located in the states of Arizona and New Mexico. Its qualities are cooperation, harmony, and peace; its Ray Force is blue; and its Master Teacher is El Morya.

Golden City Gateway Lei-line: An electromagnetic, arterial lei-line that exists across the outer span of the directional gateway of a Golden City Vortex. The length of this Golden City arterial lei-line is 64 miles.

Golden City Vortex: According to the prophecies, these large Vortex areas are havens of safety and spiritual growth during the Time of Change.

Gold Ray: An important Ray Force that is currently influencing the spiritual growth and evolution of the divine HU-man. It is also associated with karmic justice and will instigate many changes throughout our planet including Earth Changes and social and economic change.

Grace: Neutrality, calmness, peacefulness.

Great White Brotherhood and Sisterhood (Lodge): This fraternity of ascended and unascended men and women is dedicated to the universal uplifting of humanity. Its main objective includes the preservation of the lost spirit, and the teachings of the ancient religions and philosophies of the world. Its Mission: to reawaken the dormant ethical and spiritual spark among the masses. In addition to fulfilling spiritual aims, the Great White Lodge has pledged to protect mankind against the systematic assaults—which inhibit self-knowledge and personal growth—on individual and group freedoms.

Harmony: The first virtue of the Twelve Jurisdictions based on the principle of agreement.

Harmony of the Spheres: An esoteric term that refers to an exacting form of balance and synchronization often realized through the hidden geometric and mathematical perfection of all created forms. The movement of the heavenly bodies is said to be timed to such mathematical precision and perfection that the planets create a celestial music.

Hermetic Law: Philosophical beliefs and principles based on the writings of Hermes Trismegistus, the Greek sage who is analogous to the Egyptian God Thoth.

Hitaka: "So be it."

Holy Christ Self: Another name that identifies the presence of the I AM, or the great ambassador to the Oversoul. Esoteric teachings refer to the Christ Self as the higher, refined Astral Body.

Holy Spirit: An individual manifestation of the light and spiritual energy of the I AM Presence. Collectively, this same energy is known as the "Holy Comforter." The Holy Spirit is also known as the Higher Self.

HU-man: The God-Man.

I AM: The presence of God.

I AM Presence: The individualized presence of God.

I AM That I AM: This Hebrew phrase from the Torah translates into English as "I Will Be What I Will Be." In Ascended Master Teachings the I AM is known as the individualized presence of God.

Jiva: The immortal essence of a living thing that survives death.

Karma: Laws of Cause and Effect.

Klehma: The fifth United States Golden City located primarily in the states of Colorado and Kansas. Its qualities are continuity, balance, and harmony; its Ray Force is white; and its Master Teacher is Serapis Bey.

Kuan Yin: The Bodhisattva of Compassion and teacher of Saint Germain. She is associated with all the Rays and the principle of femininity.

Kuthumi: An Ascended Master of the Pink, Ruby, and Gold Rays. He is a gentle and patient teacher who works closely with the Nature Kingdoms.

Laws of Attraction and Repulsion: Like charges repel; unlike charges attract.

Laws of Cause and Effect: For every action there is another event, which is the consequence or result of the first.

Lei-lines: Lines of energy that exist among geographical places, ancient monuments, megaliths, and strategic points. These energy lines contain electrical or magnetic points.

Light: "Love in action."

Love: "Light in action."

Maltese Cross: A symbol often used by Saint Germain that represents the Eight-Sided Cell of Perfection and the human virtues of honesty, faith, contrition, humility, justice, mercy, sincerity, and the endurance of persecution.

Malton: The second United States Golden City located in the states of Illinois and Indiana. Its qualities are fruition and attainment; its Ray Force is ruby and Gold; and its Master Teacher is Kuthumi.

Map of Rings: This Map depicts Earth covered with a worldwide grid of interlocking circles. The circles portray the elements of Earth: air, water, fire, and earth. Their interaction with one another results in the physical manifestation of Earth and her many alchemical and spiritual processes.

Master Teacher: A spiritual teacher from a specific lineage of teachers—gurus. The teacher transmits and emits the energy from that collective lineage.

Mastery: Possessing the consummate skill of command and self-realization over thought, feeling, and action.

Mental Body: A subtle light body of the Human Aura comprising thoughts.

Mind: The aspects of consciousness manifested as thought, perceptions, true memory, will, and imagination.

New Age: Prophesied by Utopian Francis Bacon, the New Age would herald a United Brotherhood of the Earth. This Brotherhood/Sisterhood would be built as Solomon's Temple and supported by the four pillars of history, science, philosophy, and religion. These four teachings would synergize the consciousness of humanity to Universal Fellowship and Peace.

Northern Door: The North side of a Golden City gateway, also known as the *Black Door*.

Om Manaya Pitaya or **Om Manaaya Patiya:** This Ascended Master statement has several meanings. Two spiritual translations are: "I AM the Light of God" and "I AM the Seer of the Lord." The Sanskrit translation means: "Amen, honored Lord."

ONE: Indivisible, whole, harmonious Unity.

Oneship: A combination of many, which comprises the whole and, when divided, contains both feminine and masculine characteristics.

Open Ears, Open Eyes: The ability to see and hear spiritual truths.

Oversoul: This refers to the soul in its relationship to the ONE, which is infinite and from which finite souls draw sustenance and light.

Peak Adjutant Lei-line: This arterial lei-line of a Golden City is formed through energies surging from two points within the Golden City Gateway.

Peak Adjutant Point: This power point is energetically defined by the merging of both masculine and feminine Gateway Adjutant Points. The Peak Adjutant Point is also referred to as a *Golden City Child Point*, as it contains and expresses a pure and concentrated energy of both points of the Golden City Doorway.

Perceive: To observe, feel, sense, and have awareness of.

Point of Perception: A certain position of understanding that allows for immediate or intuitive recognition.

Portia: The Goddess of Justice and Opportunity. She represents Divine Justice on Earth. Her action is balance, expressed as the scales. Harmony holds balance. Some say her electronic pattern, a mandala, is the Maltese Cross.

Prana: Vital, life-sustaining energy.

Prophecy: A spiritual teaching given simultaneously with a warning. It's designed to change, alter, lessen, or mitigate the prophesied warning. This caveat may be literal or metaphoric; the outcome of these events is contingent on the choices and the consciousness of those willing to apply the teachings.

Rainbow Bridge: The esoteric term that describes the human aura, which contains a spectrum of light bodies, similar to a rainbow. A perfect rainbow of color, with definition and brilliance, is often seen in the aura or light field of an Ascended Being.

Ray: A force containing a purpose, which divides its efforts into two measurable and perceptible powers: light and sound.

Refreshing Drink: A metaphor for the Universal Supply of Life.

Rose: The Western symbol of the maternal creative mystery—the feminine. It represents the chakra as a spiritual Vortex; a garland of roses typifies the seven chakras and their unfolding and attainment. In Eastern culture the symbology of the lotus is similar to the rose.

Rosicrucian: An ancient mystery school with its teachings rooted in the study of Western esoteric teachings. Also known as the *Rose Cross*, its foundation is the study of alchemy through Hermetic-Christian traditions.

Sacrifice: The spiritual ideal that through giving selflessly, or taking a short-term loss, that a greater long-term return for others is created.

Saint Germain: Ascended Master of the Seventh Ray, Saint Germain is known for his work with the Violet Flame of Mercy, Transmutation, Alchemy, and Forgiveness. He is the sponsor of the Americas and the I AM America material. Many other teachers and Masters affiliated with the Great White Brotherhood help his endeavors.

Sananda: The name used by Master Jesus in his ascended state of consciousness. Sananda means joy and bliss, and his teachings focus on revealing the savior and heavenly kingdom within.

Sanat Kumara: One of the original Lords of Venus who founded the Great White Brotherhood at Shamballa. He is also known as *Lord of the World*. The Bible refers to him as *Ancient of Days*.

Sea of Consciousness: A refined state of higher consciousness, developed through the individual practice and application of the Twelve Jurisdictions, which allows one to enter into a state of Unity Consciousness, or the ONE.

Seamless Garment: The Ascended Masters wear garments without seams. This clothing is not tailored by hand but perfected through the thought and manifestation process.

Serapis Bey: An Ascended Master from Venus who works on the White Ray. He is the great disciplinarian—essential for Ascension; and works closely with all unascended humanity who remain focused for its attainment.

Shalahah: The fourth United States Golden City located primarily in the states of Montana and Idaho. Its qualities are abundance, prosperity, and healing; its Ray Force is green; and its Master Teacher is Sananda.

Shamballa: Venusian volunteers, who arrived 900 years before their leader Sanat Kumara, built Earth's first Golden City. Known as the City of White, located in the present-day Gobi Desert, its purpose was to hold conscious light for Earth and to sustain her evolutionary place in the solar system.

Simultaneous Realities or Experiences: A transmigratory experience based on a nonlinear perspective of time. It holds all the possibilities of past, present, and future events. Simultaneous realities maintain the capacity for multiple experiences and outcomes. Each reality exists side by side. A person could consciously open himself or herself to these scenarios to gain insight and self-knowledge.

Soul: The self-aware immortal essence unique to every living being.

Southern Door: The South side of a Golden City gateway, also known as the *Red Door*.

Spirit Guide: A spiritual ancestor or teacher who gives individual guidance and teaching at critical junctures for spiritual growth and evolution.

Spiritual Awakening: Conscious awareness of personal experiences and existence beyond the physical, material world. Consequently, an internalization of one's true nature and relationship to life is revealed, freeing one of the lesser self (ego) and engendering contact with the higher (Christ) self and the I AM.

Spiritual Hierarchy: A fellowship of Ascended Masters and their disciples. This group helps humanity through the mental plane with meditation, decrees, and prayer.

Spiritual Liberation: The Ascension Process is also known as *moksha* in Hindu tradition.

Spiritual Migration: The process of moving to and living in certain geophysical areas to purposely integrate and assimilate Earth's sacred energies for spiritual growth and evolution.

Star: The apex, or center of each Golden City.

Sympathetic Resonance: A physical phenomenon where a passive material (stringed instrument, glass, and tuning forks) responds to an external vibration from an altogether different source, as the two share similar and harmonic likeness.

Terra: Earth.

Third Eye: The inner eye, referring to the *ajna* (brow) chakra.

Thought, Feeling, and Action: In Ascended Master teachings and tradition, thought, feeling, and action are the cornerstones of the creation process. Thought represents the mental (causal) body and the Yellow Ray. Feeling represents the emotional (astral) body and the Pink Ray. Action represents the physical body and the Blue Ray.

Thought Transference: Telepathy—the process of a person randomly or intentionally, feeling or knowing the thoughts and emotions of another person.

Thousand Eyes: This term refers to the endless rounds of death and rebirth the soul encounters before entering the Ascension Process of spiritual liberation.

Time Compaction: An anomaly produced as we enter into the prophesied Time of Change. Our perception of time compresses; time seems to speed by. The unfolding of events accelerates, and situations are jammed into a short period of time. This experience of time will become more prevalent as we get closer to the period of cataclysmic Earth Changes.

Time of Change: The period of time currently underway. Tremendous changes in our society, cultures, and politics in tandem with individual and collective spiritual awakenings and transformations will abound. These events occur simultaneously with the possibilities of massive global warming, climactic changes, and seismic and volcanic activity—Earth Changes. The Time of Change guides Earth to a new time, the Golden Age.

Time of Testing: The Time of Testing is a period of seven to twenty years which began around the turn of the twenty-first century, following the time period known as the *Time of Transition*. According to Saint Germain and other Ascended Masters, the Time of Testing is perhaps one of the most turbulent periods mankind will experience and its first seven years is prophesied as a period of change and strife for many. As its title suggests, the Master Teachers claim this timeframe may challenge students by testing their spiritual acumen and inner strength.

Transmutation: Alchemy and the transformation of a lower energy into a higher energy, nature, or form.

Twelve Jurisdictions: Twelve laws (virtues) for the New Times that guide consciousness to Co-create the Golden Age. They are Harmony, Abundance, Clarity, Love, Service, Illumination, Cooperation, Charity, Desire, Faith, Stillness, Creation/Creativity.

Unana: Unity Consciousness.

Unfed Flame: The three-fold flame of divinity that exists in the heart and becomes larger as it evolves. The three flames represent Love (pink), Wisdom (yellow), and Power (blue).

Violet Flame: The Violet Flame is the practice of balancing Karmas of the past through Transmutation, Forgiveness, and Mercy. The result is an opening of the Spiritual Heart and the development of bhakti—unconditional love and compassion. It came into existence when the Lords of Venus first transmitted the Violet Flame, also knows as Violet Fire, at the end of Lemuria to clear Earth's etheric and psychic realms, and the lower physical atmosphere of negative forces and energies. This paved the way for the Atlanteans, who used it during religious ceremonies and as a visible marker of temples. The Violet Flame also induces Alchemy. Violet light emits the shortest wavelength and the highest frequency in the spectrum, so it induces a point of transition to the next octave of light.

Violet Ray: The Seventh Ray is primarily associated with Freedom and Ordered Service alongside Transmutation, Alchemy, Mercy, Compassion, and Forgiveness. It is served by the Archangel Zadkiel, the Elohim Arcturus, the Ascended Master Saint Germain, and Goddess Portia.

Vortex: A Vortex is a polarized motion body that creates its own magnetic field, aligning molecular structures with phenomenal accuracy. Vortices are often formed where lei-lines (energy meridians of Earth) cross. They are often called power spots as the natural electromagnetic field of Earth is immensely strong in this type of location.

Wahanee: The third United States Golden City located primarily in the states of South Carolina and Georgia. Its qualities are justice, liberty, and freedom; its Ray Force is violet; and its Master Teacher is Saint Germain.

Western Door: The West side of a Golden City gateway, also known as the *Yellow Door.*

Witness: An aspect of the soul, which has seen, heard, and experienced firsthand all of the events, incidents, and encounters involved throughout numerous lifetimes, and this includes the timeframe that is said to exist in-between lifetimes.

Bibliography

Besant, Anne. "The Laws of Higher Life." *Theosophy: The Laws of the Higher Life by Mahatma Annie Besant*. Accessed August 22, 2016. http://www.anandgholap.net/Laws_Of_Higher_Life-AB.htm.

Betz, Martha, and Keith Betz. "The Betz Ephemeris, 1940 to 2040," Laytonville, CA: Production Werks, 2001.

Blavatsky Theosophy Group, "What Exactly Is the Monad?" UK. https://blavatskytheosophy.com/what-exactly-is-the-monad/.

Browne, Sylvia. "Psychic Sylvia Browne's Near-Death Experience Revelations." 2016. Accessed October 26, 2016. http://www.near-death.com/paranormal/psychics/sylvia-browne.html.

Cardall, Elaine. "Ceremony of Songs." Malton, 2016.

Campbell, Joseph, and Bill D. Moyers. "Sacrifice and Bliss." *The Power of Myth*. New York: Doubleday, 1988.

Chia, Mantak. "Awaken Healing Energy through the Tao: The Taoist Secret of Circulating Internal Power." New York, NY: Aurora Press, 1983.

"A Common Belief System Founded in 1844." 1844-Founding. Accessed July 02, 2016. http://www.oversoul1844.org/1844-Founding.html.

Darton, Robert. "5 Myths about the Information Age." Lecture, Council of Independent Colleges' Symposium on the Future of the Humanities, Washington, D.C.

Emerson, Ralph Waldo. "Compensation." http://www.emersoncentral.com/compensation.htm.

Frawley, David. "Cycles of Humanity; Ascending and Descending Cycles." *Astrology of the Seers: A Guide to Vedic/Hindu Astrology*, 59-62. Salt Lake City, UT: Passage Press, 1990.

"The Great Sacrifice." Accessed August 22, 2016. http://sociedadteosofica.es/?tribe_events=european-school-of-theosophy-the-great-sacrifice.

Hall, Manly. "Atlantis and the Gods of Antiquity." *The Secret Teachings of All Ages*, 35. Diamond Jubilee Edition. Los Angeles: Philosophical Research Society, 1988.

Hall, Manly. "The Human Body in Symbolism." *The Secret Teachings of All Ages*, 75. Diamond Jubilee Edition. Los Angeles: Philosophical Research Society, 1988.

Hall, Manly P. "The Theory and Practice of Alchemy." *The Secret Teachings of All Ages*, 203. Los Angeles: Philosophical Research Society, 1988.

House, Jeanne M. "The Bhagavad Gita: A Primer." Accessed July 09, 2016. http://www.reversespins.com/gita.html.

Innocente, Geraldine. "Archangel Michael." Accessed August 22, 2016. http://www.ascension-research.org/michael.html.

Jenkins, John Major. "What Is the Galactic Alignment?" Accessed July 09, 2016. http://alignment2012.com/whatisga.htm.

Jessa, Tegga. "What Are Photons—Universe Today," December 24, 2015. Accessed November 14, 2016. http://www.universetoday.com/74027/what-are-photons/.

King, Godfré Ray. "The Magic Presence." Schaumberg, IL: Saint Germain Press, 1982.

"Masonic Compendium: Rose of Sharon. " Accessed August 12, 2016. http://masonic.wikidot.com/rose-of-sharon.

Myss, Caroline. "Taoism at a Glance." Caroline Myss. Accessed August 22, 2016. https://www.myss.com/free-resources/world-religions/taoism/taoism-at-a-glance/.

O'Connell, Cathal. "What Shape Are Photons? Quantum Holography Sheds Light." Cosmos Magazine. July 20, 2016. Accessed November 14, 2016. https://cosmosmagazine.com/physics/what-shape-is-a-photon.

Osuji, Ozodi. "Can an Unhealed Healer Heal Igbos Tendency to See Themselves as Victims?" http://chatafrik.com/articles/us-affairs/can-an-unhealed-healer-heal-igbos-tendency-to-see-themselves-as-victims#.V3fzv6JCZII.

Pratt, David. "The Monad: One and Many." http://www.davidpratt.info/monad.htm.

Randall, Stephen. "Mastering Linear Time." *A New Vision of Reality: Time, Space, and Knowledge*. Accessed August 12, 2016. http://www.tskassociation.org/mastering-linear-time.html.

Robson, Catherine. "Calling Your Blue Flame Angels to You." http://www.angeliclight.co.uk.

Serrano, Ricardo. "Physical Death and Spiritual Liberation through Soul Realization." July 16, 2007. Accessed July 02, 2016. http://www.qigonghealer.com/soul.html.

Simmons, Ilana. "The Four Moral [Emotions]." *Psychology Today*. November 15, 2009. Accessed July 20, 2016. https://www.psychologytoday.com/blog/the-literary-mind/200911/the-four-moral-emotions.

Sivananda, Sri Swami. "Thought Power." Accessed August 22, 2016. http://www.dlshq.org/download/thought_power.htm.

"Telepathy or the Ability of Thought Transfer: Our Ultimate Reality." Accessed August 22, 2016. http://ourultimatereality.com/telepathy-or-the-ability-of-thought-transfer.html.

"To Plunge into the Ocean of Bliss." http://www.boldsky.com/yoga-spirituality/spiritual-masters/sri-ramakrishna/eternal-bliss-swami-vivekananda-160609.html.

Toye, Lori. "Gem Elixirs by Saint Germain." August 10, 1998. *I AM America Archive,* Payson, Arizona.

Toye, Lori. "I AM America United States Golden Cities Map." Map. Payson, AZ: I AM America Seventh Ray Publishing, 1998.

Toye, Lori. "New World Wisdom: Book One." Payson, AZ: I AM America Publishing, 2016.

Toye, Lori. Points of Perception: Prophecies and Teachings of Saint Germain. Payson, AZ: I AM America Publishing, 2008.

Toye, Lori Adaile. "Spiritual Hierarchy." *Divine Destiny: Prophecies and Teachings of the Ascended Masters,* 37-46. Vol. 3. Golden City Series. Payson, AZ. I AM America Publishing, 2016.

Toye, Lori Adaile. "The Seventh Manu." *Points of Perception: Prophecies and Teachings of Saint Germain,* 31. Vol. 1. Golden City Series. Payson, AZ. I AM America Publishing, 2016.

Wong, Eva. "A Master Course in Feng-Shui." Boston: Shambhala, 2001.

Zell, Holly. "Earth's Atmospheric Layers." *NASA.* July 30, 2015. Accessed November 14, 2016. http://www.nasa.gov/mission_pages/sunearth/science/atmosphere-layers2.html.

Discography

This list provides the recording session date and name of the original selected recordings cited in this work that provide the basis for its original transcriptions.

Toye, Lori
Sacred Energies of Mother Earth, One, I AM America Seventh Ray Publishing International Audiocassette. ℗ No. 031600, 2000. © March 16, 2000.

Alignment, One, I AM America Seventh Ray Publishing International, Audiocassette. ℗ No. 032300, 2000. © March 23, 2000.

Flood of Consciousness, I AM America Seventh Ray Publishing International, Audiocassette. © March 30, 2000.

Understanding Time, I AM America Seventh Ray Publishing International, Audiocassette. ℗ No. 041900, 2000. © April, 19, 2000.

Secret Teachings on the Map of Rings, I AM America Seventh Ray Publishing International, Audiocassette. © April 27, 2000.

Alignment, Two, I AM America Seventh Ray Publishing International, Audiocassette ℗ No. 051100, 2000. © May 11, 2000.

Sacred Energies of Mother Earth, Two, I AM America Seventh Ray Publishing International, Audiocassette ℗ No. 051800, 2000. © March 18, 2000.

Integrating Golden City Energies, I AM America Seventh Ray Publishing International, Audiocassette. © May 10, 2000.

Golden Ray Compassion, I AM America Seventh Ray Publishing International, Audiocassette. © June 22, 2000.

Index

A

abundance
   and consciousness   160
acceptance   96
Adjutant Points   200
   definition   201, 249
Age of Information   76
Age of Transportation   189
agreement   153
Agreement Formation   153
   definition   167, 249
ahimsa   38
Akasa   124, 217
Akashic Records   26, 34
   and the sixth and seventh light bodies   233
   definition   143, 249
   of Wahanee   30, 44
Alaska
   hidden civilizations   55
Alchemy
   definition   107, 249
   inner   186
alien genetics   149
alignment   221
   and Saint Germain's teachings   162
   definition   249
   planetary   54
angels
   Blue Flame Angels   150
      written request to   165
anima   133
Animal Kingdom   177
animus   133
appearance of Master Teacher   33
Archangel Michael   164
   Blue Flame Angels   150
Archetypal Knowledge
   definition   132
archetype
   definition   249

Ascended Master
   and light bodies   233
   and thought transference   161
   creation myth   238
   definition   46
ascending civilizations
   definition   70
Ascending Culture
   definition   249
Ascending Cycle
   and the Golden Cities   70
Ascension   23, 25, 37
   and genetics   149
   and releasing fear   196
   and the Golden Ray   220
   and the oversoul   33
   and the Stars of Golden Cities   214
   and the Twin Ray   218
   and the White Ray   28
   and Violet Flame   183
   assisted through planetary alignments   64
   Christ or Quetzalcoatl energies   138
   preparation in Shalahah   179
Ascension Process
   and the eighth light body   233
   and the Twin Ray   237
   definition   189
   prayer for Ascension   190
Ascension Valley   179
Astral
   body   232
      and Christ Self   47
      and specific Golden Cities   221
      and the Violet Flame   148
   plane
      and Ascended Masters   47
      and spiritual liberation   37
astral light
   through the Violet Flame   160
Atlantis   56
   and Earth Changes   70
   Hall of Records   176
Atman   235
at-one-ment   37
   Shalahah   178

Aura
  and the Violet Flame 173
  Electronic Blueprint 229
  layers of the field of the human aura 230
Auric Template 232
avatar
  and sacrifice 24
  definition 249
Awakening to Love
  decree 187
Awakening to the I AM
  decree 108
awareness of the environment 76

B

Babajeran 125, 143, 174, 220
  and Golden Cities 26, 41
  and Shamballa 25
  and the Ascending Cycle 70
  and the Crystal Cities 194
  and the Gold Ray 230
  definition 249
Babaji 110
Ballard, Guy and Edna 167
belief systems 94
Bhagavad Gita
  and the playing field 73
Bliss of the Eternal Ocean
  definition 40, 249
Blue Flame 175
  invoking the Blue Flame for protection 227
  within the Violet Flame 223
Blue Flame Angels
  definition 164, 249
Blue Ray
  and Gobean 29
  and the mysteries 30
Bright Hall
  cascading 212
  construction 209
Brotherhood
  and the Gold Ray 86
Brotherhood and Sisterhood of the Light 93
Buddha
  followed the teachings of Jesus Christ 216
Buddha Body 233

C

Campbell, Joseph
  sacrifice and bliss 40
Causal Body 233
Causal Plane
  and Ascended Masters 47
  and spiritual liberation 37
causeless cause 67
Celestial Light Body 232
celestial music 142
Chakra 147
  definition 250
Chakra System 159
  and the Violet Flame 148
Change
  "from within." 151
Chela
  definition 250
chemtrails 104
chi
  definition 250
Choice
  and duality 162
  and the Golden Ray 78
  and the soul 81
  negative into positive 110
  pivots and moves consciousness 99
Christ
  birth within 102
  consciousness 37, 116
    and Shalahah 157
    and Shalahah Southern Door 44
    and the Map of Rings 138
    beyond politics 160
    definition 250
    development of 109
    definition 250
    the Rose of Sharon
      definition 115
    "Unites the dual forces" 96
    Unity Consciousness 122
Christ Self, Holy
  definition 47
circle
  symbology 136
City of White 25

coalesce
  definition 205
Co-creation
  definition 250
Collective Consciousness 79, 93
  definition 250
commitment 155
communion
  with the inner self 26
compassion 216
  heart of
    definition 237
Consciousness
  and Ascension 149
  and immortality 66
  and intolerance 57
  and simultaneous experience 95
  and the soul 34
  and Unana 69
  connects all worlds 108
  definition 250
  descending 25
  freed from duality 182
  "Grows beyond the limits of the flesh." 217
  of disease, death, decay 104
  Sea of Consciousness 95
  shift within 152, 160
  telepathy and lucid dreaming 215
Cosmic Wave Belts 99, 110
  definition 114
Cosmic Wave Motion
  definition 250
courage
  and spiritual development 97
creation myth 238
Crown Chakra
  and HU-man development through the Golden Cities 241
Crystalline Cities 122, 194
  and the Map of Rings 121
Cup
  definition 250
Cycle of the Elements 138
  creative-nourishing 140
  definition 250
cycles of time 99

D

dark rift, or great rift
  definition 65
  stirs past life memory 51
Darton, Robert 86
death
  "Down with death, immortal consciousness arise!" 97
Death
  consciousness
    erasing 100
decree
  for anger and hostility 187
  for apprehension 224
  for the Gold Ray 76
  for the I AM Presence 215
  for the ninth light body 234
  for the Violet Ray and assimilating the Golden Ray 80
  for Violet and Gold Ray 215
  to expand the Violet Flame 127
  to release fear 196
  to reprogram consciousness 97
  to unite with the I AM Presence 94
  to use in a Golden City Western Door 175
  Violet Flame for Ascension 183
descending civilizations 56
  definition 70
Descending Culture
  definition 250
desire
  and experience 94
  definition 250
Devas
  and the Map of Rings 121
  definition 250
Diamond Mind 235
diet
  and the Ascension Process 38
Dimensional
  Shift 50, 160
Dimensional leaping 54
  definition 68
Dimensional Rifting
  definition 250
disease
  and vibration 29

distraction
   "Do not become distracted by the crowd." 62
Divine Blueprint 234
Divine Complement 217
   and the Ascension Process 237
   definition 238
Divine Feminine 135
Divine Inheritor 25
   beyond karmic retribution 159
   defintion 40, 251
   the true self 216
Divine Intervention 120
   and the Golden Cities 60
   and the Violet Flame 24, 101, 174
Divine Love
   definition 114
Divine Man 141
Divine Mind
   definition 114, 251
Divine Mother 133
   Kuan Yin 139
Divine Order 221
   98
Divine Plan 35
Divine Will
   31, 79
   definition 114, 251
Divinity
   definition 251
DNA
   and the Violet Flame 161
   changes 69
doorways of Golden Cities 29, 157, 158, 192
   and CMYK (colors) 201
   and the HU-man Energy System 184
dream state
   and telepathy 162
duality 125
   and the Law of Attraction 67
   and Unana 102
   as limitation and lesson 151
   definition 113, 251

E

Eabra
   Golden City of 177
Earth
   energies 191
   white fire 192
Earth Changes Prophecies 50
   and changes in Galactic Light 70
   and new civilizations 56
   and the role of the Golden Cities 72
   definition 251
   Texas 60, 72
   the intent 23
Earth Plane
   definition 251
Eastern Door 174, 178, 180, 193, 211
   definition 251
ego
   and the playing field 73
   relinquishing through love 50
Egypt
   provenance with Atlantis 57
   relationship to Gobean's Western Door 176
eighth light body 233
Eight-Sided Cell of Perfection
   and healing 44
   and the Monad 236
Electronic Blueprint 230
Elemental Kingdom 176
   and the Map of Rings 121
   and the western four elements 141
Elementals
   definition 251
elements, five 140
El Morya 133, 176
   and meditation 30
   definition 251
Elohim
   definition 251
Emerson, Ralph Waldo
   and the oversoul 41
emotion
   and the Violet Flame 52
Emotional Body 230
   and desires 27
   definition 251

energy bodies
   recharging in Shalahah 31
energy-for-energy 47
"Energy goes where attention flows." 180
enlightenment
   and tolerance 96
etheral energies
   mirror to our Earth 192
Ethereal Mirror
   definition 198
Ever Present Now
   definition 251
Ever Present Soul
   definition 66
evolution
   and the Golden Ray 81
   through the heart 23
experience 216
   and consciousness 96
   and the aggregate body of light 102
   and time 99
   "Experience is the greatest of all teachers." 94
   the teacher 104
Eye of Providence 44

F

Faith
   the Tenth Jurisdiction 44
family
   "Must come first" 156
fear 50, 196
   teachings by Saint Germain 159
feminine
   definition 251
feminine energy
   and Eastern Doors of Golden Cities 184
   and the Map of Rings 138
   as negative energy 123
Feng Shui 206, 210
   cycle of the elements 140
Field of Awakening 233
Fifth Chakra
   and HU-man development through the Golden Cities 241
Fifth Dimension 143
   and spiritual liberation 37
   definition 252
fifth light body 232

Fire Mystery 107
First Chakra
   and HU-man development through the Golden Cities 240
first light body 230
Flower of Life
   as the Map of Rings 140
Forgiveness 83
   and the Violet Flame 38
   and vibrational shifting 30
   collective 160
Fourth Chakra
   and HU-man development through the Golden Cities 240
Fourth Dimension
   and Christ Consciousness 37
   and healing 43
   definition 252
fourth light body 232

G

Galactic Center 114
   and Earth Changes 70
   and Ray Forces 192
Galactic Light 70
Garden of Existence 218
   definition 239
gardens
   creation of Bright Hall 210
Gateway
   definition 252
Gateway Adjutant Points 200
   definition 202, 252
Gateway of Healing Formulas 43
global warming 55
Gnosis 40
Gobean 27
   definition 252
   Golden City of
     and healing 43
     Eastern Door 175, 185
     Northern Door 42
     spiritual migration 169
     Western Door 176, 185

God
- as the Law of Love 55
- "I shall rest with the Plan of God." 103

Golden Age 69, 143, 155
- and abundance 28
- and the growth of consciousness 75

Golden Age of Kali Yuga 85

Golden City Elixirs 193
- essential oils 208
- recipe and technique 206

Golden City Energies
- and vibrational shifting 29

Golden City Gateway Lei-line
- definition 203, 252

Golden City Vortex 41
- absorbing energies 193
- activation and humanity's spiritual evolution 198
- and healing 29
- and Spiritual Awakening 25
- apex (Star)
  Map of Rings 123
- definition 252
- doorway 156
- elevation 201
- gateway 202
- living in 193
- migration 154
- migratory pattern 156
- momentum of growth 195
- of Eabra 177
- of Gobean 27
- of Klehma 28, 157
- of Malton 27, 30, 155
- of Shalahah 28, 30, 157, 221
- of Wahanee 28
- pyramidal infrastructure 194
- Saint Germain's teachings 198
- through the dimensions 199

Golden City Vortices
- and Akashic Records 143
- and Babajeran 220
- and Divine Intervention 60
- and HU-man development 240
- and instant-thought-manifestation 42
- and the Gold Ray 76
- and the Map of Rings 120
- and the Western Shamballa Tradition 70
- as the Crystalline Cities 131
- Chakra Cities 242
- doorways 175
- formation through the Map of Rings 136
- the five initiations 169
- the Star
  and Ascension 220
  and the Gold Ray 214

Gold(en) Ray 75, 149
- and the Age of Information 76
- and the evolution of our Sun 160
- and the Twin Ray 219
- decree with Violet Flame 215
- definition 85, 226, 252
- ends the limitations of Kali Yuga 76
- "Many readied in vibration." 213
- next step within the Violet Flame 82
- Ray
  for acceptance and tolerance 90
- use in Golden City Stars 214
- with the Violet Flame for spiritual growth 162

Golden Thread Axis 144
- and the Golden Ray 80
- and the seventh light body 233

grace
- and the Golden Cities 184
- definition 252

Great Central Sun
- and Ray Forces 50
- and the Golden Cities 156

Great Mystery 131

Great Purification 31, 69
- and the role of the Golden Cities 72

Great Sacrifice
- definition 170

Great White Brotherhood
- definition 252

Green Ray
- and Shalahah 28, 179

H

Hall, Manly 141, 142
  and the fire mystery 107
Hall of Justice
  Golden City of Wahanee 188
Hall of Records
  definition 189
Harmony 152, 162
  definition 252
  The Tao 163
harmony and cooperation
  and the Golden City Vortex 41
Harmony of the Spheres 123
  definition 142, 253
healers
  and Shalahah 31
healing
  and desires 28
  and shift of perception 29
  and Southern Doors 30, 43
  and the Nature Kingdoms 30
  "healing is vibrational" 29
  the past 52
Heart
  and Ascension technique 181
  "Go within and listen to the heart." 60
Heart Chakra
  and HU-man development through the Golden Cities 240
Heart of Compassion
  definition 237
Heart of Love
  "When all is said and done, all that remains is love." 190
Helios and Vesta
  and use of the Gold Ray 227
Hermetic Law
  and the Law of Attraction 67
  and the pairs of opposites 113
  definition 253
  Yin and Yang 163
Hilarion 133
hitaka
  definition 253
Holy Christ Self
  definition 253
Holy Comforter 33
Holy Spirit
  definition 47, 253
householder
  definition 170
HU-man 142
  and light bodies 233
  Chakras and the Golden Cities 240
  definition 253
  development 42
  HU-man Energy System and the Four Doorways 184
  Mental Body 234
HU-man Chakras
  and the Golden Cities 242
human energy system
  and the Gold Ray 89

I

I AM
  definition 253
  Presence
    and Ascension 37
    and inner guidance 32
    and spirit guides 46
    and the Holy Spirit 47
    and the oversoul 41
    and Unana 95
    decree to unite with the true self 94
  the presence of 47
  Universal Mind 151
I AM America Teachings
  how to study 71
I AM Presence 233
  decree 215
  definition 253
I AM That I AM 33, 103, 150
  definition 166, 253
  meaning 151
  the Atman 235
  the unity of "All That Is" 95
I AM the Healing Heart
  decree 188
immaculate conception
  the Christ 129
immortality
  of consciousness 66

Industrial Age 76
Information Age 149, 213
   definition 85
   new communication methods 159
initiation
   and telepathy 215
inner garden 61
inner guidance 32
Inner Self
   and Golden Cities 41
   communion in Golden Cities 26
Innocente, Geraldine 166
instant healing
   in Shalahah 31
Instant-Healing-Manifestation 44
Instant-Thought-Manifestation 27
   and Golden City Vortices 42
interruptions 49
intolerance 57

J

Jiva
   definition 253
Joseph, father of Jesus 135
journey
   within 222
judgment
   and developing compassion 217
Jurisdiction
   definition 39

K

Kali-Yuga 25, 148
   and the Violet Flame 160
   ends 75
karma
   and desires 42
   and forgiveness of self 30
   and transmutation 38
   definition 253
   group, or collective karma 222
   shedding karma and the Gold Ray 88

Klehma
   definition 253
   Golden City of 28, 157, 180
   and healing 44
   Eastern Door 180, 189
   Northern Door 42
   Southern Door 31
   spiritual migration 169
   Western Door 189
Kok Sui, Choa
   and spiritual liberation 37
Kriya Yoga 38
Kuan Yin 135, 139, 247
   definition 253
Kundalini
   and North and South Golden City Doors 184
   and planetary alignment 51
   and the Violet Flame 148
Kuthumi 30, 133, 176
   definition 253

L

Lady Master Venus 135
Law(s) of
   Attraction 52
      "All things are pulled to their own vibration." 53
      and Law of Vibration 72
      definition 67
   Attraction and Repulsion
      definition 253
   Balance 79
   Cause and Effect
      definition 253
   Duality
      definition 190
   Forgiveness 23
   Love 181
     and the Melting Pot 71
     and Unana 57
   Polarity 67
   Rhythm 213
     definition 225
   Sympathetic Resonance 219, 228
   Unity
     definition 239

Vibration
   sympathetic resonance 142
lei-lines
   definition 254
   formation of Golden Cities 198
Lemuria
   and Earth Changes 70
library of light
   Akashic Records 124
Light
   definition 254
   expansion 175
   of the I AM Presence 33
limitation
   definition 239
lineage of gurus 46
Lord Macaw 133, 135
Love
   and dimensional shift 50
   definition 254
   of God 103
   the first initiation 155
lucid dreaming 215

M

Maltese Cross
   definition 254
   science of 200
Malton
   definition 254
   Golden City of 155
     and desires 27
     and healing 43
     Eastern Door 176, 186
     Northern Door 42
     spiritual migration 169
     Western Door 177, 186
Manas 235
Manu(s) 239
Map of Rings
   a map of Elemental Life Force 120
   definition 136, 254
   extends force throughout the solar system 126
   sympathetic vibration 126
masculine energy
   and the Map of Rings 138
   and Western Doors of Golden Cities 184
   as positive energy 123

Master
   "When the student is ready, the Master appears." 222
Master Teacher
   and appearance through the Rays 129
   and non-interference 59
   and spirit guides 46
   appearance 33
   definition 46, 254
   Grandfather Teacher 131
   Jesus Christ 132
Mastery
   definition 254
maya 37
   definition 190
melting pot
   and spiritual evolution 57
   definition 71
memory 51
Mental Body 230
   definition 254
Mercury 134
mind
   definition 254
   "Mind has always been the builder." 105
mind control 223
   decree for apprehension 224, 244
   definition 244
   overcome through the path of the heart 216
Mineral Kingdom 177
moksha 37
Monad 218
   definition 235
Mother Earth
   and the Map of Rings 131
Mother Mary 133
Muhammed 40

N

Nada 135
Native American culture 180
Nature
   Kingdoms 30
New Age 147, 159
   definition 254
New Consciousness
   decree for the Gold Ray 88

New Dimensions
  changes in DNA and RNA 69
New Time(s)
  Universities and schools of higher learning 188
ninth light body 234
Northern Door 27, 209
  definition 254
  formulas 42

O

obstacles
  use of Violet Flame 187
OM
  definition 167
omkara
  definition 167
Om Manaya Pitaya Hitaka
  definition 92, 254
OM Sheahah 157, 188
ONE
  "All things work together for the ONE!" 90
  and Klehma 157
  and the group 222
  and the Monad 236
  definition 254
  "God control is ONE mind." 223
  I AM that I AM 151
  "We are indeed a Oneship." 95
Oneship 150
  and the Golden Cities 143
  definition 255
Open Ears, Open Eyes
  definition 255
order
  Divine Order 98
Osuji, Ozodi
  and the unhealed healer 45
oversoul 26
  and the I AM Presence 33
  definition 41, 255

P

past life
  and the Gold Ray 228
  memories 160
  memories and dark rift 51
Peace 103, 175
  "Make peace within." 152
Peak Adjutant Lei-line
  definition 205, 255
Peak Adjutant Point 200
  definition 204, 255
perceive
  definition 255
Perception 53
  and healing 29
perfection
  and healing 44
persona 133
photon
  hologram 201
  Maltese Cross 200
planetary alignments 50, 54
  and kundalini 51
planetary conjunctions
  Jupiter and Saturn 64
Plant Kingdom 177
playing field 62
  definition 73
Point of Neutrality
  definition 117
Point of Perception
  definition 255
pole shift 184
Portia 133
  definition 255
prana
  definition 255
Prayer for Ascension 190
Prophecies of Change 159, 184
  and planetary alignment 67
  and technology 76
  and the Gold Ray 91
  and the New Times 69
Prophecy
  definition 255
puja or yagna 39

purification 214
  and Earth's cycle of light 100
  and Klehma's Southern Door 31
  through the Violet Flame 53
Pythagoras
  and the Harmony of the Spheres 142

Q

Quetzalcoatl 135
  energies 37

R

Rainbow Bridge
  definition 108, 255
Randall, Stephen 112
rapture 69
Ray Force(s) 129
  and Golden Cities 28
Ray(s)
  and humanity's evolution 56, 122, 148
  and the I AM Presence 32
  definition 255
Refreshing Drink 38, 163
  definition 255
  the drink of freedom 150
Rhythm of the Spheres
  definition 226
righteousness 122
Ring of Blue Flame Angels 150
  definition 164
Robson, Catherine 166
Root Chakra
  and HU-man development through the Golden Cities 240
Rose
  definition 255
  spiritual teachings 115
Rose Cross 115
Rosicrucian
  definition 256
Rosicrucian Rose 116
Ruby and Gold Ray
  and Malton 30

S

Sacrament of the Fire 207
Sacred Fire 148, 160
  alchemy 107
sacrifice 24
  definition 39, 170, 256
safe places
  and Eastern Doors 35
safety
  "Safety is a matter of the heart." 60
Saint Germain 133
  alchemist and magician 137
  and the Golden Cities 41
  and the Violet Flame 38, 160, 247
    for spiritual liberation 66
  as Divine Father 137
  definition 256
  on fear and prophecy 159
  on planetary alignment 63
  on the Blue Flame Angels 166
  on the Golden Cities 198
  teachings on desire 108
  teachings on spiritual alignment 162
  teachings on the Gold Ray 87, 228
  teachings on the Great Rift 65
  Violet Flame 144
Sananda 30, 135, 148, 149
  as Jesus the Christ 216
  definition 256
Sanat Kumara 119, 133
  as Divine Father 136
  definition 256
  Prophecies of Change 143
  teachings of the Map of Rings 131
satellitium
  definition 63
sattva
  definition 225
Schrodinger, Erwin 200
Seamless Garment
  definition 256
Sea of Consciousness 95
  definition 112, 256
Second Chakra
  and HU-man development through the Golden Cities 240

second light body 230
self-development
  and the Master Teacher 33
self (individualization) 132
Serapis Bey 31
  definition 256
seven chakras 231
Seven Rays of Light and Sound
  for alignment and balance 148
  service to I AM That I AM 151
Seventh Chakra
  and HU-man development through
    the Golden Cities 241
seventh light body 143, 233
Seventh Manu 222
  definition 239
Sexual-Creative Chakra
  and HU-man development through
    the Golden Cities 240
sexual energies
  higher expression 177, 186
shadow (dark side) 132
Shalahah
  definition 256
  Golden City of 157
    and healing 44
    Eastern Door 178, 188
    Northern Door 42
    spiritual migration 169
    Western Door 188
Shamballa 25
  creation of 41
  definition 256
  Western Tradition 70
Simultaneous
  embodiment 26
  reality 96
    definition 114, 256
Sivananda, Swami 161
Sixth Chakra
  and HU-man development through
    the Golden Cities 241
sixth light body 232
slope of land toward Golden City Lei-line 209
sojourn of the soul 81

Solar Plexus Chakra
  and HU-man development through
    the Golden Cities 240
Soltec 133
Soul
  definition 257
  learns 102
Source
  consciousness to the ONE 108
Southern Door 28, 30, 31, 211
  and Gateway of Healing Formulas 43
  definition 257
  Klehma 31
spiral of time 110
Spirit Guides 32
  definition 46, 257
Spiritual
  Awakening 26, 192
    and the Golden Cities 25
  definition 257
  Hierarchy
    and the Gold Ray 77
  definition 257
spiritual development
  and courage 97
spiritual expansion
  and the Violet Flame 127
spiritual intelligence
  and discovery of past civilizations 70
Spiritual Liberation 37, 52
  and the Golden Cities 61
  and the Violet Flame 66
  definition 257
Spiritual Mental Body 233
Spiritual Migration 175
  definition 257
  Saint Germain's teachings 168
spiritual seeker 101
Star
  and the Gold Ray 228
  and the Map of Rings 123
  definition 257
  retreating to a Golden City Center 193
steward
  definition 225
Subjective Energy Bodies 43
Sun
  evolution through the Golden Ray 160

super senses 95
survival
  moving beyond spiritually 24
sympathetic harmony 122
sympathetic resonance 127
  definition 142, 257

T

Tao, the
  Chinese Philosophy of Harmony 163
technology 76
  and ancient civilizations 55
  and the New Consciousness 85
telepathy
  and the New Times 149
Temple of Mercy 247
tenth light body 235
Terra
  definition 257
tests
  as experience only 53
Third Chakra
  and HU-man development through the Golden Cities 240
Third Eye
  and HU-man development through the Golden Cities 241
  definition 257
third light body 230
thirty-third degree
  Golden City Star 212
thought transference 149
  definition 161, 257
thousand eyes 182
  definition 190, 257
Three-Fold Flame 238
Three Refuges 44
Throat Chakra
  and HU-man development through the Golden Cities 241
Time 98
  and consciousness 97, 108
  linear
    definition 111
  linear into experience 110
  the different experiences of time 110

Time Compaction 120
  definition 258
Time of Change
  Cosmic Wave Belts 114
  definition 258
  follows the Time of Testing 107
Time of Testing 93, 119, 124
  and the opening of the Akashic Records 143
  definition 106, 258
tolerance
  "*To know the Source*" 96
  "*Work to obtain tolerance of all beliefs*" 98
Transmutation
  definition 258
Transportation Vortex 179
Triple Gem, the
  and the tenth light body 235
truth 103
Tube of Light 144, 227, 233
Twelve Jurisdictions 112
  definition 258
Twin Flames 217
Twin Rays
  and the Gold Ray 228
  definition 237

U

Unana 109, 149
  and leaps in consciousness 69
  and the Golden Ray 78
  and the Law of Love 57
  and uniting with the I AM Presence 95
  definition 258
Unfed Flame 44
  and the Christ Consciousness 113
  and the Monad 236
unhealed healer 30, 43
  definition 45
Unity
  and the Gold Ray 230
  Consciousness 93
    and sacrifice 39
    and teachings of the Christ 144
    Crystalline Cities 121

V

Vastu 206
Venus 134
Vibration
  and growth of the soul 34
  and healing 29
  and the Yugas 77
  definition 71
  Earth enters new vibration 69
  "Seeks its own level" 59
Vibrational
  Shifting 29, 43
victim
  and karma 39
Violet Flame 148
  and Ascension 38, 149
  and detachment 51
  and momentum 39
  and opening Akashic Records 217
  and sacrifice 40
  and spiritual refinement 158
  and the Gold Ray 82, 162, 214
    daily use 227
  and the messiahs and avatars 39
  and worries 23
  calling forth the consuming fire 227
  Decree
    for anger and hostility 187
    for perfection 187
    for Wahanee 178
    to release fear 196
    to remove obstacles 187
    use with Gold Ray 215
  definition 258
  for Ascension 183
  for business 173
  for expansion of consciousness and spiritual understanding 127
  for spiritual liberation 66
  invocation at sunrise, sunset 247
  reprogramming consciousness 109
  Saint Germain's teachings 144, 160
  Spiritual Lineage 247
  to harmonize relationships 186
  to release fear 196
Violet Flame and the Golden Ray
  like Yin and Yang for spiritual growth 162

Violet Ray
  and Divine Intervention 80
  and healing 30
  and higher consciousness 221
  definition 259
  for mind control 224
  reprograms the consciousness 97
Vortex
  definition 259

W

Wahanee
  definition 259
  Golden City of 28, 30, 155
    and healing 44
    and the Violet Ray 177
    Eastern and Western Doors 186
    Hall of Justice 178
    Northern Door 42
  Western Door 175, 178, 180, 211
    and new technology 179
    definition 259
Western Shamballa Tradition
  the Golden Cities 70
Wheel of Karma
  and spiritual liberation 37
White Fire 192
  and the Rays 198
White Ray
  and Klehma 28
Witness
  definition 46, 259
Write and Burn 43

Y

Yugas, cycle of 77

Z

Zero Point 117
  Golden City Star 212

About Lori and Lenard Toye

Lori Toye is not a Prophet of doom and gloom. The fact that she became a Prophet at all is highly unlikely. Reared in a small Idaho farming community as a member of the conservative Missouri Synod Lutheran church, Lori had never heard of meditation, spiritual development, reincarnation, channeling, or clairvoyant sight.

Her unusual spiritual journey began in Washington State, when, as advertising manager of a weekly newspaper, she answered a request to pick up an ad for a local health food store. As she entered, a woman at the counter pointed a finger at her and said, "You have work to do for Master Saint Germain!"

The next several years were filled with spiritual enlightenment that introduced Lori, then only twenty-two years old, to the most exceptional and inspirational information she had ever encountered. Lori became a student of Ascended Master teachings.

Awakened one night by the luminous figure of Saint Germain at the foot of her bed, her work had begun. Later in the same year, an image of a map appeared in her dream. Four teachers clad in white robes were present, pointing out Earth Changes that would shape the future United States.

Five years later, faced with the stress of a painful divorce and rebuilding her life as a single mother, Lori attended spiritual meditation classes. While there, she shared her experience, and encouraged by friends, she began to explore the dream through daily meditation. The four Beings appeared again, and expressed a willingness to share the information. Over a six-month period, they gave over eighty sessions of material, including detailed information that would later become the I AM America Map.

Clearly she had to produce the map. The only means to finance it was to sell her house. She put her home up for sale, and in a depressed market, it sold the first day at full asking price.

She produced the map in 1989, rolled copies of them on her kitchen table, and sold them through word-of-mouth. She then launched a lecture tour of the Northwest and California. Hers was the first Earth Changes Map published, and many others have followed, but the rest is history.

From the tabloids to the *New York Times*, *The Washington Post*, television interviews in the U.S., London, and Europe, Lori's Mission was to honor the material she had received. The material is not hers, she stresses. It belongs to the Masters, and their loving, healing approach is disseminated through the I AM America Publishing Company operated by her husband and spiritual partner, Lenard Toye.

Lenard Toye, originally from Philadelphia, PA, was born into a family of professional contractors and builders, and has a remarkable singing voice. Lenard's compelling tenor voice replaced many of the greats at a moment's notice—Pavarotti and Domingo, including many performances throughout Europe. When he retired from music, he joined his family's business yet pursued his personal interests in alternative healing.

He attended *Barbara Brennan's School of Healing* to further develop the gift of auric vision. Working together with his wife Lori, they organized free classes of healing techniques and the channeled teachings. Their instructional pursuits led them to form the *School of the Four Pillars* which includes holistic and energy healing and Ascended Master Teachings. In 1995 and 1996 they sponsored the first Prophecy Conferences in Philadelphia and Phoenix, Arizona. His management and sales background has played a very important role in his partnership with his wife Lori and their publishing company. Other publications include three additional Prophecy maps, thirteen books, a video, and more than sixty audio tapes based on sessions with Master Teacher Saint Germain and other Ascended Masters.

Spiritual in nature, I AM America is not a church, religion, sect, or cult. There is no interest or intent in amassing followers or engaging in any activity other than what Lori and Lenard can do on their own to publicize the materials they have been entrusted with.

They have also been directed to build the first Golden City community. A very positive aspect of the vision is that all the maps include areas called, "Golden Cities." These places hold a high spiritual energy, and are where sustainable communities are to be built using solar energy alongside classical feng shui engineering and infrastructure. The first community, Wenima Village, is currently being planned for development.

Concerned that some might misinterpret the Maps' messages as doom and gloom and miss the metaphor for personal change, or not consider the spiritual teachings attached to the maps, Lori emphasizes that the Masters stressed that this was a Prophecy of choice. Prophecy allows for choice in making informed decisions and promotes the opportunity for cooperation and harmony. Lenard and Lori's vision for I AM America is to share the Ascended Masters' prophecies as spiritual warnings to heal and renew our lives.

Books and Maps by Lori Toye

Books:

NEW WORLD WISDOM SERIES: *Book One, Two, and Three*

FREEDOM STAR: *Prophecies that Heal Earth*

THE EVER PRESENT NOW: *A New Understanding of Consciousness and Prophecy*

I AM AMERICA ATLAS: *Based on the Maps, Prophecies, and Teachings of the Ascended Masters*

GOLDEN CITY SERIES
 Book One: Points of Perception
 Book Two: Light of Awakening
 Book Three: Divine Destiny
 Book Four: Sacred Energies of the Golden Cities

I AM AMERICA TRILOGY
 Book One: A Teacher Appears
 Book Two: Sisters of the Flame
 Book Three: Fields of Light

Maps:
 I AM America Map
 Freedom Star World Map
 United States 6-Map Scenario
 United States Golden City Map

I AM AMERICA PUBLISHING & DISTRIBUTING
P.O. Box 2511, Payson, Arizona, 85547, USA. (928) 978-6435

For More Information:
www.iamamerica.com
www.loritoye.com

I AM America Online Bookstore:
http://iamamericabookstore.iaabooks.com

About I AM America

I AM America is an educational and publishing foundation dedicated to disseminating the Ascended Masters' message of Earth Changes Prophecy and Spiritual Teachings for self-development. Our office is run by the husband and wife team of Lenard and Lori Toye who hand-roll maps, package, and mail information and products with a small staff. Our first publication was the I AM America Map, which was published in September 1989. Since then we have published three more Prophecy maps, thirteen books, and numerous recordings based on the channeled sessions with the Spiritual Teachers.

We are not a church, a religion, a sect, or cult and are not interested in amassing followers or members. Nor do we have any affiliation with a church, religion, political group, or government of any kind. We are not a college or university, research facility, or a mystery school. El Morya told us that the best way to see ourselves is as, "Cosmic Beings, having a human experience."

In 1994, we asked Saint Germain, "How do you see our work at I AM America?" and he answered, "I AM America is to be a clearinghouse for the new humanity." Grabbing a dictionary, we quickly learned that the term "clearinghouse" refers to "an organization or unit within an organization that functions as a central agency for collecting, organizing, storing, and disseminating documents, usually within a specific academic discipline or field." So inarguably, we are this too. But in uncomplicated terms, we publish and share spiritually transformational information because at I AM America there is no doubt that, "A Change of Heart can Change the World."

With Violet Flame Blessings,
Lori & Lenard Toye

For more information or to visit our online bookstore, go to:
www.iamamerica.com
www.loritoye.com

To receive a catalog by mail, please write to:
I AM America
P.O. Box 2511
Payson, AZ 85547

Awaken to the Change Within

FROM THE BESTSELLING AUTHOR OF THE I AM AMERICA MAPS

THE
Ever Present Now

A NEW UNDERSTANDING OF
CONSCIOUSNESS AND PROPHECY

LORI ADAILE TOYE

The Ever Present Now
ISBN: 9781880050507

loritoye.com
iamamerica.com

Or, call 928-978-6435
or Amazon.com

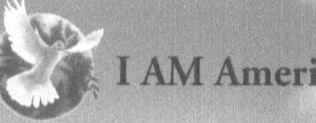

I AM America Trilogy
The contemporary Spiritual Journey

A Teacher Appears
ISBN: 9781800050446
254 pages

Sisters of the Flame
ISBN: 9781800050262
216 pages

Fields of Light
ISBN: 9781800050613
310 pages

This series of insightful books, written by the creator of the acclaimed *I AM America Maps* shares a fresh and personal viewpoint of the contemporary spiritual journey. Lori Toye was just twenty-two years old when she first encountered Ascended Master teaching. The *I AM America Trilogy* takes us back to the beginning of her experiences with her spiritual teachers and includes insights that have never been disclosed in any previous books or writings. In "A Teacher Appears," learn how true wisdom and the inner teacher is within all of us. "Sisters of the Flame," continues an initiatory passage into the feminine with the Cellular Awakening. "Fields of Light," explains how to integrate and Master our spiritual light through soul-transcending teachings of Ascension. Lori's personal story is interwoven throughout the *I AM America Trilogy* in a rich tapestry of spiritual techniques, universal wisdom, and knowledge gained through a life-changing spiritual journey.

I AM America Atlas

Contains all of the
I AM America Maps
Full color
108 pages

New World Wisdom Series

Spiritual Teachings from
the Ascended Masters
Books One, Two, and Three

Spiritual Teaching for the New Times

For more information:
loritoye.com
iamamerica.com
or call (928) 978-6435

www.ingramcontent.com/pod-product-compliance
Lightning Source LLC
Chambersburg PA
CBHW031059080526
44587CB00011B/751